CW00505840

"Never have I read a book so thought-provoking, that made me cry so many tears, as I realised that I had fallen so desperately 'out of love' with my very own self. The Art of Self-Love is the wake-up call, comforting hug, and message of hope that you have been looking for."

Kelli Dawson

"The Art of Self-Love is a tender reminder that challenge comes to us all, and that in those moments, our behaviour matters beyond belief. It is both an invitation and challenge of self-enquiry, and self-expansion. It teaches us how to step into life's curve-balls with grace, courage and love. Kim Morrison is a gift to human-kind. She lives and breathes her message of self-love and personifies kindness. She shares her learnings from a full life, the ups and downs, gifting us the self-love circle. A framework to help us to make sense of the confusion of life, together with the physical, mental, emotional, and spiritual tools to implement. The Art of Self-Love is a must-have, hands-on manual to guide us back into self-love and into full expression, whilst still accepting our imperfections and those bathroom floor moments!"

Erin Barnes, Next Generation Wellness

"I have laughed, and I have cried reading this beautiful book. Thank you so much, Kim, for pouring your heart and wisdom into these pages. This is a fantastic, practical guide for anybody to use on a daily basis to keep bringing you back to the circle of self-love. Thank you."

Hillary Wallace

"Some books you will want to keep permanently on your bedside table – this is one of them. Kim Morrison is raw, honest, real, and draws on her own life experiences to share her knowledge and tools for living a happier, more peaceful, and loving life. Congratulations Kim! It is brilliant."

Christin Plint

"The Art of Self Love and the self-love circle is going to shift the way I look at life, the world, my relationships, and myself. A lack of self-love is at the root of every challenge we face in our lives. This book provides the insights and tools to stop falling into the same self-sabotaging situations and offers solutions for how to stop listening to that inner critic! Kim Morrison is a true teacher, who shares from what she herself has learned. She is honest, raw, and real as she teaches the path of self-love. Kim's passion for essential oils shines through and provides insight on how to make self-care practical in your everyday life. Finally, a book that will empower you to act. Thank you, Kim for sharing your knowledge and experience, but most importantly for sharing your heart!"

Liz Sefton

"Thank you, Kim, for sharing your wisdom and deeply personal insights to create an inspiring resource into the art of self-care! Having the courage and confidence to keep going, even when you feel discouraged, absolutely shines throughout this book. When the daily bumps of life get to me, I know I only need to choose one of the many practical rituals provided within to get me back into the self-love circle."

Anna Grillo

"I have just finished The Art of Self Love, and I challenge any reader not to resonate with, at a bare minimum, ONE paragraph or sentence in this book. I found myself in tears in some parts, and realised it was time to heal old wounds. Thank you, Kim, for laying it all out there and making me realise it's time for me to put me first and love myself first and foremost, as opposed to always thinking I need to love everyone around me first."

Ada Tse

"This book is stunning! It comforts and nurtures you when you need it most. It excites you with all that is possible in life, and it completely relatable especially with Kim's infectious cheekiness always present. This is easy to read, follow, and adopt into everyday life. It's raw, real, and divine all in one. Kim, I love your work and all that you resemble. Thank you for making it so much easier to deal with all that life gives us. Now that I have the circle of self-love and tools in my life, everything has changed for the better. Thank you so much!"

Simone McDouall

"An inspiring read on the importance of taking time to look after yourself. This book shows the passion you have in creating a ripple effect among women to love and respect themselves. The framework of the self-love circle is a brilliant tool, along with the inclusion of specific oils for each section. I could easily relate to some of your personal experiences and was at times moved to tears as it brought back my own memories of challenging times. You have an amazing soul, and a beautiful heart. Thank you for reminding me to live life with love and passion! Congratulations!"

Debbie Williams

"Kim, I dream that one day your wisdom, inspiration, and tools for self-love will be taught in our education system. I can only imagine the phenomenal change it would have on our society and how it could empower the generations to come to live the life they desire. This has truly helped both myself and my family immensely. After being on a huge healing journey with a sick child, this information was the missing piece that our family so desperately needed. When I began to spend time on myself and love myself again, the healing effect it also had on my family was unbelievable."

Claire Holmes, Founder of Nourishing Me

"This book is brilliant and bound to be another best seller! Thank you Kim for your openness and authenticity. You highlight how normal it is for all of us to fall out of the love circle, and you help the reader, a) to become more aware of when this happens, and b)armed with this knowledge, to have an array of skills on hand to get oneself back inside! Love, love, love this book! And with the lists of essential oils to enhance one's mood, this book should definitely be on everyone's 'essential reading' booklist!

Leonie Wallace

Fall in love with taking care of yourself:
mind, body, and soul.

THE ART OF

KIM MORRISON

From the author of the internationally acclaimed,
best seller 'Like Chocolate for Women'

Disclaimer

The advice provided here is general in nature and is not intended to replace clinical, medical or psychological direction or advice. In the event that you or your loved ones are in danger of self harm, we recommend calling Life Line on 13 11 14 and Kids Helpline on 1800 55 1800 in Australia, or in New Zealand call Life Line on 0800-543-354

For a more comprehensive list of supportive centres please go to page 302

The Art Self-Love: Fall in love with taking care of yourself; mind, body and soul

© Kim Morrison 2018

ISBN: 978-1-925833-12-6 (paperback)
          978-1-925833-13-3 (eBook)

The Cataloguing-in-Publication entry can be viewed at the National Library of Australia. Reference NLApp77822

Ocean Reeve and Jason Smith - Publishing Managers

Carren Smith - Creative Editor

Kristy Hoffman, Leona Fensome, Mona de Vestel - Editors

Julie Bebbington - Cover Design and layout

Becky Rui - Cover Photo of Kim Morrison

Sarah Wilder - Self-Love Mandala on cover

Printed in Australia by Ocean Reeve Publishing

www.oceanreeve.com

Published by Kim Morrison and Ocean Reeve Publishing

www.oceanreeve.com

www.Twenty8.com

Danny, Tayla and Jakob, you are my true beacons of light.
I love you all to the moon and back, and back again xxx

LOVING THANKYOUS...

There are so many incredible souls who have trail-blazed inspiration into my heart, and who I feel indebted to for the creation of this book.

Carren Smith and Cyndi O'Meara, you are my greatest role models, mentors, best friends, and most incredible examples of pure love. Not to mention the dream team, fellow Up for A Chat podcasters. Thank you Carren for helping me to draw these words from my heart, and thank you both for writing such heartfelt forewords. Our friendship is admired by many; none more so than me.

Fleur Davis, it all began with you my beautiful friend, to say I love you is an understatement. Lizzie McPhail you amazing soul, thank you for gifting me with an adventurous and cheeky spirit. I'm sure Ray is up there smiling with his red tie on, super proud of us both.

To the team at Ocean Reeve Publishing, how did I get to be so lucky that you jumped on this ride? Ocean, Jason, and Kristy, you have all been nothing short of magnificent. It's thanks to you we actually finished this, and I'm beyond grateful.

To Carren Smith, Leona Fensome and Mona de Vestel, thank you for your endless inspiration and editing hours.

To Becky Rui for our amazing photo shoot in Paris and the cover photo, you are the best. Sarah Wilder for the self-love Mandala, you nailed it. Thank you both for your incredible artistry.

Julie Bebbington what a blessing you are. Your insight, contribution and incredible talent has created a cover we all feel very proud of. Thank you for understanding the precious contents of this book.

Claire Burness, thank you for recognising the need for this book, I pray it has been worth the wait.

To Matt Greenough and Jayne Wiklund, such caring souls, you made a place we can genuinely call our home. I am especially grateful that this is where I got to write the bulk of this book.

To everyone who has been involved, and is a part of the Twenty8 dream, I salute you and truly honour you. This full-on crazy blonde has created chaos at times, with a vision that has required everyone to constantly step up. It never goes unnoticed. I especially want to thank you Alan Perkinson and your beautiful wife Marnie, for believing in me enough to keep me in the game and to not ever give up. Our champagne moments mean the world to me.

How do I ever thank you, my reader, our cherished customer of Twenty8, attendees of my workshops over the years, and all the participants in my beloved Health & Lifestyle Education program? You are the real souls I rely on for inspiration. I owe you a massive thank you, because it is you who enables me to keep doing what I do. It is you who is ultimately responsible for keeping this dream alive.

To my aromatherapy teachers from the late eighties through to today, I sincerely thank you all. Essential oils have been a part of my world since I was nineteen, and my deep love and respect for plants, herbs, and these precious extracts has constantly been inspired by you. Judith White and Karen Downes, you two were pioneers of this industry in the '80s and '90s, and I cannot thank you enough for believing I could carry this beautiful light.

Cliff Young, thank you for taking the time with such a young soul and teaching her the true meaning of persistence, tenacity, determination, and self-belief.

To four very special men Brett Hill, Damian Kristof, Laurence Tham and Marcus Pearce, for the work you have done for thewellnesscouch.com and bringing so many amazing podcasts to the airwaves, is nothing short of amazing. I cannot thank you enough, for your love and friendship and for having me a part of your worlds.

Thank you Bruce Campbell for introducing me to so many business concepts, extraordinary people, and for coaching me into believing I can do this. You know I will continue to challenge you on 'gut' thinking!

Jacqueline Trost you are my saviour, my light. You taught me the greatest gift which came from your teacher Sathya Sai Baba; Love all. Serve all. Help ever. Hurt never. It is an honour to know you.

To my dearest girlfriends you will never ever fully appreciate just how much your love of me and your belief in what I do gives me courage and a desire to love even more each day. I seriously adore you.

To my precious, crazy-good family, I love each of you so dearly. Through all the highs, the lows, the joys, and the challenges, you have held and inspired me, and I want you to know it is thanks to you I have learned the true meaning—the essence—of love. This book is a tribute to each of you.

Zhara I hope you are dancing up there beautiful, we miss you more than you will ever know.

To the best mother in law anyone could ask for, Sandi Morrison, you delicious soul. I think it's fair to say we dreamed each other up.

To my late, sweet grandmothers, Myrtle Rose Millicent and Dorothy May, thank you for teaching me the art of kindness. I hope I can sprinkle just an ounce of what you gave to me.

Dad and Trudy, thank you for always loving me.

To my sister Keri and brother Aaron you are the best. I love the fact you both make me laugh so hard it hurts. And if you think my birthday cards have way too much writing, good luck with this baby!

Mum, you extraordinary being, I want to thank you especially for gifting me with the power of self-love. I love you.

To my beautiful children Tayla and Jakob. I thank my lucky stars every day that you chose me, I simply cannot articulate what it means to be your mumma. You are my greatest joy, my world; you are the reason I do what I do.

And finally my incredible husband, Danny you are my rock, my best friend, and my soul mate. I cannot even begin to thank you for all you do for our family. I love this amazing adventure we are on and I look forward to many, many more runs, meals, fine wines, kombuchas, laughs, and hugs. You, my gorgeous man, have taught me the incredible power of unconditional love: the greatest love of all.

FOREWORD
Carren Smith

The Art of Self Love is an exploration of what it means to turn our attention towards ourselves, in a world that demands so much from us.

Filled with stories, anecdotes, and wisdom, the journey of this book will have you laughing, crying, and reflecting from one page to the next, as you begin to look at the relevance and similarities in your own life. You'll see that so much more possibility exists for you and your family when you fill your own cup with love, compassion, joy, and self-care. It's your divine responsibility and there is no better time than right now to begin a new relationship with yourself!

As Kim Morrison reveals her own struggles with family, work, money, and life in general, she also shares her appreciation for the challenges she faces as a mother, business woman, wife, and friend. She points out that when we can see our challenges and short comings as opportunities to grow, we can embrace the learning being offered, and this book gives you the HOW TO tools every step of the way.

Our society today is asking us to do more with less, commit more of ourselves, and run our tanks dry before refueling, and while we can't avoid the endless demands, we can learn how to refuel while we are on the run! The Art of Self Love shows us that by stealing 'micro-moments' we can become more present to the beauty and joy of life, as opposed to it rushing past us as we simply hope for the best.

Enjoy this ride and embrace the tools offered here before you run yourself to the point of burnout. Self-love is an art, and you are the artist. It's time to take the palette of life and design the masterpiece you've dreamed of!

Carren Smith
www.carrensmith.com
www.spirithive.org

Spirit Hive, is a non religious, no denomentaitonal, not for profit organisation exploring the spiritual nature of human potential, mind, body, spirit and beyond!

FOREWORD
Cyndi O'Meara

To be in the presence of someone who has self-love, self-confidence, respect for themselves, and humility is so very easy, there are no hidden agendas in what they say or do. They shoot straight from the heart. They usually love their life, what they do, and the company they keep. Their life seems filled with ease and they are not affected by someone else's opinion of them.

Their confidence and leadership are palpable, they are someone you want to spend time with; you want to learn from them, and you want to find out what they know, and do.

This book, *The Art of Self Love* by Kim Morrison—who walks her talk—will teach you the principles and art of self-love.

I was on a bus the other day and I heard a young boy tell his friends what he had achieved on the ski slopes. Everyone cheered him on but one boy, whose statement was cutting: "Show off!" he yelled out for all the people on the bus to hear. The young boy didn't seem to flinch, he knew that he was okay, and had probably learnt the art of self-confidence and love. He may not have known it as that, but he displayed it beautifully, by holding his head high and not being affected by the comment. On the other hand, as I stared at the young man who made the disparaging comment, my first thoughts were that he was mimicking his parents or guardians, and instantly I felt sorry for him. His self-loathing could be seen by his comment and the cutting put-down of his friend, who was proud of his achievement. Fancy living your life hating yourself and the only way to feel better is to put someone else down.

We have a responsibility in this world to turn the art of bullying into the art of self-love. It is imperative to learn this to pass it on to our children and future generations, for a world that is more forgiving, more loving and more respectful.

Every single one of us are unique, amazing human beings. We have a stunning intelligence that lives within us, that keeps our heart beating and our cells communicating together to make us human and incredible. I have studied the human body, biochemistry, and biology my whole life, and I'm in awe of the gift of life we have been blessed to live. Everyone, as they wake up, should scream with delight at the magnificence and miracle they are.

The art of self-love is the art of self-care, which is the art of self-respect. Be your best friend that you would do anything for, this will give you a hint as to how to treat yourself. If you promise that you will do something for yourself then do it. Take time for you so that you can take time for others. Fill your own tank, so you can help others fill theirs. Respect who you are so that you have total respect for all who you meet. When you respect and love yourself and the body you have been given, then you nourish it with the best of food, care for it with the best of skin care, exercise it with the best intentions, and rest it so it can continue your mission in life. This in turn honours the people around you, the planet you inhabit, and all those who live in your presence

This way of thinking becomes infectious, where every part of your life begins to change. It's the most empowering thing you can do.

Don't expect others to change to change your life and attitude, this is all about you: for things to change, you must change, take responsibility for your actions and life. And the coolest thing of all is that you are the only one you can change with certainty. You cannot change your partner, children, friends, community, country, or planet, but you have total power over yourself.

So, with love and respect, empower yourself, read this book, do the exercises, and watch your life change. And remember, just reading the book and knowing it is not good enough, you must act on this knowledge, and this in turn will cause a ripple effect – perhaps even a tsunami of change. That will be incredible.

With love and respect
Cyndi O'Meara
Founder of Changing Habits
Founder of the Functional Nutrition Academy
Producer of the documentary, *What's with Wheat?*

THE ART OF SELF LOVE

If your greatest responsibility is to love yourself,
And to know you are enough.
Why is it we get consumed by life,
And struggle with the concept of self-love?

If I could be a voice of reason and give you,
A talking to, heart-to-heart.
You know I would say you're a masterpiece,
A precious, and amazing piece of art.

I would want you to see just what I see,
And to feel my unconditional love, too.
To know your talents and gifts are unique,
And that there is no-one quite like you.

But yes, in life there is pain and suffering,
And let's face it, no one is excluded.
Some days you may question what it all means,
And how life can become so secluded.

It's when this happens, and we hurt inside,
That our love is replaced with self-sabotage.
We doubt ourselves more, our confidence goes,
And negativity is one hell of a montage.

Mistakes will happen, wrong choices made,
We have to remember perfection is an illusion.
When you mess up in life you just pick yourself up,
And let go of the drama and confusion.

But the world will feed you all sorts of lies,
Around people, money, beauty, and self-worth.
These are judgments and perceptions at best,
Which we are conditioned to from birth.

So, it's ok to feel lost and numb at times,
Fall in a heap by yourself and conceal it.
To hide from the world is to question why,
After all, to heal it one must truly feel it.

To know how to get up and on with your life,
Is to become in tune and more self-aware.
Realise that we are all just a work in progress,
And the way up and out is with self-care.

Small daily rituals with a loving intent,
Will put your trust and love to the test.
It's doing these often and when you need it most,
That will get you back to your beautiful best.

Self-care takes a deep commitment of course,
The discipline to never ever give up.
Connecting with nature and the gifts she bestows,
Is what will guide you to fill your own cup.

It's when we accept the challenges we face,
Are the times to go within and re-connect.
After all these lessons are opportunities for you,
To build more compassion and self-respect.

To honor and truly accept yourself,
With commanding and authentic authority.
Micro-moments of mindfulness are what it takes,
And to make your self-care a priority.

What a powerful gift to know you possess,
The divine responsibility and grace from above.
With regard for your happiness and wellbeing,
Is the undeniable, unshakeable art of self-love.

Love Kim xx
© 2018

CONTENTS

Introduction

SELF-LOVE: REGARD FOR ONE'S OWN WELL-BEING AND HAPPINESS

What would it take for you to embrace the power of self-love and take responsibility for all that occurs in your world? What if all that occurs in your world is driven or controlled by something bigger than you? Something cosmic, something universal, something that encompasses all that is love; divine love?

Imagine then, that the divine responsibility you possess for your own well-being and happiness could, in fact, be mastered? This doesn't mean regard for someone else's well-being or happiness, or your kids, or your family, or friends. It means consideration for *your own* mind, body, and soul. What would it take to accept this responsibility: A disaster, a mistake, death, or trauma? A shock? A loss?

Often, it's not until we experience an unexpected event or situation, or something that brings us to our knees, that we are inclined to review how we are living our lives. One thing I've learned on my journey is that we are not paying enough attention to the things that matter, often enough. We are almost 'absent' from the one and only personal responsibility we have that is essential to our lives, and the lives of those around us: *self-love*!

I've fallen to my knees more times than I can remember. I've had what I call 'bathroom moments', where the only comforting spot feels like the chill of the tiles on the floor against my cheek, while rising to my feet feels like mission impossible. My tears have filled the bathtub and my cries have echoed off many a mirror over the years. The one thing I've come to discover, thanks to the secrets in those walls, is that self-love is the way to get through, up, and out!

Quite a few years back, I was hit with a curve ball that I didn't see coming in my relationship. I subsequently questioned my marriage, my existence, my self-belief, the meaning of life and love, and it rocked my family, and me, to the absolute core.

My husband and I had been married for twelve years; we had what I would call the perfect marriage. Since retiring as a professional sportsman (Danny played cricket for New Zealand from 1987-1997), he had been trying to find his new calling, his niche. It wasn't easy for him, and I have seen many great sportspeople wonder who they are, often feeling like they have been chucked onto the junk heap of life when they finish their playing days.

Sadly, in the midst of his own self-questioning, Danny's beautiful sister tragically died. This took him into a very dark place; alone, and in solitude. He hid it from me, from everyone. I had no idea of the internal dialogue and struggles he was facing. And yet, despite Danny's inner turmoil, it was still the biggest shock when I finally found out that my beautiful husband had become lost in a world of loneliness, self-loathing, drugs, and alcohol, whenever he was on the road as a cricket commentator.

At the time, I felt that things would never be the same between me and my husband Danny, ever again. My grandmother had just passed away in the same week, and I was also scrambling to raise the money to launch my business and release a self-published book I co-authored with Fleur Whelligan (Davis), *Like Chocolate for Women*. Everything hit me at once. This external chaos and turmoil all felt insurmountable and no matter how I tried to reason or convince myself that I could cope with all of this, nothing made sense anymore. I felt helpless.

With my cheek pressed firmly against the bathroom floor and a flood of tears collecting underneath me, my beautiful daughter Tayla, who was eleven at the time, came in to me saying, "It's OK mummy, just smell this rose oil, it will make you feel better." It still staggers me how our children learn and absorb so much from us along the way. I shouldn't have been surprised, though, as this is what I had always done for her whenever she was upset.

While my husband, Danny, rubbed my back in an attempt to soothe the desperate pain that was tearing my stomach to shreds, my ten-year-old son, Jakob, would sit next to me saying, "Mum, what's wrong?" This inner turmoil, along with everyone else's worry of my struggle, was simply too much. I felt so humiliated that I was in such a state in front of my kids, and so confused as to how life would ever be normal again after so much hurt. I asked them all to just leave me alone and to leave me in my world of pain. I just needed space to breathe.

I do not recall how much time had passed before I pulled myself up and crawled into my bedroom, only to find my Jakob laying on his stomach on my bed, looking right at me, resting his chin in his hands. "You'd better tell me what's wrong mum," he demanded.

"I'm just really upset, Jakob," I replied. "I'm upset with Daddy. Grandma has gone, and it has left a hole in my heart, and I'm trying so hard to get this book and business out there, so I can make a difference to people." I cannot even begin to explain. I mean, how do you say to a wide-eyed ten-year-old that your world as you knew it has come crashing right down on top of you. Even though my pain was raw, and visible, I was feeling even sicker inside. Despite this, I didn't want my sweet, innocent son to lose out of sight of the feeling that life is still wonderful.

Then, without flinching or hesitating, my son launched into a response that blew my mind. "Mum, the problem with you is that you're trying to get to a massive diamond in the middle of a massive mountain. But you're chipping away at it using just tiny little nail clippers!"

I was a bit shocked. I looked at him, puzzled, wondering where these words of wisdom were headed. He continued, "Mum, if you get up, I promise, people will arrive with shovels and picks and help you chip away at that mountain with you. And then, Mum, I promise, if you get up then there will be diggers and bulldozers. And then, Mum, someone will come along with a stick of TNT dynamite for you to blow that mountain up completely! And then right in front of you, you'll just see the diamond shining so brightly in the middle of that mountain. And then, Mum, your job will be to help other people to see their own diamonds, because you've seen yours. You just have to get up and stay up!"

I could not believe it. "Jakob, are you for real?" I asked this small person who had come out of my body a decade earlier. "Are you kidding me? Where on earth did you get this from?"

Again, without hesitation, and looking very pleased with himself, Jakob said "Well, actually Mum, it's this new PlayStation game and I was wondering if I could get it?"

I felt myself burst out laughing in shock. It was comical that such a profound analogy was really my son's bid to get a new game! But I was also still very taken by the sheer wisdom and truth that had just so innocently come out of the mouth of this babe; my babe. Kids have a way of offering us such amazing truths when we are at our most fragile state, leading us to a turning point. He related to what he knew—which ultimately became his message of love—which changed my state, altered my direction, and became the foundation for the work I've done ever since.

Like Jakob's message to me, this book is my message of love. My strategy, my go-to teacher every time I find myself, my family, or friends in need of direction, clarity, and a way to reconnect to the vital force that is our saviour in times of need.

I am yet to meet anyone who has evaded bathroom moments such as this, or indeed challenges, problems, grief, hurt, heartache, or fear. Every single one of us will be confronted with moments that literally bring us to our knees, or times when we question ourselves, or our reason for being. If that is the case, then my question is this: how on earth do we get up, get through it, and get on with it? And how do we do all of this without losing ourselves in the process, or becoming a victim of such occurrences?

Within this book I will be sharing what I have discovered works for me. It is a step-by-step process, so I do not lose sight of myself through life's challenges. I can then work out how I use those challenges to help me grow, expand, and hopefully, love even more. I never want to *not* love; to feel that love is lost, or impossible, when I am suffering.

My invitation to you right here, right now, is to begin the journey of regard for your own well-being and happiness, and know that through this book, I have your back, and I'm walking right alongside you every step of the way.

So, what's the journey? What am I suggesting here?

We've heard a lot when it comes to self-love and the practice of being kind and gentle to yourself and others. Over the years, there have been thousands of books, videos, articles, television shows, and documentaries created that seek to explore the power of kindness. Throughout the years, this message has resonated with me, and I have tried to incorporate it into business, my daily life as a wife, a mum, and as a friend. One of the most simple and influential books I've read was Don Miguel Ruiz' *Four Agreements*. If you haven't had a chance to read it, here is a summary:

1. BE IMPECCABLE WITH YOUR WORD: Speak with integrity. Say only what you mean. Avoid using the Word to speak against yourself or to gossip about others. Use the power of your Word in the direction of truth and love.

2. DON'T TAKE ANYTHING PERSONALLY: Nothing others do is because of you. What others say and do is a projection of their own reality, their own dream. When you are immune to the opinions and actions of others, you won't be the victim of needless suffering.

3. DON'T MAKE ASSUMPTIONS: Find the courage to ask questions and to express what you really want. Communicate with others as clearly as you can to avoid misunderstandings, sadness, and drama. With just this one agreement, you can completely transform your life.

4. ALWAYS DO YOUR BEST: Your best is going to change from moment to moment; it will be different when you are tired as opposed to well-rested. Under any circumstance, simply do your best, and you will avoid self-judgement, self-abuse, and regret.

If we could just truly embrace these four agreements on a daily basis, the world indeed would be a better place.

Armed with these and many other contributors to my personal philosophy, I've taken my passion for the planet, humanity, and love, and created my Aromatherapy-based business, Twenty8.

Twenty8 is a place of business, but also a place where we exemplify our gratitude towards the bounty provided by our plant world. We have created a working environment that is compatible with the harmony of nature by playing music to our oils, and bless each parcel with a divine intention that the recipient will open their hearts and minds to the power of self-love. These incredible gifts from the universe, in the form of essential oils, are drops of inner strength, well-being, transformation, and inspiration. At every step of the way, throughout our existence, we are loved by the universe mentally, physically, spiritually, and emotionally. And with every deliciously fragrant application of our oils, we are giving ourselves permission to let a little more light into our lives, and love into our hearts.

I easily get lost in the magic that is created by Mother Nature, and as a result I have embodied self-love through my love of life and essential oils for more than three decades now. And not a day goes by when I don't look to my team, my workplace, and my essential oil kit, and know that our amazing plants are the platform from which we launched our love and healing to the world. Through these gifts of nature, we are reminded that harmony and balance are always within reach for us, through the practice of self-love.

At home, my self-love rituals have been ingrained in my two incredible children, Tayla and Jakob, since they were born. As my children begin their own journey as adults, it always brings a tear to my eye to see them spritz or light a vaporiser when the world gets on top of them, or to witness their unshakable commitment to improvement and kindness, or their ability to express themselves for the purpose of un-derstanding rather than complaining. I have to admit that I am THAT mum who embarrasses their kids with pride! Jakob has been known to say, "Mum, it's OK when we're at home, but when I'm out with the boys can you just keep how much you love me on the down low?" If you're a mum and think the sun truly shines out of your kids, even when they are rat-bags, you will know that keeping the love on the 'down low' is almost impossible!

For me, learning to respect and care for myself was almost thrust upon me from when I was very young. While growing up, I faced many challenges, even though I was also blessed with a loving family home. I still knew from way back then, however, that if I was going to live a great and empowered life, love, and self-love, had to develop from deep within myself.

It was my mother who taught me that no one will look after you like you do. She always said, "Count on no-one but yourself". She embodied this, and I have always admired her grit and determination.

I share all these insights throughout the book as an example of what self- love can look like in the day to day life of an average home and most importantly, to introduce the very tool that has been the foundation of my personal philosophy through all of the highs and lows of my life.

The day when my then sixteen-year-old son, Jakob, came to me in desperation after making a silly teenage mistake and was facing possible expulsion from school, I realised that this information needed to find its way into the hands of more people.

I was in our bedroom; my husband Danny and I were just about to turn out the lights when Jakob slinked in and sat on the edge of our bed looking like he'd taken a beating. "Mum, what's wrong with me? My mum and dad are famous athletes, my sister dances in the Queensland National Ballet and what do I do? I'm just a fuck up."

Seeing the tears roll down his face and hearing my son's cry for help clicked my brain into immediate 'mum-to-the-rescue' mode. As he sobbed into his hands with a muffled recount of how the teachers at school hated him, how certain ones treated him like he was a no-hoper, and how much he now hated himself for the mistakes he had made, I reached for the journal I had been keeping and asked if he wanted to see what I had discovered when I found myself feeling as hopeless as he did right now.

I stroked my son's head as I had when he was a little boy, and I reassured him that this situation was just a small episode in the entire long series of Jakob Morrison, the riotous rat-bag and lovable larrikin. This certainly was not the whole show.

After a moment, Jakob lifted his head to see that I had drawn a heart on the page as I said, "Nothing is wrong with you Jakob, you've just fallen out of love with yourself. It happens to all of us and sometimes, when tough times strike, we feel helpless. I promise you sweetheart, that if you can embrace what I'm about to show you, you will never be at the mercy of circumstances again."

With interest, Jakob looked and listened as I escorted him through the gifts I now refer to as the self-love circle and by the end of our conversation, I witnessed my broken boy stand up, flex his manly shoulders, and take back the power he had relinquished to his mistakes, teachers, friends, and to this entire experience. Even though my son is an amazing human being, life had just temporarily gotten on top of him in the way that it sometimes does for all of us.

I felt so proud to see him regain control the instant he realised how he felt about himself. After all, the process of changing our attitude about ourselves is purely an inside job!

After about fifteen minutes of listening to me explain this entire message to him, Jakob finally said to me, "Mum, you have GOT to get this stuff out into the world. I've never heard it explained like this before. It's really good!"

I'm now committed to not just sharing the impact these tools can have on your life but also HOW you can introduce rituals, exercises, activities, contemplations, and meditations into your world, and begin to take back the control you may feel you've lost so you can thrive instead of merely surviving.

I am not talking about spending huge amounts of money, or hours upon hours taking care of yourself. I am talking about micro-moments of self-care. A three second aromatherapy spritz, a barefoot walk to the letterbox, a five minute 'Workout of the Day', turning on your essential oil diffuser, or putting on a face mask while you attend to your emails. Self-care does not mean self-indulgence—although I wouldn't say deny yourself, if you have the chance—it's about doing the small things and doing them often, and well. Call it accumulation; deposits into the well of self-love.

So, if self-love is our ultimate goal, we know that for some of us it is not just a click of our fingers and *voila*, we love ourselves. The journey of self-love involves discipline; it is a practice, an art, something that requires constant attention to being in the present moment, and being mindful of what is required, especially on those challenging, dark days, and those bathroom floor moments.

In my research over the past decade, I have noticed that for the people who practice self-love, a pattern arises out of their practice. And it is inside the groove of this pattern that these practitioners can find themselves again, and access the benefits of this practice, no matter where they are in life, or how low they may be feeling.

To embrace the art of love, there is a pattern—a six-step pattern—that I have used over and over. I have found it incredibly helpful when life is weighing me down, and I feel

I have nowhere else to turn. I use these six steps for the big challenges I have faced in life, such as death, trauma, grief, loss, and break-ups. And I use it for the everyday struggles like hurtful comments on social media, differences of opinion, and even road rage.

What I love most about this work is it is such a simple, quick, and profound way to get up, get through it, and get on. It's not about hiding feelings or burying them, it's about honouring how you truly feel. It's not about avoiding pain, but rather working through it with care. It's not about pretending life is grand, it's acknowledging that sometimes it's just plain hard, but you will survive. And most of all, it's about knowing that there is a way to navigate through all the difficulties.

There are six basic steps to self-love, three of which are about *doing* the work required and the remaining three are about *being* the work. If life ever brings you to your knees in a big way, or challenges you in a small way, you can use the same framework. It's a simple process.

In summary, this journey is to build a relationship with your own self, and the magic of the journey is its ease! When you begin to feel heavy, out of flow, resentful, or rejected, you're out of the self-love circle. But the minute you acknowledge you're out of the circle and become self-aware, you're immediately back in the circle and from there, you can move to the next step of self-care, and with self-discipline you will see you have more self-control which leads to greater self-respect and the ultimate self-accep-tance. Do the work in the first three steps and the rest will just fall into place.

This is your invitation to the restorative power of self-love.

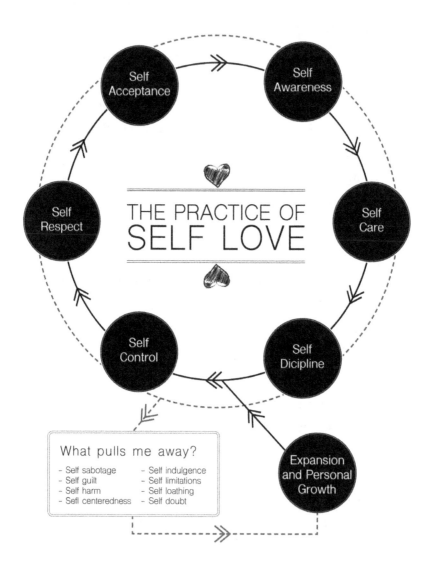

THE PRACTICE OF
SELF LOVE

Self Acceptance

Self Awareness

Self Care

Self Dicipline

Self Control

Self Respect

Expansion and Personal Growth

What pulls me away?

- Self sabotage
- Self guilt
- Self harm
- Sefl centeredness

- Self indulgence
- Self limitations
- Self loathing
- Self doubt

HOW TO USE THIS BOOK

This book is interactive and provides you with online downloads, PDFs, recipes, questionnaires, and meditations. At the end of each chapter, you'll find a list of essential oils that you can introduce to your daily rituals to support the changes you might like to focus on. If you feel a little overwhelmed by the list of oils I've outlined, don't worry. You can effortlessly select any one of the oils from the list and use it to 'anchor' your emotional states. These anchors, which are just like 'reminders', keep you on track and help you to prioritise self-love when you're in the midst of challenges that feel overwhelming.

How essential oils will help in the art of self-love.

If you are new to aromatherapy, as the word implies, it can be summed simply as a therapy using 'aromas'. As a general statement this means aromas which are highly concentrated, pure potent, plant extracts also known as essential oils are said to have been used for thousands of years medicinally, therapeutically and spiritually.

Salvatore Battaglia, author of The *Complete Guide to Aromatherapy*, and honorary member of the International Federation of Aromatherapists (IFA), says aromatherapy is hard to define. It has been stated as a branch of phytomedicine that uses essential oils as its principal therapeutic tools. He says the term has also been abused, for example, skin and hair care products, often promise to introduce the user to benefits of aromatherapy. The fact that these products contain essential oils does not mean they will have the efficacy of essential oils used by a professional aromatherapist. Another definition of aromatherapy is the use of pure essential oils to seek influence, to change, or modify, mind, body, or spirit; physiology, or mood. Robert Tisserand, one of the world's leading experts in aromatherapy, lists five fields in which aromatherapy is practiced: medical, nursing, holistic, psychotherapeutic, and aesthetic.

The National Association for Holistic Aromatherapy (NAHA) defines aromatherapy as, 'The therapeutic application or the medicinal use of aromatic substances (essential oils) for holistic healing'.

Whatever level you are, from novice to experienced, it is important to understand the complexity of essential oils, and this book is a guide to using oils in an everyday way for the benefit of self-care.

Many books have been written on this topic, some more reliable than others, and there are some that now delve into the science and evidence-based research available. It must be noted that it is still quite difficult to obtain scientific evidence on the effectiveness of all essential oils, and as far as hard data is concerned, aromatherapy could still be considered in its infancy.

It is thanks to many teachers, practitioners, and medical experts that more research on essential oils, and their health benefits, is being carried out. While this research gains momentum in the scientific community, we can refer to the great volume of anecdotes supporting the benefits of aromatherapy, dating back centuries and across many different cultures.

As someone who has been a therapist for almost three decades, and has used essential oils daily, I cannot underestimate their power. Even if you were to use them just because you loved their smell, or they have more of a placebo effect, I would still encourage you to use them.

In this book I share with you what I have learned and found helpful to me. My purpose here is to share my knowledge, not only as an aromatherapist, but as a mum and a busy woman.

There are a many amazing teachers and authors I look up to including Robert Tisserand, Salvatore Battaglia, Shirley Price, Daniel Penoel, Kurt Schnaubelt, Dr Eric Zielenski, Pat Princi-Jones, Robbi Zeck, Megan Larsen, Jennifer Jeffries, Liz Fulcher, Farida Irani, Valerie Ann Worwood, Sabrina Zielenski, Vanessa Megan Gray, Patricia Davis and Bo Hengden. I look to these people and many more for guidance and knowledge, which in turn helps me to share my passion of these precious substances.

I will often refer to essential oils as 'aromatic anchors', as we know smells can link or anchor us directly to certain feelings, moods, memories, experiences, or situations. Essential oils are known to support healing, balancing, and overall well-being. They come from a vast array of plants extracted from Mother Nature's extraordinary medicine cabinet. As mentioned previously, their use dates back thousands of years. Their potency can be up to one hundred times more concentrated than the plant or source they come from.

According to world leading aromatherapist Shirley Price, essential oils are known to be active; they gain access to cells by being fat soluble and are metabolized by the body. They can be applied to the skin, ingested or inhaled, and all are harmless unless used incorrectly. Essential oils have multiple actions and effects. For example, some may be antiseptic and anti-inflammatory; they can support the immune system and can be considered as pro- and eubiotic, as opposed to synthetic antibiotics.

I am particularly fond of the traditional ancient wisdom handed down from generation to generation. I love to understand the science, but I also love to appreciate their incredible, unexplainable magic. They are a wonderful connector to Mother Nature herself.

We are often told to get outdoors to recharge, reconnect, and heal ourselves. A walk in the park, going barefoot on the beach, or swimming in the river or ocean can do wonders for the mind, body, and soul. In a busy world where we are time-poor, aromatherapy is one of the best ways to bring nature directly to us. Not only can essential oils support our physical wellbeing, with oils like eucalyptus and tea tree useful for the common cold, and lavender and orange for insomnia, it can also rejuvenate the spirit with oils that can calm and soothe like chamomile and patchouli, or energise and uplift the mind, like frankincense and orange.

As mentioned, high quality essential oils are all antiseptic and antibacterial to a degree. They are also highly concentrated, volatile substances that need to be used with care. Unfortunately, approximately seventy per cent of the aromatherapy industry is adulterated, so it is important that you purchase your oils from a qualified source.

The tips given in this book are based on everyday concerns and ailments and are no way seen as a replacement for traditional medical and psychological advice. I would err on the side of caution if well-meaning oil lovers start telling you to take oils internally. Personally, that advice should only come from a qualified and professional therapist who understands your history, the biochemical reactions that occur in the human body, and the complex structure of essential oils.

Having said that, there are so many ways you can use essential oils in a fun, easy, and highly effective way. My advice always is, less is best. You do not need many drops to make a difference. Make sure you do your own research on the individual oils, and as you experiment more, learn to trust your intuition and nose. For the journey of self-love and self-care, starting with three oils is perfect. Remember, they are the tools for you to practice the art of self-care, so let's just understand how that might work for you.

When I suggest oils within each chapter that could help with certain conditions, you can choose any three oils to make a blend. One way of making a blend is to choose one of each of these three aromatic categories

1. Woody

2. Floral, herbal, or spicy

3. Citrus oil

For example, blended together could help calm the mind, balance the body, and help clear negative thinking.

Essential oils work in two ways. Firstly, when we inhale a high-quality, complex, organic essential oil, the chemical constituents of that oil travel up the olfactory system and into the limbic part of the brain, which is the centre for emotions, memory and sexual arousal. This often explains why they have such a profound effect on the way we think and feel, and a change can often occur within seconds.

Secondly, when an essential oil dilution is applied to the skin, because of their solubility in the fats found in the stratum corneum (the outer most layer of the skin) lipophilic substances like essential oils are easily absorbed. Once the minute molecules have passed the epidermis and enter the dermis, which houses blood vessels, nerves, sweat and oil glands, lymph, and elastin, they are carried away in the bloodstream and throughout the body. They can help stimulate the immune system, support the circulatory and lymphatic systems and can help promote healing and detoxification. Each essential oil has its own characteristics and qualities, and no two oils are the same. This makes it a remarkable therapy for combining a number of essential oils together, creating what we call a synergy blend. Three oils in a blend is a great starting point.

As you read the suggested oils at the end of each chapter, you will note the physical conditions related to that oil. If any of these physical conditions are present in your body, take note as there could indeed be an emotional correlation that you can also work on.

You can easily experience these messages by reading this book from cover to cover, however, as you become more familiar with the self-love circle you can dive straight into sections based on what is going on for you in your world and find comfort and clarity in a more spontaneous way. Whichever way you devour these words, I encourage you to look deep inside yourself and be willing to try something new. You may have already heard some of the suggestions in this book, while others may be a surprise.

If you are struggling in life, and want to improve where you are right now, or simply generate more love in your life, perhaps promise yourself that you will try the suggestions in each chapter and if they don't benefit you, leave them aside. If they do work, you can look forward, your heart resonating, your spirits lifting, and your mind waking up to new possibilities and vitality.

I'm excited to share this self-love journey using essential oils with you. We will all encounter adversities, challenges, or troubles at some point in our lives. Not one of us will escape tough times. This is not a book suggesting those tough times will never happen again or advising how to avoid them. It is a guide, a pathway to help navigate the shaky ground we sometimes find ourselves on, and know that with awareness, self-care and self-discipline at the forefront, we can get through anything. It does not matter what your age is, or where you are in life right now, the self-love circle is a tool you can incorporate at any time.

I have created an interactive quiz for you here that will help you to see where you're currently situated in the self-love circle. Through the results of this quiz, you will immediately see the triggers that cause you to fall out of love with yourself. Jump on in and take the quiz online at www.twenty8.com/selflovequiz now and get ready for an eye-opener.

Chapter 1:

WHY WE FALL OUT OF LOVE WITH OURSELVES

Ok, before we jump into loving ourselves, we need to go back to the part where we fell out of love in the first place. The following section in this book is designed to outline the common sabotaging behaviours that often show up when we feel that the love and happiness is missing. These are the times in life when everything appears to go wrong.

Life can be going smoothly, you feel content… and then the next minute…. wham, bam, there you are…. on your knees wondering what freight train just ran you down. You didn't see it coming, you were unprepared, and suddenly you are unsure how to react, cope, or move forward. You could be having one of my 'bathroom moments'.

I think we all accept that life is going to throw us curve-balls. Our subconscious beliefs, along with challenging situations, or our relationships with other people are going to put our strongest will to the test from time to time, as are unfulfilled dreams, disappointments, challenges, health concerns, loss, and tragedy.

Over the years, there have been many self-help strategies offered out there and yes, I've read a lot of them, especially when confronted with one of those 'bathroom moments' mentioned earlier. This book however, I would like to think, is different. We are not only focusing on WHAT happens in life and WHY you feel the way you do, we are unveiling the illusive HOW to reconcile, resolve, reason, and heal.

In my explorations, I've found it's the step-by-step HOW TO that I have craved, which is maybe why, collectively, we keep consuming more and more information without achieving the results we're all searching for. We don't have to look too far to see how the people around us, including ourselves, are struggling through some aspects of life, feeling helpless, and sometimes hopeless.

I know it's impossible to wish for everyone to be happy all the time. I also know that in order to appreciate happiness we need to understand and maybe even experience its opposing force. After all, how can we understand light without knowing dark? How can we appreciate high if we do not understand low?

The reality is, every single person I have ever met or known has experienced some form of hardship, suffering, or challenge. In fact, in a weird kind of way, it seems that suffering is an important—maybe even essential—part of being happy. After all, it is often through our greatest discomforts that change and growth occurs; that we are most vulnerable and have a stronger sense of empathy for self and others. We may not feel so good about this when we are experiencing heartache or faced with a challenge, but in hindsight we realise these challenges have made us into the person we are today. For many, they have helped shape their direction in life with even stronger meaning and purpose.

I was driving down the highway with my then ninety-one-year-old grandmother. She would often say to me, "Penny for your thoughts" when we were together. She must have picked up on my internal dialogue and the thoughts that were battling around in my mind. I was in a dilemma and told her I didn't think I should tell her. She reminded me that a problem shared is a problem halved. I proceeded to tell her quietly, so that my young children in the back seat could not hear me clearly, as it was quite disturbing.

"Grandma, I have these terrible thoughts that I am going to have a head-on collision when I'm driving. I keep feeling how hideous it would be. Since reading a book called *The Secret* by Rhonda Byrne, I now worry myself sick thinking about the laws of attraction. That what you think, you attract. I cannot get that out of my head. What if I attract this and make it happen?"

My grandmother lovingly put her hand on mine. "Oh dear," she said. "That's terrible." She empathised and continued to tell me something I have never forgotten. "Sweetheart, when you have thoughts like this, does it occur to you that your angels are talking to you?"

"Well no, it hadn't, and if it had, why would they be saying things that were so disturbing?"

Grandma continued, "When you have a terrible thought like a head-on accident, it's just your angels reminding you to drive more carefully." I confided that I had not thought about it like that. Grandma believed that we would only pay attention when thoughts were uncomfortable.

"If you are worried about your children, it's your angels reminding you to take a breath and send out a loving white light, and visualise them being protected. If you sense a frightening scenario that you might fall or hurt yourself, it is a message to pay more attention to what you are doing. If you are worried what someone thinks about you, it's a sign to send out a white light and love all around them. If you ever feel like you have no control over a certain outcome and are worried about what may be, it's a reminder to surrender, hand it over, be present and mindful to what is going on right now."

Gosh, this one thought process, and understanding a way to handle negative thoughts, has helped me with hard times and challenges. It has helped me stay in the circle of self-love, or at least get back into it when I fall out.

I have often questioned why we must suffer or have negative thoughts or bad experiences.

According to Clifford Nass, a professor at Stanford University, there is sound reason. "There is a general tendency for everyone to zero-in on negative experiences, more than positive. Some people do have a more positive outlook, but almost everyone remembers negative things more strongly and in more detail." There are physiological as well as psychological reasons for this.

"The brain handles positive and negative information in different hemispheres," said Professor Nass, who co-authored the book, *The Man Who Lied to His Laptop: What Machines Teach Us About Human Relationships*. "Negative emotions generally involve more thinking, and the information is processed more thoroughly than positive ones," he said. "Thus, we tend to ruminate more about unpleasant events—and use stronger words to describe them—than happy ones. Bad emotions, bad parents, and bad feedback have more impact than good ones."

Well, no wonder we have bad thoughts then, or angels coming to visit as Grandma would say. We pay more attention to those thoughts than positive ones. It's natural, after all. It's normal, and what's more, maybe it's nature's way to keep us in check with our own sense of self when times are challenging or tough.

But here's the thing, if we know that suffering and hurt, trials, and challenges are all part of the human experience, what is it that causes us to fall out of love with ourselves? And worse than that, stay out of love?

I remember when Danny and I were in the middle of our heartache. I remember sitting with him at our counsellor's office. I could hardly breathe let alone talk. I was broken. I was not sure I would ever feel normal again. Our counsellor looked at us both.

"Your marriage will never be the same," she said. "But if you work on yourself (as she pointed to Danny), and you work on yourself (as she pointed to me), then your marriage could be better than it ever was." When I pleaded with her, "But what about our children?" she told us it was not our job to hide our pains from our children, or lie, or pretend. It was our job to show our children how to get through tough times.

So, before we head into how to get through tough times, let's see what behaviours hold us back and keep a strong hold of us outside the circle of love, all of which can come under the heading of self- sabotage.

~ Self-Sabotage

"Self-sabotage is when we say we want something
and then go about making sure it doesn't happen."
– Alyce P. Cornyn-Selby.

All of my school life, I can remember dreaming of playing netball and representing New Zealand. I had pictures on my wall of the girls that were selected every year, and I used to go to bed at night with the most excited feeling deep in my soul that I would one day be up there just like them. I had been selected to play in the state Auckland Under 16 side in 1984 and was selected to play in the Under 18 team in 1985, which was so exciting, I knew I was destined to rise further up through the ranks.

I was thrilled when selected. Inside I secretly knew I was always going to be a part of the team because I felt deep down I had the skill and the ability to really make a career out of this sport. I knew I could go a long way and I loved it. Night after night, day after day, I dreamed about the game, where I could improve, how I could train harder each week, and it occupied my every waking thought. It was a passion, and I was willing to work harder and faster than anyone I knew. I truly believed that anyone who worked that hard, and with that much commitment, was bound to have their dreams come to true.

We trained hard during that 1985 season, we started bonding as a team through the pre-season build up. After we'd played our first few competition games, I remember walking off the court one sunny winter's morning feeling completely spent, yet so incredibly proud of the effort I'd given to our winning game. We all congratulated each other, hugged, and shook hands with the other team, then I walked over to the side of the courts to grab my towel and water bottle. All the other girls were chatting on the court when I overheard our coaches talking on the side-line.

I hadn't noticed that I was the only 'white' girl on the team up until that point. As I bent down to wipe my forehead I heard the manager say "She's just not one of the girls. She's a 'honky'". 'Honky' is often a word used to describe white people.

I was shocked and didn't know how to interpret what I had just heard. It felt like a hot knife in my gut, and at the same time I was confused, lost, and bewildered. *What were they saying? Were they talking about me? Was it because I wasn't a good player? Why else would they be talking about me? It must be me... I am the only white girl, I must be hopeless. Oh, my goodness, have I been kidding myself all this time?*

These thoughts raced through my mind at a rate of knots and I didn't know what to do with them or how to begin even making sense of what I had just heard.

As it turns out, when I stopped to notice, the team I had been selected for were all strong, tall, and powerful women who had come from either Pacific Islander or Maori descent. When I took a closer look at the differences between them and me, not only was I the shortest, I was the whitest, and the wiriest of the team. Those differences had never even occurred to me until that day, when I heard what sounded like disappointment in my manager's voice.

I didn't hang around to hear the rest of that conversation. I walked off feeling like I had lost my entire life—my dream—right there. If they didn't believe in me, why was I bothering to believe in me? I felt like I must be the worst player on the team and I had no chance of ever fulfilling what I had been dreaming of. I mean, these guys were the experts and maybe I *had* just been kidding myself all along.

The next game we played, I had completely lost my confidence. Then the next game, and the next game. I could feel inside of myself that the wind had been knocked out of my sails, but no matter how hard I tried, I just couldn't bring myself back to playing a great game. Maybe I was trying too hard? As much as I loved to play, from that moment on I felt like I was second rate and didn't measure up to the standards of the rest of the team. I'd almost psyched myself out of a good game before we got on the court, thinking there was no way I was going help my team mates win. I felt like I was more of a hindrance to the team than a help. To be honest, I was devastated to say the least. My position in the team remained unworthy, in fact, I hardly had court time from then on. I felt like I had proven them all right.

The following year, surprisingly, I was selected to trial for the Auckland Under 21s and as suspected, I was cut from the team in the final trial. I was gutted as you can imagine, and, in my mind, I blamed myself for being white. I knew that it had sown a seed in my mind that I just couldn't shake, and from that one comment in the previous year, my dream to be a top netballer felt destroyed.

Pretty soon after that I gave up on my dream of ever playing netball seriously, and just accepted that I would play for the fun of it without ever expecting myself to be any good. In the end, I played the game right up until I was forty years of age, but never again felt the same euphoria or the rush that I used to get, thinking about the possibility of life as an elite athlete.

Of course, I enjoyed playing for fun and who knows, maybe all things work out for a reason, given that I went on to run a twenty-four-hour marathon instead, and set a world record! Maybe I would never have made it, after all, so many don't. Who knows? One thing I'm absolutely sure of, is that a comment from someone I looked up to created, in my mind, a self-sabotaging thought cycle that cost me a dream and also the potential reality of representing my country. If nothing else it cost me the energy to pursue my goal, and my personal self-worth.

Sometimes you know you are in full self-sabotage mode; you can sense old, familiar patterns creeping up and taking over, and it feels like Groundhog Day, only you have no control over it. You want so badly to create your dream outcome or to bring your vision to life on one hand, but on the other, it's as if you're working against yourself and you can't stop it!

Other times, you're oblivious as to why your attempts at success are not working, and you feel frustrated at best, apathetic at worst. You try harder, switch directions, move the goal posts, or seek independent counsel, and no matter what you do, nothing changes the outcome.

It's not your fault; it's been your subconscious mind having its way with you, trying to protect you from threats, and unfortunately, in doing that, working against all the incredible desire and effort.

It's funny, actually, as I write this last statement. I'm sitting, scratching my head thinking, *Why on earth would anyone want to work against themselves?* It seems bizarre, doesn't it?

The thing we've been inspired to do, or have a desire to create, is being hijacked by the greatest mystery of human kind; our very own mind! We are sabotaging our success with hurtful behaviours.

It seems we are not alone. Most us are doing the same thing to ourselves with everything from making money, finding love, being healthy, to raising kids.

As we explore the nature of self-sabotage, we discover it's not just mental; it's physical too. It's not until we bring our awareness to what is actually going on inside that we stand even the slightest chance of healing, so let's take a look at what self-sabotage is all about.

Self-sabotage is a cycle of negative beliefs about ourselves that sneak up on us without us even knowing they are coming, and inevitably, they cripple the outcomes for goals that we are attempting to create or achieve. Interestingly, self-sabotage enlists our emotions, thoughts, habits, and our motivation. Often it will kick in when we feel like something is challenging our beliefs about our ability or capability to do what it is we would like.

> *Behaviour is said to be self-sabotaging when it*
> *creates problems and interferes with long-stand-*
> *ing goals. The most common self-sabotaging*
> *behaviours are procrastination, self-medication with*
> *drugs or alcohol, comfort eating, and forms*
> *of self-injury such as cutting. These acts may seem*
> *helpful or provide relief in the moment, but they*
> *ultimately undermine us, especially when we engage*
> *in them repeatedly.*
> www.psychologytoday.com

This description of self-sabotage highlights that these behaviours are largely subconscious, which leads us to question, where did these come from? How did they originate?

Try thinking back to your childhood and how you felt about yourself. From your own perspective, how did your family feel about you? What did your friends, teachers and employers feel about you? Each of these is a contributing factor to how you feel about yourself today. Like it or not, we are a product of both nature and nurture.

Psychologists also suggest that we begin to form our 'identity' (who we think we are) at a very young age and when circumstances push up against the boundaries of our identity, the subconscious mind will try to halt the threatening situation (through self-sabotage) just to make sure the status quo is maintained and in its innocent lack of wisdom, it believes it is keeping us safe by maintaining the identity we've established for ourselves since childhood.

Self-sabotage is a huge threat to our ability to maintain self-love and throws us off course instantly as we blame, shame, and judge ourselves, while our inner dialogue becomes a toxic waste dump of negativity, chastising us for everything we've done wrong, or failed to achieve.

As a mum, I've explored the triggers in myself and with my kids, and I've discovered some surprising beliefs that lurk beneath the surface, but are covered up by inauthentic behaviours, simply because we are just too scared to share our vulnerability. I have compared my mothering skills to other mums. Whether it was about sleeping routines, food choices, or disciplinary measures, there were times I was judged—sometimes quite harshly-with comments or actions, which just reinforced a belief that I was simply not good enough.

As you read of my own journey, self-sabotage definitely had an effect on me. Those negative thoughts and beliefs lay quite dormant within me for many years. Whenever something didn't go the way I dreamed or believed, I lost confidence, assuming once again that I wasn't 'good enough'. It wasn't until I discovered the gifts of the self-love circle during the past decade that I was able to look at my beliefs and recognise where they originated from, and how they were hindering my success, my netball dream falling apart, for instance. Maybe even how it has sabotaged other goals.

Armed with this new knowledge, and a little willingness and attention, I was able to forgive what I presumed that manager said, and forgive myself for allowing what could have been an innocent and benign comment to sabotage my dreams.

As a mum, I aim to set an example for my kids every step of the way. At some point, I had to decide to stop carrying silly beliefs around with me and allow myself to thrive. To allow a self-sabotaging belief to live inside me for so long had not served me in the best way, and the sooner I could let go of a sad, maybe even ridiculous memory, the better I would feel, and the better I could teach my kids how to build resilience in the face of their own self-sabotage or unrealised dreams.

I knew that my own self-mastery in shedding limiting beliefs was a crucial step in my ability to empower my kids and allow them to bring their biggest dreams to fruition. Both of my children have big dreams and yet already Tayla has had some setbacks in her dancing career due to injury. Without her resilience and refusing to take on sabotaging thought systems, she could be at risk of missing opportunities, resources, or appreciating the beautiful gifts she was born with, and that is just not okay. I have had to teach my children that no matter what life throws your way, you can rise above and beyond it if you choose to, in favour of being your absolute best.

Having shared my story, let me assert that you don't have to be a mum to understand self-sabotage. This can affect people of all ages, and in different phases of life. I honestly believe that we've all sabotaged ourselves at some time in our lives, and unless we look back and analyse how and why we've done this to ourselves, as well as what it has cost us, we may not be able to truly heal the hurt or end subconscious patterns of behaviour that created the sabotage in the first place.

So, to give you a start, let's explore how you can recognise when self-sabotage has a grip on your hopes and dreams. As you explore this list, never fear; all self-sabotaging behaviours are learned. Contrary to how it feels sometimes, you are NOT born with them, which is great news. Anything that has been learned can be unlearned, and our behaviours modified. It's important to first identify the feelings, beliefs, and actions that trigger self-sabotaging behaviour. Once we establish these triggers, and with the benefit of clarity, we will use the self-love circle to reconcile them and quickly kick those suckers to the kerb!

1. You will find yourself procrastinating to avoid a big project or task. This is number one on the list for a reason! It is the gap between what you intend to do, and what you actually do!

2. You're easily distracted by everything OTHER than the thing you should be doing.

3. You feel guilty because you're not paying proper attention to what you've promised yourself you will do.

4. You judge yourself harshly for not achieving what you'd set out to do.

5. You judge or blame others for what they could or should have been doing to support you.

6. You notice that you're belittling yourself in your thoughts and striking out at your self-worth and self-esteem.

7. You avoid people or places that could question your actions.

8. You may find yourself turning to food, drugs, sex, shopping, alcohol or self-harm for comfort and to make yourself feel better after you've given yourself an emotional beating for what you have done.

9. You may find yourself 'catastrophising' the situation and thinking, *Poor me, why me?*

10. You may become upset about being upset (the double-whammy). "I hate feeling this upset about my relationship".

11. You look for the easy way out or the path of least resistance.

12. When you take a good look, you will recognise that your actions are not consistent with your goals.

13. You may lose confidence in your ability to make the right decisions.

14. You are excessively seeking reassurance and acceptance from others and as it drives people away, your self-doubt is exaggerated.

15. You constantly put off tomorrow what you can do today.

Self-sabotage denies possibility. Whilst it clearly plays a role in our lives—remember, we have to understand dark before we can appreciate light—it can rob us of life itself if we let it control us for too long.

I remember hearing my beautiful friend Carren Smith tell her story for the first time. Carren was a survivor of the Bali bombing terrorist attack in 2002. She lost her two best friends in that incident, after losing her fiancé a year earlier to suicide. Carren was in a world of pain, and that pain—which she blamed herself for—caused her to suffer from depression for six years. If you ever want to read an incredible story, her book, *Soul Survivor*, is one of the best. What Carren describes took her six years to come to grips with. Now, if she finds herself in a whirlwind of pain or challenge or self-sabotaging behaviour, it can take her just six minutes to navigate her way through that behavior and find her way back to self-love. It is only after years of studying, researching, and exploring the human psyche that she now openly shares how harbouring self-sabotaging thoughts caused her to believe that her fiancés death, and the deaths of her friends, were all her fault. As she tells her story, she asks her audiences, "Do you think it was all my fault?" And, of course, her audience always says no. But she says she lived in that belief for six whole years and it didn't matter what anyone would say or how they would try and comfort her, she stayed committed to her belief.

Thanks to her partner finally snapping one day and saying she was doing this to herself, she was forced to wake up and begin working on her healing. Her dad helped her further with this beautiful story from her book, *Soul Survivor*. He lovingly refers to her as 'Boofy'.

'*Think of the humble caterpillar,*' he started. '*The caterpillar doesn't go around questioning what his purpose is or why he's here. He just does what he does and goes about life as a caterpillar. Then one day, instinct tells him to spin his cocoon – so he just does it. He doesn't question why he has to spin a cocoon or get all depressed about it, he just does it because that is the way life is for him. Now think of what is about to happen to that caterpillar. He is about to be trapped, tied up, and squashed in that cocoon where he will be miserable for months. Now Boofy, it feels like that for you right now, Daddy knows!*' he exclaimed. '*It's horrible and you're going through a horrible time, just horrible. In fact, I'm in awe of how you're coping with it all, I really am,*' he continued. '*After a little while, the caterpillar has gone through his change, his terrible time, and his transformation. But you know what, it's still not over yet, not even close! Now, he has the fight of his life on his hands. He has to break through that cocoon, and do it quick, otherwise he will die. No one can help him, no one can do it for him. Nature just has to stand by and watch. Then, if he has enough strength, stamina, and guts, he bursts out of the cocoon as the most beautiful butterfly, and within seconds, life takes on a whole new perspective for him as he catches the breeze under his new and very strong wings.*'

Recognising what a powerful analogy my dad had just given me, I still had one burning question, 'Yeah, that's all very *well father, but the butterfly dies three days later! So, what's the point of all of that?'*

Laughing, Dad said, 'Boofy, you've missed the point. Isn't it far better to have experienced the beauty of the butterfly, even if it is just for three days, than to never have experienced it at all?' With that, we both chuckled, and I promised to give it more thought and explore how I could become the butterfly he knew I could be.

She lovingly reminds us to not let a self-sabotaging belief like guilt rule your life for as long as she did. In her powerful talks, Carren reminds us that she took one for the team, and to let her story be a reminder that you do not need a bomb to go off for you to wake up and get living.

In our beautiful, self-love circle, you will see that by following the steps, no matter what life throws at you, and no matter how hard you feel spat out of that circle, you can always get back in. I am not saying that by following these six steps that you will never have a bad or self-sabotaging thought again, or that life will be joyous forever more. What I am saying is, this could give you the framework, be a guide and a tool to support you when you are not coping. It could become the tool you use to help you feel, heal, and quickly move on from.

Self-sabotaging behaviours can include: Guilt, self-loathing, self-doubt, self-judgement, limiting self-beliefs, negativity, and drama. If you are questioning any of these within yourself, we will be taking a closer look at these in the next chapter.

Remember, I have not met anyone yet who does not do this in some shape or form so if you have any suspicion that you too are a self-saboteur in any way, type this URL into your browser and watch my Master Class on self-sabotage. It may just help fast track your understanding.

LINK: www.twenty8.com/selfsabotagemasterclass

Essential Oils for Self-Sabotage:

If ever you are not in a good space, if you are sabotaging your life and letting it consume you, there are some wonderful essential oils that can support you. In the chapter on Self-Care on page 159 you will find the best ways on how to use these remarkable oils.

Grapefruit Oil: Call on this oil with euphoric properties when you're feeling tense, overwhelmed, under pressure, defeated, depressed, weary, or frustrated. Enjoy the feelings of focus, clarity, joy, positivity, trust, and strength, as you're gently uplifted by the delightful citrus scent.

Application: Compress, inhale, massage, or spritz this zesty, uplifting, and revitalising oil.

May Also Benefit: Oily, congested skin, acne, weight loss, cellulite, muscle aches and pains, headaches, insomnia, and muscle tension.

Lemon Oil: This fresh and stimulating oil is an instant pick-me-up, leaving you with energy and mental clarity. You'll feel less confused, defeated, disheartened, exhausted, weary, and worried.

Application: Massage, compress, diffuse or spritz. This oil makes a refreshing addition to your bath, opening the heart, alleviating exhaustion, and creating self-confidence.

May Also Benefit: Anti-aging, nausea, cellulite, weight loss, oedema, varicose veins, warts, colds, flu, immune support, and a liver tonic.

Note: Avoid exposure to the sun after using lemon in a massage or bath as it is phototoxic (will cause a sunburn-like skin condition when exposed to sunlight).

Oregano Oil: A beautifully purifying oil that warms to the skin during massage. Feelings of frustration, hopelessness, lethargy, impatience, negativity, procrastination and rigidity will be replaced with clarity, openness, protection, safety, and strength.

Application: Massage, compress, inhale, and spritz this warm and stimulating oil.

May Also Benefit: Staving off colds, flus and sore throats, digestion issues, urinary tract infections, asthma, bronchitis, and bacterial and fungal conditions.

Peppermint Oil: This fresh, minty oil is both warming and cooling at the same time! A perfect remedy for chaos, confusion, depression, fatigue, procrastination, and forgetfulness. Instead, experience being alert, clear, connected, enthusiastic, motivated, and vital.

Application: Inhale, massage, compress, massage, vaporise, or spritz.

May Also Benefit: Indigestion, flatulence, colds, flus, coughs, fever, headaches, nausea, muscle aches and pains, asthma, bronchitis, and sinusitis.

Note: Be careful with topical application if you have hyper-sensitive skin, and within twenty minutes of taking any homeopathic remedies.

Pine Oil: This cleansing, refreshing, and invigorating oil can have the same effect as if you were standing in a pine forest. A fabulous oil for clearing the air, improving alertness, and increasing inspiration.

Application: Inhale, vaporise, bathe, spritz, and compress this motivating and intuition-enhancing oil.

May Also Benefit: Coughs, colds, flu, asthma, cystitis, pyelitis, inflammation, muscle aches and pains, headaches, arthritis, rheumatic pain, and liver detoxification.

Rosemary Oil: Known to have a very stimulating effect on the mind, a cleansing effect on the emotions, and is renowned for being the oil for memory. This energising oil improves mental clarity, focus and intuition while calming exhaustion, mental fatigue, neglect, procrastination, and feeling overwhelmed.

Application: Enjoy this delightful oil in a bath, compress, diffuser, spritzer, or massage.

May Also Benefit: Liver detoxification, weight loss, cellulite, muscle aches or pains, respiratory conditions, sinusitis, heart palpitations, circulation, and hair growth.

Note: Be careful with topical application during first trimester of pregnancy as the high level of camphor may be neurotoxic.

Rosewood Oil: Uplifting and enlivening, this oil is wonderful for meditation and can help restore emotional balance and enhance spiritual healing. Trade your depression, insecurity, procrastination and moodiness for balance, confidence, courage, energy, peace, and joy.

Application: Massage, diffuse, inhale, compress, bathe, or spritz this regenerating and balancing oil.

May Also Benefit: Acne, dermatitis, sensitive skin, dry mature skin, bronchitis, respiratory conditions, headaches, nausea, and inflammation.

Wintergreen Oil: The sweet and minty scent of Wintergreen is a powerful antidote to stressed muscles and head tension. Replace feelings of hurt, negativity, procrastination, and rigidity, with energy, endurance, motivation, positivity, relaxation, and heal those deep-down emotional wounds. As an added bonus, this oil has the ability to act as a natural pain reliever! It is also antiseptic, anti-arthritic, and an astringent.

Application: Massage, compress, diffuse, spritz, and bathe in this relieving and warming oil.

May Also Benefit: Colds, flu, muscle aches and pains, digestion issues, inflammation, bacterial, and fungal conditions.

Note: Avoid topical application during pregnancy due to the high levels of methyl salicylate, which may cause dermatitis. Always use diluted as the methyl salicylate content can cause other skin sensitivities, too.

~ Guilt

'Guilt is always hungry, don't let it consume you.'
- Terri Guillemets

I remember when I was younger, I used to get frustrated I had a curfew when it came to going out. I was a typical teenager who didn't like being told she couldn't do something. It's not like I was a huge party girl, after all, I loved sport, and netball was my life, but I still craved the freedom all young people want. One weekend, I begged my mum to let me go to a party out in West Auckland, up in the Waitakere Ranges; the hills. It was quite far from home. Remember, we did not have mobile phones in those days.

My mum was the immovable object though, and no matter how hard I tried to manipulate the situation in my favour, her commitment was clearly about looking after me, and my welfare: Not that I thought that at the time. No, at the time I thought her commitment was to hold me back! I was frustrated, disappointed, even angry with her, but there was a perspective I was not seeing, because I was only looking through the eyes of an inexperienced teenager.

In the end, I'm not quite sure what I said, but I was given permission to go to the party, but I had to be home by midnight. My friend Tony, who was twenty-one and working, had a company car. There were five of us and we all piled in. It was going to be an amazing night, and it certainly started out that way. That is, until the drugs started being shared, alcohol was flowing, and I realised by 10pm that all I wanted to do was get home.

Finally, I convinced Tony and my other friends to leave. It was 11.30pm and already I knew I was going to be late home, given it was a fifty-minute drive. I was already in trouble. Tony had been drinking so I insisted I drove, but he would not let me. Stupidly, we all got into the car.

As we descended the Waitakere Ranges my heart was in my mouth as Tony was driving erratically. I wanted to get out, but before I knew it the back of the car clipped the rock face on the opposite side of the road. Suddenly, we ricocheted, bounced, and the car started sliding down a sideways slope until it came to an abrupt stop. A tree branch lodged right through the front passenger window, almost taking out both the passenger and Tony's head. My two girlfriends and I were piled on top of one another (unbuckled, I might add) in the backseat. The engine had stopped and all I heard were the wheels still turning outside the vehicle.

We all climbed rather hazily out of the upside-down car, through the driver's door and back right passenger door. Crawling up the slope, the five of us finally made it up to the road. We looked down through the darkness, where the car was just visible, and saw that our car was hanging precariously on the side of a fifty-metre cliff face. Shocked realisation washed over us: The tree branch that had almost decapitated the two front-seat passengers had actually saved our lives.

We searched for a house with a light on and asked the occupants if we could call a tow truck. I also asked if I could call my mum. When I finally got her on the line, I told her what had happened—playing it down, of course—and that I was going to be late. She was worried and angry in the same breath. I knew I was in big trouble. And I felt so goddamned guilty.

By the time the tow trucks arrived we were all quiet and in shock. We could have all died. It was that obvious. No one was speaking.

I would not call myself a religious person, but in that moment, I believed in God. My mum worked three jobs to raise us. I would like to say I was her right-hand person. The reality of her protection of me struck with incredible force, not only that she really needed me, and relied on me to help out (being the eldest of three), but also the devastation that could have been.

Later, when I was finally able to put the puzzle pieces together, I felt so guilty that I could have ever been so selfish, frustrated, and rude. During those years, guilt and I built a close companionship as both my mother and I used it as a weapon to keep me in check. The feeling of self-guilt, fuelled by frustration, would reach into the pit of my stomach, and render me completely powerless at times. I realise I have engaged with self-guilt often, especially when I feel I have let people down.

You know that feeling when you've done or said the wrong thing, knowing there are consequences, and then you feel ashamed of yourself for getting yourself in that position in the first place? You wish you had thought it through or better yet, not done 'it' at all! Sound familiar?

I am seriously convinced that none of us escape the sensation of guilt during our early childhood years, and now, as a parent, I can see why sometimes my mother and I would use guilt to get what we wanted or needed. I have to confess; I've caught myself using guilt as a last resort to motivate my kids when they have been stubborn, immovable objects as well! What I've discovered though, is that we all do the best we can with the resources we have, as there are no rulebooks to download on the internet on *How to Be a Perfect Person and Parent, or How to Perfectly Manage Guilt*. Let's face it, if you are a people-pleaser this one is especially difficult for you.

Self-guilt can be paralysing if left unchecked. Long-term self-guilt appears as an internal dialogue that leaves us feeling lonely and sad. Worst of all, it's happening right there inside of us; right between our own two ears. Our thoughts about what we have or haven't done are creating these emotions, and there is just no escape. The more we think about it, the worse the feeling becomes, and no amount of justification can seem to pull us through. We can't run, we can't hide, and for the most part, we can't even talk ourselves out of it, because somewhere inside we truly believe we deserve to feel this way. It's our inner punishment, and it hurts.

Now, before we all throw in the towel, there is an upside! Guilt, like all emotions, is an internal and very private event. And that is a good thing because no matter what we have experienced, it's not the experience that hooks us into self-guilt, it's our interpretation of that experience, and if we are willing to become our very own problem-solvers, we can talk ourselves out of what we have talked ourselves into.

Let's take a look at what manifests as guilt and the sorts of experiences that can bring it on, so you can easily identify the need to enter the self-love circle for help.

Two Types of Guilt: Rational and Irrational

According to research, there are two types of guilt, rational and irrational. To keep this simple, rational guilt is when you go against your own personal values, your own morals, wishes, and desires, and is very self-oriented.

Irrational guilt is based on should and shouldn't, conditioned thoughts, childhood belief systems, and/or societal norms, which are rules that are not really your own. These are the beliefs that your parents had about right and wrong, or what you determined was going to work for you when you were a child, and you're still carrying it around subconsciously. As we become adults, sometimes these 'strategies' can cripple us with anxiety or misplaced responsibility for things that are ultimately out of our control.

Name the Problem

Whether your guilt is rational or irrational, it's still inside of you. You feel it; it's very real for you and shaking it off feels impossible. One of the best ways to bring rationality to an emotional situation is first to name the problem. Get clarity on what it is, where it came from and then begin to seek out solutions. So, what are the ways guilt manifests in our lives?

We Feel Guilty for Something We Did

This seems logical, right? We did something we feel wasn't right, either against ourselves and our own values, like lying or cheating, or maybe just face-planting a chocolate cake when we were trying to reduce our sugar intake! Or we feel we've done another person wrong, either physically or emotionally. This is totally normal and, in a way, an opportunity to re-evaluate what is important, what we want, and maybe set ourselves on a new course: It can be helpful to reassess our behaviour. Sometimes, decisions must be made in a personal relationship or a business sense that will hurt and affect others. You may feel guilty for having to make such decisions, but you also need to hold yourself accountable and ask the question: Is this for the greater good? If it is, then trust that you have made the right decision, regardless of how someone responds. Just remember that spending too much time beating yourself up over a perfectly normal emotion is only adding fuel to an already burning fire.

We Feel Guilty for Something We Didn't Do

You promised you'd pick the kids up and you didn't. Or worse, you didn't realise your partner was struggling and didn't offer to pick the kids up to help. Either way, you're destined for the guilt train.

More significantly, you may have had thoughts of doing something, but didn't do it, and now you feel guilty about just having the thoughts. It feels so real–almost shameful–because the mind doesn't know the difference between what is real and what is imagined, so it feels as bad as if you had committed the act and you've violated your own standards with the thoughts.

> *A human being is part of a whole, called by us the*
> *"Universe," a part limited in time and space. He*
> *experiences himself, his thoughts and feelings, as*
> *something separated from the rest - a kind of optical*
> *delusion of his consciousness. This delusion is a kind*
> *of prison for us, restricting us to our personal desires*
> *and to affection for a few persons nearest us. Our*
> *task must be to free ourselves from this prison by*
> *widening our circles of compassion to embrace all*
> *living creatures and the whole of nature in its beauty.*
> - Albert Einstein

Guilt that You're Doing Better than Someone Struggling

This can be a really tough situation. Often, this guilt is driven by feeling bad because you're succeeding in a certain area, and someone you know or care about isn't experiencing the same success. You may find yourself dulling down your own excitement or enthusiasm just so you don't make them feel bad. I know at times this was significant for me, especially when Danny was doing so well at the peak of his career. We had a new house, money in the bank, no kids, we were free;

travelling the world and genuinely having an amazing time. I wanted to scream from the rooftops how exciting it was to live in our bubble, but at times I found myself feeling guilty that others were going through challenges or not experiencing the same joy.

Survivor's guilt falls under this heading too so let's not leave out how it feels when you survive an accident or horrific situation, and others do not. Families of suicide victims often grapple with why they are still alive, when their children or siblings are no longer around. "What if I had done more?" is a common thought, along with "How could I not have seen the signs?" Having been here myself and asked the same questions, I soon realised they were unanswerable and left nothing but a residue of guilt that plagued me for a very long time.

Mother or Father Guilt

This one is so challenging for parents and my heart goes out to each and every one of you; especially my own parents. You can't get anything right, you're never a good enough parent, you're second-guessing yourself at every turn (and it doesn't matter what anyone else tells you), you're still caught in the merry-go-round of trying your best, and never measuring up to what you want and envision for your children. Argh! Often it is not until we become parents ourselves that we can fully appreciate how tough it must have been for our own parents. Teenagers are particularly good at finding your Achilles heel of guilt, and unless you learn to stand up and be strong, they will use it to get what they want, or find a way to make you feel bad. I have had many parents tell me how hurtful their kids can be, with comments like, "Why can't you just be like so-and-so's parents?" or, "You are sooooo dumb", "You are embarrassing me; you are the worst parent ever", "You never let me do what I want", and the worst one; "I hate you".

Danny and I have learnt that the best thing we can do when a not-so-nice comment is directed at us is to not react; almost laugh it off. Let it wash over like water off a duck's back and realise that those frontal lobes are not fully developed, and comments like that are just a teenage version of a two-year-old's tantrum. It was explained to me many years ago that the reason why teens can be so challenging is to give parents—and teenagers—a reason to fly the nest, so to speak. It's a way of cutting that umbilical cord and making it easier for our children to move out of the family home. Harsh as it sounds, it may well be a necessary part of growing up, and of parenting. The important thing is the parent hopefully has more maturity to deal with it. And if not, they've just fallen out of the circle into self-sabotage and need to follow the first three steps to get back into the Circle of Love. If really struggling, some good counselling or courses on how to deal with your children growing and or leaving home can be helpful too.

One thing my girlfriend Simone taught me when my children and I have struggled with guilt is to remind them that I have never been the mother of a seventeen-year-old girl or a fifteen-year-old boy (or whatever age they are). Remind them this is all new territory for me too, so I might make mistakes or say the wrong things. At the same time, they have never been a seventeen-year-old girl or a fifteen-year-old boy, so they too might make mistakes, or say things that don't serve anyone well, especially themselves.

Growing up, parenting and being a functional family takes work; it takes guts and it takes strength to not let Mother or Father Guilt consume you and take away the joy of watching your babes enter the world of adulthood.

Shame

This is a BIG one. And according to Brené Brown, the author of *Daring Greatly and The Power of Vulnerability*, there is a profound difference between guilt and shame. Here is how she describes the difference:

"I believe that guilt is adaptive and helpful - it's holding something we've done or failed to do up against our values and feeling psychological discomfort.

I define shame as the intensely painful feeling or experience of believing that we are flawed and therefore unworthy of love and belonging - something we've experienced, done or failed to do makes us unworthy of connection.

I don't believe shame is helpful or productive. In fact, I think shame is much more likely to be the source of destructive, hurtful behaviour than the solution or cure. I think the fear of disconnection can make us dangerous.

I believe the differences between shame and guilt are critical in informing everything from the way we parent and engage in relationships, to the way we give feedback at work and school."

We can certainly feel shame for all sorts of reasons. From a pimple on our face keeping us indoors out of embarrassment, all the way to the other end of the spectrum of shame for doing something we wished we hadn't, or worse, for being a victim of abuse. No matter what the underlying cause of the shame, this gripping feeling is always an invitation to return to the self-love circle.

So, what to do with feelings of guilt or shame? When you explore your own self-guilt, I encourage you to look at it with an open heart and mind, and explore how this feeling can be turned around and made to work for you. Diving into the tools of the self-love circle, you'll see how every experience and emotion is providing us with contrast and if we look, we can find the lesson it's trying to teach us.

I often find myself questioning the gut reaction of guilt. You know, that feeling in the pit of your stomach that goes up into your heart. That feeling is often a good barometer to determine whether next time you could do something a little better, or to see if that guilt is being driven by your own response to someone else's behaviour. And we all know that sense of control when you make someone else feel guilty for not doing what you want. Well, sometimes it may well happen to you, too.

Research shows that we, collectively, spend on average up to five hours a week, at a minimum, in a state of guilt, so let's not waste another moment. Let's embrace the remedy, see what oils can serve us, and become an example of what can be possible for everyone in our lives.

Essential Oils for Self-Guilt:

Cardamom Oil: When you feel like you're in a rut, cardamom reminds you of all that is possible, leaving you feeling content, fulfilled, generous, and warm. Leave behind feelings of depression, disheartenment, mental fatigue, judgement, lethargy, and tension. This precious oil eliminates fears, worries, and helps to restore your appetite for life.

Application: Massage, compress, inhale, diffuse, bathe and spritz this supporting and inspiring oil.

May Also Benefit: Digestion issues, flatulence, monthly feminine balance, immune support, coughs, bronchitis, nausea, circulation, and it is even an aphrodisiac!

Clary Sage Oil: Considered the 'champagne' of essential oils, clary sage calms anger, anxiety, irritation, judgement, nervousness, stress, and feeling overwhelmed. Strengthening and fortifying the mind with clarity, creativity, enthusiasm, inspiration, intuition and strength, this oil can help you become joyful and intoxicated with life.

Application: Massage, compress, bathe, diffuse, and spritz.

May Also Benefit: Keep this oil on hand for monthly feminine balance, labour, childbirth and infertility, asthma, bronchitis, muscle aches and pains, and even oily hair.

Lavender Oil: This oil is like having your 'dream mum' in a bottle. Comforting you with generosity, gratitude, kindness, love, nurturing, protection, and relaxation, your feelings of anxiety, hurt, irritation, judgement, neglect, worry, sadness, shock, stress, vulnerability, and feeling overwhelmed will melt away with ease.

Application: Inhale, massage, spritz, compress, direct application, diffuse, and bathe.

May Also Benefit: Coughs, colds, catarrh, and fever. Great for burns, bites, stings, and rashes (direct application works well here). Keep handy for headaches, muscle tension, asthma, respiratory conditions, and all skin conditions.

~Self-Loathing

*"I managed to achieve a depth of self-loathing that
usually takes a night of drinking to achieve."*
Anthony Bourdain

My dear husband, Danny, went through a period of self-loathing. This highly talented, incredibly charming, and attractive international athlete seemed to have the world in the palms of his hands from his teens and through his twenties. He played cricket for New Zealand for ten years. He was at the top of his sport; a professional athlete; he loved every minute. He gave his life to the game and lived and breathed it. Whilst he always appreciated that it was a privilege, and always knew not many players got to write their swan-song (the way they retire), he still held big hopes for how he would leave the game.

So, when his career ended suddenly aged thirty-one with absolutely no warning, following a national radio announcement that he had been dropped from the national side, his heart broke and he allowed this major challenge to slowly, over time, penetrate his soul. The news was so wounding Danny felt he had been thrown out and left on the junk heap of life, with a sense of failure, a lack of control, and a terrible feeling of not being good enough.

As that penetration deepened over the next few years, it felt like that amazing bubble we had been in was going to pop. And it all began to crumble. We lost our home in a property deal that went wrong. And a year after that, we tragically lost

Danny's beautiful sister to suicide. A year after moving our family to the Sunshine Coast to start afresh we freakily lost the rest of our equity in a financial institution that collapsed during the 2008 share market crash. It felt as though every aspect of our world had crashed, leaving us, including Danny, who kindly allowed me to share his story with you, vulnerable and wounded.

To put it mildly, Danny derailed. He questioned what life was all about and he felt no good to anyone. His heart was broken, yet he had to continue working, travelling extensively away from home for up to seven or eight months a year. He had forged a career as a sports commentator, and to his credit, created a niche for himself, and became very good at it. He had to keep providing for his family and stay on the road, even though he was feeling more and more lost and alone. As the emotional pain he was experiencing grew, so did his drinking and partying. The guilt and the shame grew, too. He lost sight of himself.

Our marriage suffered, to the point it was over at that moment when I found myself lying on my bathroom floor. We both agonised about what the future held for us, and for our family. Remember, I had no idea of Danny's anguish; I put his strange behaviour all down to losing his beloved sister. I kept trying to give him space and support him in the best way I knew how, as well as raise our two children as best I could, often in the role of a single parent, given how much he was away.

It was thanks to Jakob's wise words that had me get up, learn how to get on and decide to work on this journey together with my husband. The two of us went to counselling, discussing our challenges and to reconcile a new definition of who we were as a couple, and even though we both were struggling emotionally, we were equally committed to finding a way through the turbulence.

We continued visiting our counsellor, Jacqueline, an inciteful, spiritual, French woman who was a trained psychologist, aged in her eighties. She looked straight at both of us and asked Danny, 'Do you love this woman?' to which he replied absolutely. Then she asked me, 'And Kim, do you love this man?' and of course I said yes. 'Well', she said in her beautiful French accent, 'We have no problem. When there is love there is no problem.' I remember thinking, that's it? That's all you have to say? It was hard to take in that moment.

She then suggested we give it four whole seasons before we make any big decisions, such as deciding to stay together or part. When I asked why she said seasons and not one year she explained. "My dear, some of us are better in spring, some of us are better in autumn, it is wise to allow your full self-expression in all four seasons before making the big decisions."

I hung on to those words like you wouldn't believe. I think we both did.

With our situation weighing heavily on our hearts one morning, I looked up at Danny and noticed him staring at me with tears rolling down his face. I asked him what was wrong. He took a deep breath, met his reflection in the bathroom mirror, and then looked back at me. He said he envied me. He said he envied the fact that I was a good soul. He was battling.

He said he understood the need to forgive and love himself, in order to be a better husband and father, but it was really tough doing that when, looking at himself in the mirror, all he felt was guilt, hate, and self-loathing.

I asked him whether he felt he was a bad person. He said yes. I asked him whether he thought that I thought he was a bad person. He said yes. I asked again if he was absolutely sure that it was true; that I thought he was a bad person. He said he knew it for sure.

Isn't it interesting how blind we become when we are in the grips of our own self-loathing? We cannot see past it, not even to a bigger truth about ourselves. It's not going to take a miracle, but it is going to take a bit of inner searching.

When we get to the first step of the art of self-love in the Self Awareness chapter on page 143, we explore the work of Byron Katie, where you will be encouraged to see yourself through new eyes, because in order to see yourself through the eyes of self-loathing, it simply means you don't know yourself nearly as well as you think. Through the process of self-enquiry, you will discover there is much more to you than your experiences, and with this help, you may begin to forgive yourself as well as forgiving others.

I can honestly say that through a strong commitment during that time, along with several years of counselling, self-care and self-discipline, our marriage is indeed better than it ever was. I may have contemplated divorce at one point, but by working through our trials together we learned to forgive, love, and trust again. We have just celebrated twenty-five years of marriage and renewed our vows with our children and my brother and his wife present. It meant the world to both of us. Not only was it a celebration of twenty-five years, it was a testament to the love we shared. My advice would be this: do not let self-loathing, or indeed any of the challenges of life rob you of your happiness. Follow the self-love circle and it will help to keep you accountable and on track.

As I outline the nature of self-loathing, I can identify with the weight of past hurts creeping up to grab me in the throat, and as I swallow this lump, I take comfort in knowing that it has been the wisdom and emotional and spiritual gifts on the path to self-love that have rescued me, my friends, and family, time and time again. If self-loathing has cursed you, remember you are not alone, even though it feels that way. You are not the first person to lose your identity to self-destructive emotions. The emptiness inside that is left behind from a session of self-berating is the signal that it is time to explore what else is possible. You may not feel like you deserve any better, and I'm not here to convince you of anything. My dream for you is that you will read these words and when the time is right for you to heal, you will reach for them as a life raft, knowing that the storm is ready to subside inside.

I'm pretty sure we've all felt it to some extent, where we have moved past the pangs of guilt and graduated to self-loathing, where we are in constant judgement of ourselves for a wrong we believed we've committed either towards ourselves or someone else. We can't forgive ourselves, no one can make us feel better, and it feels a lot like mental and emotional torture with no fix or finale.

As time passes, self-loathing threatens to destroy our relationships because we can't seem to connect with others anymore. We have so much loathing for ourselves, we believe that we are no longer worthy, of value, or lovable. We can't love ourselves, so why on earth would anyone else love us?

The sneaky nature of self-loathing is that it can hide behind a smile, a cheerful face; a facade that life is all perfectly in order. The picture behind closed doors can be remarkably different, though. The internal dialogue circulates back and forth, over and over again, constantly repeating the event that caused the self-loathing, or alternatively, if this has been going on for years, we may not be repeating the vision of the event, instead, we are repeating the way we feel about ourselves. Self-loathers may feel inadequate, but they must also remember they are only seeing part of what other people see. A person's self-perceptions are not complete and they're not necessarily any more 'right' that anyone else's perception of him or her.

When we do not like ourselves, we need to have faith in how others see us, and have faith in the aspects of ourselves we may not even be aware of.

The good news is self-loathing can be overcome. It requires your care and discipline, maybe even some professional help, which is not to be underestimated, but most of all it requires your forgiveness. If you have spent years knocking yourself for being overweight, you may find you have used food or alcohol to punish yourself further;

the more weight you gain, the more you loathe yourself. When your reason to change becomes stronger than the punishment you're inflicting upon yourself, only then can you begin to separate yourself from the perils of self-loathing. Acknowledging that your body has responded to your actions is the first step. It's not the other way around, where your body has 'done' this to you. My beautiful mother-in-law Sandi always says how important it is to act, and not react, to the challenges we face.

Essential Oils for Self-Loathing

Black Pepper Oil: This revered, spicy oil helps to activate and excite the body! Think energy, endurance, enthusiasm, focus, vitality, warmth, and stimulation, as you wash away feelings of defeat, fatigue, mental lethargy, nervousness, sensitivity, and worthlessness. This oil has a powerful kick, so only small amounts are needed for great results!

Application: Inhale, massage, diffuse, spritz, massage, bathe, and compress.

May Also Benefit: Colds, flu, rheumatic pain, muscle aches and pains, bruises, oedema, circulation, liver detoxification, and digestion issues.

German Chamomile: A very calming and healing oil to ease anger, irritation, nervous tension, stress, and hopelessness, instead inducing feelings of harmony, joy, and relaxation.

Application: Massage, bathe, compress, spritz, and diffuse.

May Also Benefit: Inflammation, arthritis, dermatitis, muscle aches and pains, sensitive skin, dry skin and rashes. Great for bruises, burns, acne, psoriasis, and feminine balance. Dilute to 2.5% to help heal inflamed skin conditions. A high content of the active compound azulene give this oil its deep blue colour.

Ginger Oil: Brings clarity, confidence, courage, endurance, motivation, and strength to situations where you're feeling trapped by mental fatigue, forgetfulness, grief, lethargy, and worthlessness.

Application: Inhale, massage, bathe, compress, foot bath, spritz, and diffuse.

May Also Benefit: Digestion issues, indigestion, bruising, muscle aches and pains, cold hands and feet, arthritis, nausea, travel sickness, catarrh, coughs, and sinusitis.

Jasmine Oil: Considered to be the 'King of Flowers', you can draw on its strength to let go of the past and adapt to what is present. Become confident, content, fulfilled, grateful, passionate, positive, sensual, uplifted, and trusting. Release deception, depression, distance, disconnection, fear, rigidity, sorrow, and worthlessness.

Application: Massage, bathe, spritz, compress, inhale, and diffuse.

May Also Benefit: Muscular cramps and spasms, coughs, colds, and flu. Relieve insomnia, muscle tension, dry skin, eczema, dermatitis, infertility, and premenstrual syndrome. Can also be used as an aphrodisiac!

Lemongrass Oil: Bring balance, clarity, endurance, energy, enthusiasm, expansion, motivation, and vitality to your days as you say goodbye to apprehension, depression, mental fatigue, impatience, lethargy, negativity, stress, vulnerability, and feelings of worthlessness.

Application: Massage, compress, bathe, spritz, inhale, diffuse.

May Also Benefit: Muscle aches and pains, bruising, oedema, inflammation, indigestion, fever, headaches, weight loss, and cellulite. Works wonderfully as an insect repellent and air freshener, and when used in massage, boosts energy and endurance.

Myrrh Oil: Rejuvenate yourself with rituals that include Myrrh to create a feeling of abundance, connection, expansion, patience, grounding, peace, trust, and wisdom. Allow neglect, sadness, vulnerability and feelings of worthlessness to fade away.

Application: Massage, bathe, foot bath, spritz, compress, inhale, diffuse and direct application (to mouth ulcers and cold sores only).

May Also Benefit: Bacterial and fungal conditions, dry, aging, mature skin, eczema, acne, diarrhoea, flatulence, respiratory conditions, arthritis, mouth ulcers, and cold sores. Blend myrrh with frankincense, pine and orange and use as a perfume or add to your facial regime to reduce wrinkles and preserve youth.

Myrtle Oil: Cleansing, positive, harmonious, and peaceful, kindness and sensuality replace anxiety, chaos, fear, tension, hurt, hopelessness, and feelings of worthlessness. Supporting deep inner wisdom and knowing, calm the busy mind, and feel reassured that we are all supported and connected.

Application: Inhale, diffuse, spritz, massage, bathe, compress, and hair rinse.

May Also Benefit: Bronchitis, catarrh, coughs, urinary tract infections, haemorrhoids, acne, oily skin, open pores, hormone support, and head lice.

Neroli Oil: Considered a wonderful rescue remedy oil, making it an ideal choice if suffering from shock or hysteria. It is one of the best oils to enhance creativity, trust intuition, and to connect to your higher self. Enjoy calm, contentment, courage, joy, nurturing, passion, peace, strength, and trust. Support depression, fear, grief, moodiness, negativity, sadness, shock, sorrow, and worthlessness.

Application: Massage, compress, spritz, diffuse, bathe.

May Also Benefit: Sensitive and dry skin, insomnia, muscle tension, diarrhoea, digestion issues, scars, broken capillaries, stretch marks, and is even an aphrodisiac!

Pine Oil: This cleansing, refreshing, and invigorating oil can have the same effect as if you were standing in a pine forest. A fabulous oil for clearing the air, improving alertness, and increasing inspiration.

Application: Inhale, vaporise, bathe, spritz, and compress.

May Also Benefit: Coughs, colds, flu, asthma, cystitis, pyelitis, inflammation, muscle aches and pains, headaches, arthritis, rheumatic pain and liver detoxification.

Rose Oil: The 'Queen of Flowers' has long been a symbol of love. Through her nurturing properties you'll enjoy abundance, compassion, creativity, connection, courage, enlightenment, joy, kindness, love, nurturing, passion, and peace. Release anger, defeat, depression, fear, heartache, sorrow, worry, and worth-lessness.

Application: Spritz, massage, compress, bathe, diffuse, inhale.

May Also Benefit: Broken capillaries, inflammation, hormone support, menopause, dry, mature skin, wrinkles, scars, weight loss, cellulite, and even an aphrodisiac! (Have you noticed each time I write aphrodisiac, it comes with an '!'? I love it when nature nurtures the human spirit!)

~ Self-Doubt

"It's not what you think you are that is holding you
back, it's what you think you're not!"
Anonymous

About five years ago, I was fortunate enough to join forces with the incredibly brilliant nutritionist, author, and founder of the Functional Nutrition Academy, Cyndi O'Meara, along with the ever-inspiring author, trainer and Mindset mentor, Carren Smith, to create a podcast show called *Up for a Chat*. Oh, my goodness, I can still remember the day we decided to bring this show to the public, and all three of us were just so excited to not only work together on a project like this, but to potentially reach tens of thousands with our messages combined. We were 'fizzing' with excitement on the day we kicked it off!

We sat in Carren's office with our sophisticated 'recording device' (Cyndi's iPhone!) mounted on top of a coffee mug, and away we went; chatting about each of our specialties and business adventures. I was so engaged in both women's stories, backgrounds and experiences, that what was intended to be one podcast to introduce ourselves turned into a three-part show that took about four hours to record. We had so much to say!

In the third part of the introduction series, the conversation turned to me. I felt so nervous to talk about myself, and what I had achieved, but Cyndi and Carren were so interested and engaged, it made it easier than I'd expected.

A few months went by and our topics became more and more complex, as Cyndi spoke about the immune system and the micro-biome, and Carren dove down rabbit hole after rabbit hole into a world of quantum physics around mental, emotional, and spiritual welfare, that left even our listeners saying she was from another planet! I was in awe of these remarkable women. Their knowledge and understanding of the human body, mind, and soul blew me away, and I began to doubt myself—my value—and question why on earth I was even part of this show. I felt so unworthy that one day it became an internal barrier for me.

I arrived at Cyndi's office for our show after we'd been recording for about six months, and just as I sat down, Carren and Cyndi made a joke about me being late and I lost it! I found myself on the brink of tears, I was so emotional I couldn't find the breath to speak or explain what was going on.

In true Cyndi style, she was devastated to realise what was happening, because she thought it was just a harmless comment, and likewise, in true Carren style, I watched her go straight into counsellor mode and attempt to understand what was causing my mini-breakdown.

Both women, in their own loving way, tried to get to the bottom of it, but in the moment, I couldn't even see it, much less explain it to them.

We decided to do the show, but in my heart I felt so sad. I knew I had to figure it out, but at that moment I had to put it aside. I resolved to find the time and space later to deal with it. I pulled up all the energy I could muster, performed the show with a smile on my face, and then from the moment I got in my car, I set about sorting this inner turmoil out!

I got home, poured myself a cup of chamomile tea and switched on my diffuser with a soothing aromatherapy blend I created for my range called Instant Calm, and sat on my soft and comforting lounge. I began replaying the day, trying to see what was really creating my thoughts when I arrived for the podcast. As I recounted the moments, louder and clearer than I could possibly have imagined, the words SELF DOUBT rang in my ears!

Wow, I had been on the verge of telling the girls, "I quit!" just because I doubted my ability to genuinely contribute. Oh, my goodness, did I have some work to do!

My self-doubt sneaked up when I wasn't looking, and it bit me right on the nose! It was so alive in me, in that moment, that I was considering sabotaging something I really wanted to do!

This was not okay with me, so 'down the rabbit hole' I went, and the more I looked, the more I found that self-doubt had reared its head several times in my life when things were coming together in very powerful ways. I could see so clearly where I'd bypassed opportunities because I thought I wasn't smart enough, or I'd endured situations where I felt I wasn't good enough, and while on the outside I was smiling, on the inside I was suffocating under the weight of this self-doubt.

It was time I resolved this huge weight once and for all. I knew in my heart that I had great skills and experiences to add to the show, so what I felt wasn't logical at all. I knew it was an old belief pattern that didn't serve me anymore, and

I knew that with a little self-love and reassurance, I could be back on the show with all the energy and enthusiasm I had originally felt.

That day, and for the rest of that week, I made a point of telling myself all the wonderful things I did each day and reflected on what I knew, and the experiences I was drawing on to bring me confidence. I began journaling every day and anchored my 'me time' with a blend of oils I call Balance and Harmony, made up of clary sage, geranium, lavender, lemon, neroli, and rose, which I used every day in a full body massage ritual I call my daily body boost (explained more on page 331), and in one of my diffusers.

By the time our next show rolled around, I was feeling much better and way more present. Of course, Cyndi and Carren were none the wiser about the process I'd been through to comfort myself, but inside I felt like I had kicked a major goal in my life and from that day to this, the podcast has gone on to become a powerful resource which sits proudly alongside other amazing podcasts like The Wellness Guys. Together all of our podcasts have had over an amazing 2.5million downloads.

Honestly, now I look at us with so much love and respect and wonder what on earth I was thinking back then! We are a spectacular team, and while I'm sure we will always be expanding together mentally, physically, emotionally, and spiritually, it is an amazing ride to share with two women I consider to be my nearest and dearest friends. Most of us develop a healthy dose of self-doubt from the time we are little kids. We learn from very early childhood to question ourselves, as we conform to the wants and desires of our parents, our teachers and society. The influence of should and shouldn't, right and wrong, can and can't, all enter our frame of reference, and, as a result, we build neurological connections to self-doubt as we question our own 'compass', unsure of which direction is best, or most pleasing. Well, if this isn't one of the greatest tragedies to each of us, I don't know what is!

You know how it feels; it's familiar and sometimes feels like the safest place to remain, because if you do nothing, you can't get it wrong. Right? Wrong!

You'll second-guess yourself, hesitate, feel disempowered, doubt your own experience or viewpoint, feel anxious, judge yourself, your decisions and coping abilities, feel miserable and resentful as more and more opportunities pass you by, because you're paralysed by self-doubt and, worse still, you'll doubt yourself for doubting yourself!

Does this feel even just a little familiar now?

Self-doubt shapes our expectations about what we are capable of and whether or not we will succeed. It plays out almost like a self-fulfilling prophecy because we always perform and behave according to our belief system, which sadly places self-doubt as one of the major contributors to self-sabotage.

To help you explore this, I've collected some of the effects of self-doubt. My hope is they may help highlight and heal where self-doubt could be lurking in the background or the dark places of your mind.

Self-belief

If we don't believe that we are capable, then we aren't. If we don't believe that we can succeed, then we won't. The brain is just not wired to create actions or thought systems to support success, and for most of us, we don't even know we are thinking this way.

Think about any area of your life that you KNOW you can succeed in. Deep down, you know that if you put your mind to it, you can really do well. When you analyse your behaviour and the path you chose to get to where you are, you'll begin to see where you sabotaged opportunities, didn't take action where you could have, or ignored certain signs that were right in front of you. Also, think about areas you believe you could NOT succeed in. Perhaps you truly believe you're not a runner. You think there is no way you could ever run ten kilometres let alone a marathon. I cannot begin to tell you how many amazing people I have met at the end of a half or full marathon who are so damned proud of themselves for accomplishing something they never thought possible.

Burnout

We can tend to burn ourselves out when we are trying so many different ways to prove ourselves right, or others wrong. When we are unsure of our own mind, we flail around in the dark, looking for a path that we think will be most accepted by others, or at least won't ruffle any feathers. We invest so much time trying to make up our minds on both small and large matters, expending endless energy on avoiding getting it wrong, that anxiety ends up being the ultimate winner.

As the essential oil industry has exploded onto the marketplace with more and more people joining network marketing companies, or selling oils through affiliate links online, I started to doubt, and wonder if I had enough knowledge, or indeed enough of a story, to ensure that there was room for me, and my business, too. I noticed the anxiety creeping in. Was I enough? I enrolled in about five online courses to see if I was up to date with my knowledge. Alongside managing my business, and a team going through huge changes, I spent hours, days, and weeks trying to get through all of these study programs, with many late nights and early starts. I was desperate to make sure the knowledge I was sharing via my talks and online health and lifestyle education program was enough, that it was up to date, and relevant. After all, my diploma was attained way back in 1991.

And as you can imagine the lack of sleep and self-care hit hard. I burned and crashed. I got whacked so hard with a flu virus that I was literally bed-ridden, only to discover that I had pneumonia. I could hardly breathe. Everything hit me like a ton of bricks. And, to no surprise, it was the emotional side of things that I think wiped me the most. Trying to do too much or be something more than what you are can be downright exhausting and debilitating. This situation literally robbed me of being 'me' and was driven from a place of fear of not being good enough.

Stuck in a rut

Have you ever found yourself stuck in Groundhog Day? Where you want to change things up, but the sabotage of self-doubt means you can't move due to the unpredictability of the change? This can happen as a parent, in your job, and even in relationships. As a small business owner, I am always thinking of ways to grow my business, increase profits, decrease costs, and create new products. There is a constant fine line between money in versus money out. And there is a constant battle between my business owners' mindset and the 'what is viable versus what is possible' creative mind.

My business was ticking along, but I felt stuck. Online sales were slowly decreasing, and yet the costs were increasing. I was out there doing as many talks as possible to boost the business, but it never felt enough.

My business coach, Bruce, took me aside one day, "Kim you can't constantly be out there 'shooting ducks', you can't just be out there looking for the next sale, the next customer." He told me I needed a strategy that would serve customers that were already engaged. There's a well-known saying that 80% of your business comes from 20% of your customers. I needed to give my customers more, yet I felt stuck, I had no idea what to offer that was of real value.

I was honoured to speak at The Wellness Summit in August 2014. This is an annual health summit that takes place in Melbourne to honour all the listeners of the podcasts that are on www.thewellnesscouch.com, the website which is home to our podcast, *Up for a Chat*. The speakers are not paid to speak but are encouraged to share who they are and what they do. There is a market hall where the sponsors, speakers, and organisers have stalls for an engaged and interested audience. It's a beautiful event; one of my favourites.

Seventy-two hours out from the summit, Bruce rang me and asked, "So buddy, what are you selling to this audience of 600?" I replied, "My usual, a Body Boost kit, my book and the complete Essential Oil kit." He knew these packs had a value between $70.00 and $500.00, but he wanted to know if I had something to offer in the thousands of dollars mark? I was gob-smacked. No, I didn't. Although, I did tell him I had been contemplating an online program for almost ten years. I knew how it would look, what each of the modules would be. I knew the content I needed to provide, and I knew how I would love to deliver it. However, it was not ready. So, no, I did not have something to offer.

A business coach is like a running coach; they see your potential. They see how far they can push you to find more potential. They also know how to push your buttons to get you to fire up. As we were finishing the call Bruce casually mentioned that this would be the perfect opportunity to announce the online program. I just had to get out of my rut, believe in myself, and let the audience know it was being launched in a few months, in October.

I went into panic mode! I knew he had pushed a button. I had this voice in my head saying it was impossible, *You cannot do this. How can I do this?* And another part of me saying, *About time*. For the next forty-eight hours, I wrote out the whole structure and content of the online program. It was easy, I had been thinking about it for so long. My life's work was broken down into fourteen modules. I worked out what my student would get as a part of the $4,997.00 ticket price. This self-care program would go over six months. It would be made up of weekly modules, plus extra down-loadable e-books and content I had written or needed to write. There would be live webinars, accountability calls, plus an online coach walking right beside them. I worked out that, included in this price, would be beautiful, natural, chemical-free skincare, organic essential oils, plus books, a vaporiser, and special product surprises sent throughout the program. This program was about making self-care easy, so participants could act immediately and complete the weekly self-care rituals. There would be no reason for excuses, or to give up, or give in. And it would all culminate in a four-day face-to-face training and graduation event on the Sunshine Coast; my home. There would be two intakes per year, one in September, graduating in February, and one in March, graduating in August. It came so easily and poured out of me onto the notepad in front of me.

There were four cornerstone values I based the program on:

- Connect
- Care
- Collaborate
- Contribute

It felt so right. I could do this. I was not prepared for what was to come!

The next day I stood on stage in front of 600 wellness advocates to deliver my presentation. With seven minutes to go I saw my dear friends Cyndi and Carren at the back of the room, pointing to their watches. They knew I only had a few minutes left to share my program. Now, I am not what you would call a natural sales person. I can never remember all the sales techniques I've been taught as a speaker, and I get flustered whenever I attempt to sell. So, on this day I took a deep breath and just told them from my heart what this program meant to me. I told a story about my dream to create a community of like-minded, beautiful souls who could call on each other for support, advice, and care, and not be thought of as weird or a little crazy! I wanted a program that would give people permission to take care of themselves.

I shared that I had started my business with a mission to change the world and help women understand the importance of self-care. However, on this day, standing on that stage thinking about what this program could do for so many, I realised that's not what I wanted now. No, today, and moving on from today, my mission would be to help one person—one woman at a time-realise their incredible, innate ability to use the healing power of plants for themselves and their family. That was it.

I explained the program with the love I felt for it, and I could really see it as I imagined. I almost cried as I spoke of it. To see if there was any interest or need for such a program, and as a call to action, I offered the program at a discounted price, given that it would be the first intake. I almost cried on stage that day. It was now out in the open. I had just given birth to my dream.

The first person who approached me after I stepped off the stage was a gentleman called Simon. He was beaming, he had such a kind face, and he just looked at me and said, "My wife needs to do your course and we want to sign up!" Anna appeared from behind her husband, also grinning, and we signed her up on the spot. That is how the Health & Lifestyle Education (HLE) Program began. Anna was the first of six people who signed on that day, and another five enrolled for the first intake that was to begin in a few months. I was blown away. We had over 150 graduates over four years. It has grown into a wonderful online platform now, with students enrolling from all around the world. My business grew over 400% in just one year, thanks to the push I needed to get this program out of my head and into reality.

Every year, I wonder what I would be doing had Bruce not given me the push, and a time limit to do it. I may have just stayed in my rut and not even have a business to speak of.

It doesn't bear thinking.

Sacrifice Self-love

If we are in the throes of sacrificing self-love as we experiment and grow, then we simply cannot acknowledge our very own struggle and meet our heart with the compassion it deserves. Sometimes, we can find ourselves being too pre-occupied with being right which can lead us to berating ourselves for not seeing the hurdle we have just struck as we tried to jump it with the grace everyone else seems to possess.

When my beautiful sister in law, Zhara, passed away tragically in February 2005, we were a family in shock, in disarray, and in completely unknown territory. I cannot describe the effect it had on each of us, but it pushed and pulled us all as if we were in a washing machine, being constantly spun, wrung, drenched, and pounded.

There were so many gifts this beautiful woman etched onto our hearts before she left this world. One of the most profound for me was learning to remove my judgement of death, particularly suicide. In the past, whenever I heard someone mention the tragic passing of someone to suicide, I would have a quiet thought that whilst incredibly sad, it seemed selfish. I mean, how could they do that to their loved ones? I never stopped to think about things like psychotic episodes, medications, mental illness, and the agony someone must be in to get to that point.

When we judge ourselves, or others, we fall out of the circle of love, which in turn sabotages our ability to love ourselves. I got a massive wake-up call. We have all cried a million tears and still miss Zhara every single day.

Fast forward a few years and my daughter was dancing in a competition on the Sunshine Coast. Tayla was about to come on and perform her beautiful ballet solo. I was sitting next to Danny's mum, Sandi, and it was just the two of us. The young dancer that came on before Tayla was beautiful.

But it was when the music started playing that it really struck a chord. The song *Hallelujah*, recorded by many amazing artists but on this occasion performed by Leonard Cohen, echoed in the whole theatre. After a short time, I noticed tears rolling down Sandi's cheeks and her body shuddering slightly. I passed her a tissue and held her hand. She just quietly sobbed until the end of the routine. I knew there were no words that would ease her breaking heart. When the song ended Sandi squeezed my hand, took a deep breath, and wiped her eyes. We waited for our beloved Tayla to come on stage, and she did not let us down. Her solo was breathtaking. Her stage presence was bewildering. She was captivating. It was a beautiful performance and an amazing distraction.

Later that evening I asked Sandi if she was okay. She smiled and told me how important it is to just BE in the moment. To feel the pain, but not let it continuously consume you. Just breathe through the moment when it hits you. And remember that this too shall pass.

The one thing I have embraced is the notion that you must 'feel it to heal it'. If we do not allow ourselves to work through our emotions, they can overwhelm us. We might become bitter, angry, fearful, or consumed by guilt and shame, all of which can sabotage our ability to love others, and, in turn, sacrifice our ability to love ourselves.

Imposter Syndrome

We have a sneaking suspicion that people will one day discover we are a fraud and an imposter. We may have worked hard and achieved something great in everyone else's eyes, but in our own, we are waiting for the bubble to burst or to be 'found out'.

While some may blow their own horn without the actual achievement to back it up, the self-doubter is so worried they won't take praise or give themselves the proper credit they deserve.

For many years I have reflected on a story that I am not clever enough, or know enough, or contribute enough. I went to university for six months. I was studying law. What was I thinking? It was not for me. My mum, who had me at just seventeen years of age, always said that if there was one thing she could advise her three children was to get out, travel, and see the world before settling down. So, when a job opportunity arose for me to work in travel, I took my mother's advice and was out of that classroom in a flash.

Working in travel lead me to meet one of my best friends Lizze. We were teenagers, loved working together, and were lucky enough to win a British Airways trip for two to the city of Perth, Western Australia, in 1987. I felt like we had won lotto.

This is the city I happened to meet my husband in, while he was touring with the New Zealand Cricket team, but I will get to that story later!

I ended up living in Melbourne at the end of that year, and found my passion for health, fitness, and wellness was well and truly activated. There are no accidents; as luck would have it, right next to the gym I was working in was a Natural Therapies College. I noticed a ten-week course on massage and essential oils advertised in the window. With $180.00 in my bank account I enrolled in the $160.00 course, that's how committed I was. On top of that I bought over $700 worth of essential oils on my $1000 limit credit card. This course became the first of many. My passion for essential oils grew bigger and sparked a desire to know more. I soon realised the more I learned the more I didn't know.

Within three years I had diplomas in Remedial Therapy, Sports Massage and Fitness Leadership, Ortho-Bionomy, Reflexology, Kinesiology, and my absolute favourite, my Advanced Aromatherapy Diploma, completed on Valentine's Day in 1991. But I still didn't feel like I knew enough. And even though the feelings have subsided, I realise I have had this little inkling that, because I did not attend university and do not have a degree, I am not qualified enough to speak, or share my insights.

At times I have felt like a fraud. It has happened for me in sport, motherhood, business, and even as a wife. I mean, how could I possibly have been a cricketer's WAG (an acronym used to describe the wife or girlfriend of a famous sportsperson) when I was not a model or a celebrity? You see, imposter syndrome can lurk in all areas of life and I have half expected my bubble to burst in every single one of them.

You don't know yourself

We spend a lot of time thinking about what we can't do, what we're not good at, and what we're told we're incapable of, and let's face it, it can almost cause a 'separation sensation' inside.

It's as if we shut down our ability to experiment with life and see what is possible, and then we use our own assessment to determine our strengths, even focusing more on our weaknesses. To live life this way, shrouded in self-doubt, is simply to not know yourself.

Maybe the truth is we just don't know ourselves because we've never suspended our self-doubt long enough to try and see what else could indeed be possible.

Elizabeth Kubler-Ross weaves the most powerful message:

People are like stained-glass windows. They sparkle and shine when the sun is out, but when the darkness sets in, their true beauty is revealed only if there is light from within.

To complete my Diploma in Sports Therapy we had to log 200 hours of time at community sports events. I wanted to do this as quickly as possible so, along with Australian Rules football, cycling races, and netball events, I thought the best way to fast-track it would be to attend a couple of ultra-marathon events. The first one was in Coburg, Victoria, and I was assigned to look after a man by the name of Cliff Young. Cliffy was a sixty-six-year-old potato farmer, and a celebrity in his own right. If you don't know this remarkable human being, he surprisingly won the inaugural Sydney to Melbourne road race in 1983, aged 61, which was almost 1,000 kilometres in distance. Cliffy grew up on a farm in Colac, Victoria, where they could not afford tractors, bikes, or horses, and he would have to round up the sheep on a property of around 2,000 acres, on foot. This would sometimes take up to two or three days. It was this kind of training that had him believe he could compete in such a gruelling event.

The day the race started all the top athletes left Cliffy in their wake, possibly even laughing at the fact there was such an old person in the race. It didn't seem to bother Cliffy. He slowly and surely 'shuffled' his way down the highway at a constant and steady pace, not fazed by who passed him or who he passed. As the race progressed, his constant pace meant he began to pick each runner off, passing them all until eventually crossing the line in first place. He astounded almost everyone.

I was told he was asked what his tactics were around not stopping to rest very much, or at least sleep throughout the race. His response was, "I didn't know I could!" Whether he was joking or not, it got me thinking at a very young age that if you didn't know what you couldn't do, why would you ever question what you could do!

Cliffy became one of my greatest inspirations. During that twenty-four-hour event that I was assigned to him, he never complained once, he just kept shuffling around the track, always at the same pace, always appreciative of the massages and food I offered. At 3am during this Coburg event, he asked me what I thought of 'ultras'? I was cold and tired, and with brutal honesty I told him exactly what I thought. "Cliffy, it is the most boring thing I have ever done."

He chuckled and told me that was the perfect reason to run one and not watch one. He dared me to fill out the entry form for the next ultra.

I was so darned cold and fed up being there, I was thankful to do something. I stood up and went to the registration table, and then proceeded to fill out the form for the forthcoming twelve-hour race in a few months' time. He was right, I would much rather be participating in one than watching it.

A few months later and there I was, lined up on a 400-metre track on a cold winters morning in Coburg, with about forty other athletes. I had never run beyond ten kilometres in my life, and suddenly it hit me. I had no idea what the hell I was doing, or why on earth I was doing it. Who did I think I was kidding? Run. For twelve hours? What planet was I on? I was not a runner, I was a netballer for goodness sake.

Cliffy calmly came up to me with a big smile, asking if I was excited. He knew I was nervous and just added, "Kimmy, it's 90% mental and 10% physical, remember that." He also told me to look at the Sri Chinmoy quote on a board on the side of the track. 'The race is not always to the swift but to those that keep on running.' I didn't have to be the fastest, I just needed to keep going, he said.

I didn't know if I had it in me to run around a 400-metre track for twelve whole hours. But I decided I would give it a shot. Surely it wouldn't be too hard. Cliffy had made it look quite easy after all.

I was fine for the first few hours, but four hours into the race and this voice in my head suddenly appeared. *What the hell are you doing? What a bloody nutter. Sit down. It hurts. You're being silly. Who are you kidding? Why on earth are you doing this? There's still eight hours to go, you fool.* These comments did not stop. I could not shut them up. And what's worse, I believed them all. I did not like who I became in that moment, and it's fair to say I had a bit of a melt-down; a small tantrum. With eight hours to go, I walked off the track and into the pit-stop tent and told my team I quit the race. It was a stupid thing to be doing anyway. No one said a word. They all gave me some space. And then Cliffy appeared. He sat beside me sipping on a cup of tea or soup.

"You know, no one said running an ultra would be easy, you might notice there are not many who do them. But those who do, discover something inside of them they didn't know about themselves. Those who complete a run like this usually have the ability to dig a little deeper; they find a way to keep going and they don't quit because it hurts. They get up and get on with it. Instead of being angry in here you could at least keep moving, Kimmy. Get back out there and take it out on the track and just walk, you don't have to run, just put one foot in front of the other."

My coach came up to me and added, "You've got this. You don't have to quit. You're more than that. But, it's your choice." Cliffy finished his cuppa, stood up, and as he shuffled back out onto the track he looked at me and gently tapped his head and then his heart.

I knew I had to get my sad, sorry butt back out on the track. The guy was forty-six years older than me, and he was not complaining about how much it hurt or talking about quitting. My coach and support team had given up their entire weekend to support me.

I got back out on that track. I walked, and then jogged, and walked, and ran, and walked. It still hurt but I did not give up. And I finished that race. Remarkably, I went on to run 96.4kms, and, unbelievably, won the women's section. It was insane, really.

As I hobbled up to receive my trophy the organisers proudly told me I had won a place to run in the Victorian 24 Hour Championships being held a few months later. Everyone was clapping and cheering. I was trying to smile but inside I was going, *You're kidding? I have to do that all over again, and for twice as long?*

And indeed, I did. For the next few months I trained in Melbourne and up in the Dandenong Ranges in Victoria. I ran with Cliffy and some of the other athletes I had raced my twelve-hour event with. We would do 30km, 40km and 50km training runs. Sometimes we ran as a group, sometimes I ran by myself. The voices in my head would go from being highly supportive—almost euphoric—to completely questioning my sanity and over-riding any sense of positivity. I could be really mean to myself. But I kept pushing and training.

In February of 1989 I lined up on another 400-metre track with around thirty-five other athletes. The Victorian women's champion was in the race. She was twice my age and I figured I could probably beat her, given how old she was! Yes, at fifty now I do chuckle at that comment. The race began, and I felt better than in the twelve-hour race. For a few hours I felt amazing. And then... the voices appeared again. And were talking incessantly in my mind, louder than in the last race.

One minute I was excited to have this opportunity, the next minute complete self-doubt would cloud my mind. I kept saying to myself, *This time tomorrow, this time tomorrow it will all be over. Minute by minute, lap by lap, hour by hour I can do this.* And then I would think, *There's no way.*

To say this was one of the toughest challenges of my life is an understatement. I went through many highs and even more lows. I quit more than eight times. At one point I hid from my team in a port-a-loo toilet on the side of the track. I cried. I whinged. I hurt. I laughed hysterically. I wanted my mum more times than you could imagine. And I apologised often. You could say every emotion was present at some point in those twenty-four hours. In fact, the tantrums I had seen other runners throw in races were also present in my race. At one point, one of my team members gave me a cup of cold pumpkin soup and I was expecting a warm cup of tea. That completely threw me. It was a shocker. And in my mind, surely a strong enough reason to throw a tantrum and quit!

My support team were, quite simply, amazing. They put up with every part of me. They kept me going. They fed me, massaged me, encouraged me. They used my beloved essential oils on me at every chance. I would look up from the track to see any one of them tap their chest and point to their heart to keep me motivated and focused. Sometimes I would feel elated, other times I would see their faces and want to burst into tears. It hurt. There's no other word it was gruelling. And then there were times I could not feel anything, and it almost felt like an out-of-body experience.

Running constantly, for hours upon hours, is one of the most excruciatingly painful and yet most euphoric experiences I have ever had.

From midnight to 6am is what is commonly known as the 'graveyard shift' and it's aptly named. It's cold, it's dark, and it's quiet. Yes, some team members are awake, and the lap scorers are rugged up and keeping note of each lap the runner completes. But it is eerily quiet. It was during this time of the race that I understood what Cliffy meant when he told me that prior to the setting sun was when I would meet the real Kim.

You are alone with your own thoughts. It feels like the time will never end. At times you almost feel like you are counting each second. All I wanted was to exit the track and rug up in the pit-stop tent with my team. I desperately needed sleep. I often questioned why I was there and had so much doubt about even finishing the race. I battled constantly with my thoughts, crying out in my head to quit. I would say to myself, *Just one more lap then you can sit down for a massage and some food.* Then I would come around the next lap and say, "There you go, one more of those and you can rest." And then I would complete one more lap and say, "Gosh, in 200 metres you have completed another kilometre." I would then have an internal argument and challenge the quitting voice saying, *If I had listened to you I would still have another kilometre to catch up!*

I honestly do not know who I was talking to. I mean, who is that voice? Where does it come from? And if it is me listening, then who is doing the talking? Or if I'm talking, who exactly is listening? In my experience, to go down the rabbit hole of human questioning like this just leads to more questions, and then sometimes it is so bizarre you wonder if this life, this body, is even real. Maybe this is quantum physics at its best. I wouldn't call myself a philosopher or anything, but my goodness, did I have some serious chats with myself and someone or something else in those wee small hours on that weekend in Victoria.

As I pushed through each lap, each dark hour I hoped and prayed the sun would soon rise. As it began to peek through the clouds, one of my team members came out from the pit stop tent with a cup of warm sugary tea and gave me some stats. She told me the Victorian champion had been gaining on me through the night, but I still held onto a 2km lead. If I could at least keep the pace I was running at then I had every chance I could win the women's section of my first ever twenty-four-hour race. One of my aromatherapy teachers, Judith, arrived and used this exquisite combination of essential oils which included juniper, rosemary, cypress, lemongrass, grapefruit, black pepper, and rose in a compress on my forehead. She massaged my neck and shoulders with this blend. She kept saying amazing things in my ear like, "You can do this Kimmy. You've so got this, get out there and win this race."

I had no idea if I had it in me to push on any further. I was exhausted. But although I was physically and mentally spent, something clicked inside. Was it my team? The last massage?

Those incredible oils? I found another gear I didn't even know I had. Apparently, I ran the next few hours of this race quicker than I ran the first few hours. I don't know where that drive came from, or how I found the energy. But it's interesting for all of us to realise there is more strength and resilience inside of us than we ever give ourselves credit for.

As more people arrived to witness the end of the race, the more I was inspired to keep jogging. My energy was lifting. Everything hurt but I kept pushing, grinding out lap after lap. I passed Cliffy at one point and all I heard him say was, "Adda girl, keep that up." I did not stop. It hurt when I did anyway. And it hurt when I ran. So, I just kept running.

Finally, when the twenty-four-hour siren went off and the sandbag was placed where I took my last step, I just felt myself sink onto the track. I fell onto my back and looked up at the sky. The world felt like it was spinning. My legs were twitching. My tummy felt so empty. I had lost nearly 6kgs in this race. I was weaker than ever, and yet felt stronger than ever. It was so emotional. I had done it. I had been on that track for twenty-four hours and I was elated it was over. I wasn't sure if I had maintained first place, but I didn't care, I had given it everything I had.

My team were all beside themselves with excitement, and right there with me. They hugged me and congrat- ulated me. It was like I had run the race on their behalf, and it felt amazing. They had all believed in me. I sat up and looked around at all the other runners, and although I wasn't sure if they were tears of relief or joy, I felt nothing but love and inspiration. We had all endured something together. On that day, in that moment, I felt like I joined an extraordinary group of amazing people. Where I finished no longer mattered. It was the completion, the fact I had not given up, or given in, to the pains and demons within my head.

As I was helped into the pit stop tent, I started to analyse my performance. I know I could have spent more time on the track instead of off it. One of my support team members told me I had spent four-and-a-half hours in the pit-stop tent in total, that it was a great effort. But that just begged the question: how much further could I have run had I not been off the track for so long?

As they called for all athletes to come forward to hear the prize-winner announcements I felt like I was in another place. It was like I was a witness to the whole event. I think I was just exhausted, but I felt like I was someone seriously different. I heard the women's third place-getter's name called, then I heard the Victorian champion's name as the second place-getter. And then I couldn't believe it, they called my name, with a winning distance of 168.4 kms (104.6miles). Everyone clapped loudly. I was so elated for my team and especially for my Cliffy. As I wobbled forward to receive my trophy, they then had a further announcement. I had just set a world record for being the youngest female to run a hundred miles in less than twenty-four hours. And that due to this remarkable effort, I had won a place to represent Australia in the World Indoor 24 Hour Championships in London the following year. It's amazing recounting and writing this story. I can feel every emotion as if it was just yesterday. You could say I was completely blown away. As everyone was clapping and cheering, no one had any idea I was so excited inside. I had just been selected to represent Australia!

All that self-doubt, all that worrying I was not good enough, or incapable of running, yet here I was now standing in front of everyone as a world record holder and a national representative.

My dear friend, Marcus Pearce, a fellow podcaster and speaker always finishes his talks with, "May the rest of your life be the BEST of your life!" This moment changed my life forever. I am sure it became my anchor that for the rest of my life I could now achieve anything I set my heart on.

I also took away, and still relate to, many running messages such as:

- Never ever give up.
- Don't be surprised if your path takes you on a different journey, just be open to it being an exceptional one.
- Know that deep down there is always more in you.
- Trust that pain comes, and it goes.
- Don't stop; no matter what is happening, stay on the track.
- It's 90% mental and 10% physical.
- Winners finish, finishers win.

- The race is not always to the swift but to those who keep on running.

- And most of all, even when you least think it: you've got this.

And just as a side note, that combination of essential oils of juniper, rosemary, cypress, lemongrass, grapefruit, black pepper, and rose became a blend that I created for my business. I wanted to call it my World Record Blend but ended up calling it Detox & Strengthen. It is a beautiful blend of oils that help detox and eliminate negative thinking and give you an incredible sense of strength within.

Essential Oils for Self-Doubt

Black Pepper Oil: This revered, spicy oil helps to activate and excite the body! Think energy, endurance, enthusiasm, focus, vitality, warmth, and stimulation as you wash away feelings of defeat, fatigue, mental lethargy, nervousness, sensitivity, and worthlessness. This oil has a powerful kick so only small amounts are needed for great results!

Application: Inhale, massage, diffuse, spritz, massage, bathe, and compress.

May Also Benefit: Colds, flu, rheumatic pain, muscle aches and pains, bruises, oedema, circulation, liver detoxification, and digestion issues.

Cypress Oil: If you're challenged emotionally, mentally, physically, or feel as if you're about to fall apart, cypress will help you pull it all together. Diffuse in times of change, and transition from chaos, defeat, grief, judgement, sadness, or sorrow to acceptance, balance, expansion, protection, and vision.

Application: Massage, compress, sitz bath, spritz, diffuse, inhale this reviving and cleansing oil.

May Also Benefit: Varicose veins, hemorrhoids, acne, oily skin, broken capillaries, asthma, coughs, colds, weight loss, cellulite, bruises, oedema, and excessive perspiration.

Grapefruit Oil: Call on this oil with euphoric properties when you're feeling tense, overwhelmed, under pressure, defeated, depressed, overwhelmed, weary, or frustrated. Enjoy the feelings of focus, clarity, joy, positivity, strength, and trust, as you're gently uplifted on the delightful citrus scent.

Application: Compress, inhale, massage or spritz this zesty, uplifting, and revitalising oil.

May Also Benefit: Oily, congested skin, acne, weight loss, cellulite, muscle aches and pains, headaches, insomnia, and muscle tension.

Lemon Oil: This fresh and stimulating oil is an instant pick-me-up, leaving you with energy and mental clarity. You'll feel less confused, defeated, disheartened, exhausted, weary, and worried.

Application: Massage, compress, diffuse or spritz. This oil makes a refreshing addition to your bath, opening the heart, alleviating exhaustion, and creating self-confidence.

May Also Benefit: Anti-aging, nausea, cellulite, weight loss, oedema, varicose veins, warts, colds, flu, immune support, and a liver tonic.

Note: Avoid exposure to the sun after using lemon in a massage or bath as it is phototoxic (will cause a sunburn like skin condition when exposed to sun light)

Manuka Oil: This healing, cleansing, and uplifting oil is right there for you to call on when you're feeling emotionally low, and negative feelings are getting the better of you. When apprehension, confusion, defeat, depression, mental fatigue, irritation, lethargy, shock, vulnerability, or weariness sets in, this highly medicinal plant is at the rescue. Instantly feel more balanced, cleansed, energetic, protected, and vital.

Application: Foot bath, spritz, massage, direct application (for abscesses, ringworm, corns, warts and cold sores only). Bathe, compress, diffuse, inhale, and sitz bath.

May Also Benefit: Bacterial and fungal conditions, wounds, and bites. Healing for candida, urinary tract infections, coughs, colds, and flu.

Marjoram Oil: This oil is perfect if you're trapped in obsessive thinking and negativity. Ease anxiety, defeat, frustration, neglect, stress, and tension with ease as you ground yourself with love, openness, strength, and warmth.

Application: Massage, bathe, compress, inhale, diffuse, and spritz.

May Also Benefit: Muscle aches and pains, respiratory conditions, coughs, constipation and flatulence. Great for pre-menstrual syndrome, menopause, headaches, insomnia, and muscle tension.

Note: Be careful with topical application during first trimester of pregnancy.

Rosemary Oil: Known to have a very stimulating effect on the mind, a cleansing effect on the emotions, and is renowned for being the oil for memory. This energising oil improves mental clarity, focus and intuition while calming exhaustion, mental fatigue, neglect, procrastination, and feeling overwhelmed.

Application: Enjoy this delightful oil in a bath, compress, diffuser, spritzer, or massage.

May Also Benefit: Liver detoxification, weight loss, cellulite, muscle aches or pains, respiratory conditions, sinusitis, heart palpitations, circulation, and hair growth.

Note: Be careful with topical application during first trimester of pregnancy.

Rose Oil: The 'Queen of Flowers' has long been a symbol of love. Through her nurturing properties, you'll enjoy abundance, compassion, creativity, connection, courage, enlightenment, joy, kindness, love, nurturing, passion, and peace. Release anger, defeat, depression, fear, heartache, sorrow, worry, and worthlessness.

Application: Spritz, massage, compress, bathe, diffuse, inhale.

May Also Benefit: Broken capillaries, inflammation, hormone support, menopause, dry, mature skin, wrinkles, scars, weight loss, cellulite, and is even an aphrodisiac!

~ Self-Judgement

"The highest form of human intelligence is to observe yourself without judgement"
– Jiddu Krishnamurti

I will never forget one particularly stressful day. Tayla and Jakob were four and three years of age, respectively. We were rushing to get to kindergarten on time, so I could get to work. Both children had been mucking about, fighting, arguing, squabbling. They were tired. Tayla had spilled her breakfast, Jakob had jammed his finger in the drawer. I dropped a load of clean white sheets onto the dusty floor below the clothes line while desperately trying to hang them out speedily. I wanted all the beds made, kitchen cleaned, bedrooms tidy, teeth and hair brushed. You know, the perfect home and children, the perfect mother. Why was today so damn difficult?

I was raising my voice constantly; I was cross. I needed them to conform and do as they were asked. As I rushed them into their car seats I realised I had forgotten their lunch boxes. In the time I had raced upstairs to get them, and unbeknown to me, Tayla had yelled at Jakob and then bitten him hard, and in response, just as I returned to the car, he was angrily hitting her so hard she was screaming.

That was it. I had had enough. I grabbed his little hand, I was now yelling at him, "How many times have I told you, you do not hit people?" I smacked his hand in time with the words DO-NOT-HIT-PEOPLE. Four times, maybe five, I smacked that little hand in a rage.

As I was about to raise my hand one more time there was a moment, a split second where I was completely shocked; side-swiped, aghast. Oh, my god. I was doing exactly what I was telling him NOT to do. I looked at my children, both with tears streaming down their faces, and just slumped in horror into the driver's seat, holding the steering wheel with my hands, and my head dropped hard onto it as if I had just been handed a life sentence for abuse and neglect. I burst into tears. All three of us were sobbing; as far as I was concerned I was a complete failure. The only thing that managed to break me out of my self-hating spell was when I heard Tayla say, "I'm sorry mummy, please stop crying."

I can't believe I am sharing this story. I feel sick at the thought of it. For hours, days, weeks, and months after that moment, I found there would be times when I truly hated myself. Why did I put so much pressure on myself and my kids? Why did I let it all get on top of me and just suddenly lose it? As far as I was concerned I was the worst mother in the entire world. And far from anything that resembled 'perfect'.

That unstoppable rage frightened me. I had failed the test. I was not like all those held-together wonder-women. I was a disgrace to them, to all women, to motherhood, full stop. I was so embarrassed by my total lack of control, and the fact I had smacked my son so hard, that I didn't talk about this episode with anyone. I couldn't even tell my husband, who was away working overseas. I had let him down immensely. I was not the remarkable mother he thought I was.

It took many internal conversations, books, attempted meditations and a number of mothers' group get-togethers before I started to realise that there were a lot of mums out there who, on some days, were struggling to hold it all together. I listened to other young mums share their exhausted stories of their children misbehaving, their anger and frustrations. I didn't share my particular story for a while, but I always agreed and understood what they were saying. After all, I was the worst of the worst; I absolutely understood.

I was down on myself for months. People asked if I was okay. I would respond with the easily distracting statement, "Oh, I'm just tired." Meanwhile, inside, I would be muttering, *Actually I am an abusive, horrible, violent, abhorrent mother if you really must know. And I am trying to come to terms with my total lack of parenting skills, thank you for asking*!

For a good while I thought I was a shocking mother with no hope. This had become the catalyst for many things. Everything I did seemed useless or not up to scratch.

I went along to a talk by a gentleman called Ian Grant, a New Zealand author of several best-selling parenting books including *Growing Great Boys*, *Growing Great Girls*, and *Growing Great Families*, and it was here that I found I had the power to forgive myself (and give myself an uppercut!) I understood at that moment the healing power of forgiveness, and the undermining effects of self-deprecation. If I forgave myself, I could finally free myself up to begin healing my embodiment of the societal pressure that is placed on women, that had led me to slap my little boy's fingers. I needed to accept that I was human, and I would make mistakes.

I went along to this particular talk because I was worried that Jakob wanted to play with guns. Another worry, right? He begged me to buy him one all the time. My three-year-old needed to kill all the baddies in the world. I was sure it was because of the violence I had bestowed on him months before, in the car that day.

When I raised my hand over my gun-wielding, baddie-wrangling concerns, I noticed other mums nodding whilst Ian just chuckled. He told me to relax. With a smile on his face he said, "Let it go mum, boys will turn a carrot stick into a gun!"

He acknowledged I was a good mum, in fact he said we were all amazing parents for coming along to learn. He acknowledged me for bringing up the rather sensitive subject of violence and guns. And then proceeded to tell us that boys need three things:

1. They need to be able to fix things.
2. They need to know they can get rid of offenders and baddies, and
3. They need to know they can be a superhero and save whoever needs saving.

And, Ian reiterated that—according to boys—everyone needs saving! He encouraged us all to just get down on the floor and let our boys create a scene, play it out and be the damsels in distress so they can kill the baddies and save us. Everyone laughed.

I cannot express what a relief Ian's words were to me. My boy was 'normal'. I was 'normal'. Maybe I hadn't damaged my son after all. Maybe I was as tired as they were on that particular morning, and even though there is no excuse, I had just made a mistake. Little did I know it was just one of many more to come. And what I learned through all of this was that it was okay.

I went home after Ian's talk and lit my vaporiser. I took some nice deep breaths and looked at myself long and hard in the mirror. One of my favourite Wayne Dyer quotes is up on my bathroom mirror. It's been there for many years.

'Forgiveness is the scent the violet emits onto the heel that crushed it.'

I looked deep into my eyes and said, "I am a good mum. I am a good mum." I ran myself a long, soothing, magnesium and essential oil bath, and reminded myself that despite my months of guilt, conversations of uselessness were not serving me well; they were exhausting me and my family. I could forgive myself in that moment and promise to be an even better mum tomorrow. Yes, it was time to pick myself up, dust myself off and get on with raising my two fabulous babies. I have learned to replace the guilty mindset with curiosity and now whenever I experience it I try to remember to ask questions like: "What if I did the best I knew at the time?" and "What if there really weren't any other options?" and also (and this is my favourite) "What if there was a lesson for me to learn in that situation, and judging myself stops me from seeing it?"

You see, I do believe we all do the best we can with what we have and where we are, but the trappings of self-judgement seem to hold us accountable for an unrealistic outcome and create crushing pressure if left unchecked.

As I was researching the topic of self-judgement, I found myself astounded by how harsh we can be on ourselves. Self-judgement, like most of the other self-sabotaging behaviours we've already explored, are thoughts that are occurring in your own mind; generated by you, felt by you, and then acted upon by you. It reminded me of a book I read many years ago, *Wherever You Go, There You Are* by Jon Kabat-Zinn. He explains that no matter where we run to, or how far we travel, we always take ourselves with us, and this can be troubling at best when we are plagued with slip-ups and particularly self-judgement.

Self-judgement is always a way of shifting from the mindful present into the past or the future, and then looking to our faults and failures as a way to make us feel wrong about what have done in the past, and anxious about what we may or may not do in the future. In other words, when we judge ourselves, or others for that matter, we lose ourselves. We lose touch with who we are, who others are, and believe for those moments, hours, days, weeks, months, or years that our perceptions are a representation of reality.

I can assure you, if you're anxious about what you perceive will occur in the future, you're deceiving yourself, because you're creating future imaginary battles that most likely will never occur, and if they do, you will have the resources to support yourself when the time comes. Likewise, if you're dwelling on a past event, you're investing your energy into something you can't change and, over time, don't fully remember anyway. Let's face it, you probably can't remember what you had for breakfast last Wednesday, much less what your mother said to you when you were twelve!

I'm moved to explore what the opposite of self-judgement could be, and I wonder if it is curiosity. Try this with me: think of a scenario where you're judging yourself and deeming yourself to be at fault. Would your attitude toward yourself and the event change if you could bring a mindset of curiosity to the table, instead of judgement? Does it change the way you see yourself?

Let's examine the impact of self-judgement in your life. Please check off any of the following items that apply to you right now:

- ✔ Negative self-talk
- ✔ Stagnation: you can't move forward because your judgemental thoughts are just circulating about how you got 'it' wrong
- ✔ Habitual self-criticism
- ✔ Debilitating thought patterns

- ✔ Dwindling passion
- ✔ Non-existent vitality
- ✔ Unable to face a crisis
- ✔ Lack of self-belief and missed opportunities
- ✔ Trapped into comparing yourself to others or the alternative life you imagine
- ✔ Dwelling in the past, feeling regret
- ✔ Identifying with faults or mistakes and spiralling into a self-destructive, blaming mindset
- ✔ Judging others harshly and often (if you judge others, you're judging yourself)
- ✔ Keeping your self-judgements to yourself like a dirty little secret

If you see yourself in any of these statements, you'll no doubt take comfort that we have been judging ourselves for centuries. *The, I'm better than, worse than, equal to or not as good as...* thought systems have us saying terrible things to ourselves that we would never say out aloud, or to someone we love.

The tragedy of self-doubt is that it occurs when we don't distinguish between the actual truth and our interpretation of the truth. Let's say you jump on the scales and they read 90kg. That is the truth. The judgement then goes ahead with, "I'm 90kg and I'm so fat and ugly!" This is NOT a truth, it's the embellishment that your judgement has created in order to put you at fault.

For a moment, even if you believe your self-judgements are justified, try suspending the negative self-talk just for an hour and replace it with curiosity. As you entertain this perspective, you will see how you can easily get to the self-acceptance chapter and 'try on' a new way of experiencing yourself. It's free, it's within your reach and it's calling out to you NOW! So, "I'm 90kg and I'm so fat and ugly," could become, "Okay, wow, I have hit 90kg. Okay, it's time we found a way to reduce this. Let's make a plan." Even if you are gutted you have hit this weight, remember it's not your body's fault. What you have put into your mouth has had a remarkable effect and your body has responded accordingly. In the same way it took huge commitment to gain the weight, you could apply the same logic and commitment to losing it. Only this time you will use a food and movement program that supports weight loss, not gain.

I know for myself self-judgement has hit at various times. During one podcast for our show *Up for A Chat,* my co-hosts and I were all feeling rather vulnerable and questioning what we were all doing? I mean, was it really making a difference? Did it really matter? And did anyone really care? It was a deep and sensitive podcast and one that has received a lot of positive feedback and attention. A few days later I received this long but beautiful message from a listener, Christin, who told me she had heard me questioning if I made a difference.

Kim, I want to share a little story with you about the evolution of one of my work mates. You know, I work in the mining industry, in the port side of the operations. To paint a picture, it basically means I operate giant machines, loading huge ships up to 8,000 tonnes per hour. I am the only female some of these guys have ever worked with. It can be exhausting. The hard part is to be accepted as part of the crew while still maintaining my own feminine identity, especially as you know I have a bit of a potty mouth and know it's a struggle!

One of the better jobs is in the train unloading station. It is where I get to spend hours upon hours listening to podcasts. A few shifts a week I have this one guy come down to relieve me in the station and he always walks in and asks, "So, what are we being brainwashed with today?" I'll tell him what I'm listening to and we'll have a bit of a discussion or debate about it. It usually ends with him calling me a hippie. Apart from being a miner he grew up on a sugar-cane farm, and farms cattle, too.

One week I decided to introduce him to Kim Morrison. I played him the Wellness Guys podcast episode on chemicals that make us sick and obese. He came into work the next week and said he went home and played it for his wife and daughter. And then he said, "So, it turns out we already have some of those essential oil thingies, and now each night before I go to bed I read a few pages of my book and just before I fall asleep, I put a couple of drops of lavender on my pillow."

Me, "Oh my goodness! You have a ritual?" Him, "A what? A ritual? Nah, nah, it's just something I do before I go to bed each night."

A few weeks later he said, "That talk on chemicals really got to me. Every night I massage my wife's feet with lotion. It's something I have always done. Lately I haven't been able to do it knowing that the lotion could be so bad for her, so I went and got some bees wax and some coconut oil and made my own lotion. I've started using that on her instead."

Fast forward a few more weeks. "You're bloody sending me mad with this stuff," he said. "On my days off I found borers in my trees and instead of spraying them like I normally would, I got a pin and poked them through their holes in the tree. It was embarrassing. You know I used to sell pesticides for a living, right?" I then got him to listen to a health podcast on sugar. "You cannot play this to me," he said, "I'm a cane farmer. What am I going to do now?"

We have had many heated discussions on chemicals, pesticides, and herbicides. Roundup was one that kept coming up with him saying, "You're being brainwashed by all this hey, this is all fear-mongering. Roundup is a safe chemical, trust me, I used to sell it. I've sat through seminars on the stuff."

I played him the Up for A Chat podcast episode after the MINDD forum and another interesting podcast on wheat by The Good Doctors. The lights started to come on. He came back after a few days off and said, "It turns out I am the one that has been brainwashed. If only you knew the conferences and seminars I have sat through on Roundup. I was told it was safe, I didn't know what they were really doing with it. I didn't know it would end up in our food."

Now for the really exciting news. In the past few weeks he said, "You know I have been losing sleep because of you. My parents are getting old and they need to sell their sugar cane *farm. I would hate to see it just go to someone else but how can I invest in another sugar cane farm knowing what I know now? Also, all this talk on conservation and chemical-free living has made me realise I don't want to hand over a farm to my children one day, there's enough of them around. I want to hand them over something special. I want to regenerate that land and turn it into a nature reserve. There is already a large part of uncleared land, creeks, and a lake. I want to turn it into some form of eco retreat, so others can enjoy it and it will be there for generations to come. How freaking amazeballs is that!!*

So, Kim Morrison, never for a second question whether what you are doing is making an impact. It truly is. One thirty-minute podcast interview made a couple of years ago may lead to a nature reserve being created for generations to come. He has asked me to be his consultant on this. Maybe one day we could even host an event there with you speaking... it would be fitting, don't you think?

On my days where I wonder if I make a difference or I judge myself harshly, I pull out this message I have saved on my phone. I cannot begin to tell you how many times I have read it. My business coach calls it the Law of Precession, which was defined by the late Dr. Buckminster Fuller, as the effect of bodies in motion on other bodies in motion.

This law simply states that for every action we take, there will be a side effect arising at ninety degrees to the line of our action. We can explain it by looking at examples of this through nature.

*"The Sun and the Earth are both bodies in motion.
Despite the 180 degree gravitational pull of the
in-motion Sun upon the in-motion Earth, precession
makes Earth orbit around the Sun in a direction
that is at ninety degrees, i.e. at a right angle-to the
direction of the Sun's gravitational pull."*
– Dr. Buckminster Fuller

Dr Fuller's favourite example is that of the honey bee. As intelligent human beings, we are aware of the importance of honey bees to our ecosystem, and much research has been documented about this. If they become extinct, mankind will undoubtedly soon follow. Their purpose in this world is cross-pollination and the sustenance of life on earth.

But when they wake up each day, do you think they go about their daily business completely aware of that purpose and being driven to save the world? I doubt it! They are simply drawn towards the nectar in the flowers they seek. However, as they move from flower to flower, their body and legs 'accidentally' gather pollen, which then results in cross-pollination and fertilization.

As a precessional effect of following their innate search for food, they unknowingly fulfil their true purpose. When I look at all we do on a daily basis, I think it's fair to say we may not realise how much of an impact we can make. As stereotypical as it may sound, as a mum, it may seem like all you are doing is cooking and cleaning. As a dad it may feel like all you are doing is working. Yet at a ninety-degree angle is the incredible job you are doing raising children with strong values in a nurturing home, and a strong work ethic is immeasurable. You could be inspiring your children to believe they can be, do, and have anything they dream. It's incredible, really, and quite an amazing responsibility and privilege all at the same time.

And besides, when you think about it, who's got the time for detrimental self-judgement?

Essential Oils for Self-Judgement

Cardamom Oil: When you feel like you're in a rut, Cardamom reminds you of all that is possible, leaving you feeling content, fulfilled, generous, and warm. Leave behind feelings of depression, disheartenment, mental fatigue, judgement, lethargy, and tension. This precious oil eliminates fears and worries and helps to restore your appetite for life.

Application: Massage, compress, inhale, diffuse, bathe and spritz this supporting and inspiring oil.

May Also Benefit: Digestion issues, flatulence, monthly feminine balance, immune support, coughs, bronchitis, nausea, circulation, and is even an aphrodisiac!

Clary Sage Oil: Considered the 'champagne' of essential oils, clary sage calms anger, anxiety, irritation, judgement, nervousness, stress, and feeling overwhelmed. Strengthening and fortifying the mind with clarity, creativity, enthusiasm, inspiration, intuition and strength, this oil can help you become joyful and intoxicated with life.

Application: Massage, compress, bathe, diffuse and spritz.

May Also Benefit: Monthly feminine balance, labour, childbirth and infertility, asthma, bronchitis, muscle aches and pains and even oily hair.

Cypress Oil: If you're challenged emotionally, mentally, physically, or feel as if you're about to fall apart, cypress will help you pull it all together. Diffuse in times of change and transition from chaos, defeat, grief, judgement, sadness, or sorrow to acceptance, balance, expansion, protection, and vision.

Application: Massage, compress, sitz bath, spritz, diffuse, inhale this reviving and cleansing oil.

May Also Benefit: Varicose veins, haemorrhoids, acne, oily skin, broken capillaries, asthma, coughs, colds, weight loss, cellulite, bruises, oedema, excessive perspiration.

Lavender Oil: This oil is like having your 'dream mum' in a bottle. Comforting you with generosity, gratitude, kindness, love, nurturing, protection, and relaxation, your feelings of anxiety, hurt, irritation, judgement, neglect, worry, sadness, shock, stress, vulnerability, and feeling overwhelmed will melt away with ease.

Application: Inhale, massage, spritz, compress, direct application, diffuse, and bathe.

May Also Benefit: Coughs, colds, catarrh and fever. Great for burns, bites, stings and rashes (direct application works well here). Keep handy for headaches, muscle tension, asthma, respiratory conditions, and all skin conditions.

~ Limiting Self-Beliefs

"It's never too late to be what you might have been."
George Eliot

I've recently put one of my limiting beliefs under the microscope and found that I had just been looking at myself from the wrong angle and didn't see the magic that had always been there.

When we were kids growing up, we never had a lot of money, with my mum supporting the three of us, and the little money we did have never seemed to stretch very far. I witnessed and therefore felt that money was incredibly scarce and took a lot of sacrifice to create. I believed that money was only about providing for what we needed instead of what we wanted.

When I was nineteen I was in a relationship with a man who was much older than I was, and he was also my boss. Now, going into this relationship and job, I believed that I really had no idea about how to handle money, and that left to my own devices I'd be hopeless. So, in my naiveté, I asked my partner to bank my weekly pay cheque into an account that I couldn't touch and to just pay me the minimum I needed for food, rent, and general expenses. He very kindly agreed, as we continued with this arrangement and relationship for another few years.

When the relationship came to an end. I asked my partner for access to my account, and to my great shock and surprise, the account had never even been set up. In fact, he had spent the money on his own drinking and gambling addictions, which I'd never known were even an issue. It was all happening behind my back, and in the end, it cost me tens of thousands of dollars.

As I left that relationship, I was more convinced than ever that I was not only hopeless with money, but I was also hopeless with choosing who should manage it for me.

Fast forward, when Danny and I got back together, I discovered he was fantastic with money and saved just about every penny he made. He was careful and really had it together, so it gave me a great sense of reassurance that we were going to be okay when it came to our financial future.

Over time, together we built the equity in our home and had money in the bank, and the limiting beliefs about money seemed to dissolve into the background. That is, until I overheard a comment from a friend of Danny's saying that Danny always 'had the luck of the Gods'. Right then, my own realisation of inadequacy hit me. Danny and I weren't in the great financial position because he was good with money, it was because *he* was just plain lucky.

And there it was, and there it stayed. Left to linger and fester until sometime later when I was ready to venture into the world of property development. I'd spent months looking for just the right property to build on and when I found it, both Danny and I were so excited because there was a chance we could make real returns on our investment if we got this one right.

The next step was finding the best building company to partner our venture. So off I went, on the hunt. I began asking around, looking for recommendations, interviewing construction companies, and I even discussed it with friends from all social connections in the hope that someone could suggest a suitable building company. After a few weeks, I discovered that a friend in our young mothers' group, and her family, were in the building trade. Her husband was a builder, but had been experiencing tough times lately. On reflection, I was carrying a lot of guilt that Danny and I were doing so well, and these guys were, in a way, struggling. I offered the building project to my friend and her husband, and really felt it was a win/win situation for everyone. And deep down my conscience would be eased as the disparity between us, and our financial success, would be lessened.

I know you're anticipating what came next already, and yes, you're right. The property deal did not go as planned and let's just say Danny and I lost a lot of money. Like all challenges, it was all quite complicated but suffice it to say, we were significantly impacted, financially, after accumulating such a great nest egg. And after that episode, I was even more convinced that even when I make money, I lose it.

After Danny's sister tragically passed away, we decided to move to Australia and to take the smaller nest egg we had left and invest it somewhere that it could grow while we found our feet in a new country with two little kids.

I researched for months to find the best financial investment for our little 'stash' and when I found what I believed to be a strong financial management institution, we made the decision to transfer our money from our bank to theirs. Danny and I were excited to watch our investment grow and I really believed we had made a great decision this time.

Three months later however, I got a call from my girlfriend who was not only working for this institution but had invested everything she had with them, saying it was all gone, everyone had gone under. Everyone.

The fear, the anger, the anxiety, and a white-hot terror kicked in as I contemplated that yet again, I had lost everything. I couldn't believe I had done this to our family after we had worked so tirelessly to build up the savings we had. I couldn't believe I had done this to Danny.

Of course, we weren't the only ones to lose money. In fact, there were thousands of Australians who lost millions in the collapse and I can't even begin to imagine those who had invested their entire life savings, only to find they were left broke, with no way to recover their losses. There was one positive I guess; at least we were young enough to rebuild.

Fast-forward again to a few years ago, I was ready to close the doors on my much-treasured business, Twenty8. It seems my limiting beliefs had caught up with me. *Money is hard to come by, I'm hopeless with my money, I have no idea when it comes to money.* All of these limiting beliefs had their way with me all at once, and I was faced with some very difficult decisions that I knew I had to make.

In my darkest hour as I sat in our beautiful, rented home alone, I began to contemplate the possibility of alternatives because closing my business down just didn't feel right to me. I mean, I knew all the signs were pointing to that outcome, but something wasn't sitting right. I started to put my beliefs under the microscope to see if they were true and to see what else I had inside that could bring a different outcome. I was just exploring. I had no idea if there was an answer to this question, but I felt it was worth a look. What is that amazing saying? *"Keep doing what you've always done, you'll keep getting what you've always got."* It was time to do something different.

I began to look at what I did when the chips were down over the years and the inner strength that always seemed to get us through. I mean, I may have lost a lot of money over the years, and I may have also spent a lot, but one thing I've never experienced is poverty. The truth is that I've always had enough. I've always been able to go on holidays, enjoy wonderful experiences with my family, and I've never found myself truly scrimping and scraping like my dear mum had to in the early years.

Limiting self-beliefs are not something we are born with. We develop them or come to believe them from childhood, and then find reasons and situations in our lives to confirm that we are right about how far we can go.

Deciding on a limiting belief is a conscious process and is usually caused by an event or situation where we felt we really didn't measure up. The more we hold this thought pattern, the stronger it becomes and eventually it becomes subconscious, just like when you first learned to drive a car. At first you were very aware of the brake, the clutch, the gears (if you learned in a manual) and you were very aware of the other cars and what you had to do. The more you repeated the practice of driving though, the more experienced you became with it, and eventually the process became subconscious. So, too, with our beliefs. The more we practice them and repeat them, the more they become subconscious, and sooner or later they are driving your behaviour and results and you don't even know it's happening.

Some of our limiting beliefs are obvious. *I'm not good enough, smart enough or pretty enough; I'm too fat, I'm too slow.* These are right up there, in your face and you can hear yourself repeat them loud and clear. You don't step into adventures readily, and you find yourself second guessing opportunities.

Some are much more subtle and sneaky and have been imprinted from a very young age. How about 'money doesn't grow on trees' or 'you have to work hard to get anywhere in life' or 'people don't like chatter-boxes'. In truth, these are all limiting beliefs, and most of us have heard or carried ones like these with us from time to time. While they are subtle, and you wouldn't know that they are there, they still temper your behaviours and colour your actions.

I honestly believe that we have made bucket-loads of limiting decisions about ourselves, and for the most part, they aren't even important, but we do need to explore those crippling beliefs that lead you to defend your negative view of yourself; that you aren't limitless.

When I thought back to my own story and my own limiting beliefs about money, I had to ask myself about the part of me that stepped up when the chips were down, to bring myself, my bank account, and my inner peace back into balance.

TENACITY!

I may be a lot of things, and indeed I'll be the first to admit that I am a 'work in progress', but I think tenacity would be one of my greatest attributes. When I look back on my career, my world record, and what it's taken to raise my babes, build homes, and grow a business, I've held a deep belief that I have what it takes, and that is tenacity! It was just a case of figuring out how to apply tenacity to my business situation so that I could dismiss these limiting beliefs once and for all.

The more I analysed my past, the more I realised that when I focused my energy, attention, and efforts in the direction that matters, I can always manifest and create the outcomes that serve me and others. I discovered that I genuinely had what it was going to take to make this business work, and while it was going to take some extra effort on my part, some luck maybe, and the right team of people, there was absolutely no reason why I couldn't at least give it a try. I had everything to gain, and nothing to lose.

I knew that I had to put my energy into the numbers of my business, because making the money and managing it WAS my business! My business coach always said, "Kim, when you love the numbers, the numbers love you back." These were the most powerful words that have stuck with me ever since, and it was all I needed to set me in the right direction. I knew my business was in desperate need of help to not only get efficient systems and procedures in place, but also to take it to the next level.

Whilst I was in hospital undergoing back surgery a year later, I had plenty of time to think about what it was I truly wanted, and how I envisaged it playing out. You see, each year I choose one or two words to focus on, and last year my focused word was 'ease'. But to be honest the year felt anything but easy.

My son, Jakob, was swimming in his own world of problems and struggling in his new school environment, my daughter, Tayla, was struggling greatly with stress fractures in her back, threatening her beloved dancing career. My hubby was yet again away for months on end, and I was constantly in fear of letting down my team and the position of the business with never-ending expenses. I felt like I was drowning.

So, I meditated on it daily and then decided to try something different and take different action. My girlfriend Cyndi and I get together once a year to work through Dr Michelle Nielsen's ten-step manifestation process. If you haven't read her book *Manifesting Matisse*, I highly recommend it; her ten-step process is a game-changer. Here is a quick summary of her ten steps, for when you want to bring something to fruition in your life.

1. Clarify your vision. It must be present tense. Make your vision bigger than you can imagine, like a 400-year vision.

2. Day in your life. Write down what your day will look like when you get there, in the present tense.

3. Vision book or board. Make a vision book or board. A book is easier to transport with you, use pictures, images and words for your vision.

4. Create a plan and act. What are the key actions, key people, and practical steps needed to create your vision.

5. Declutter. Get rid of all that is not needed, clear out the things that won't add to your cause.

6. Connect with spirit. Meditate, self-care rituals, trust your innate wisdom

7. Gratitude. Create a gratitude journal and engage in a relationship with universal intelligence. Write down ten things you are grateful for at the end of each day or ask, "What was the best thing in your day?"

8. Reframe your past. Remove emotional blockages and ego as well as words like, 'I deserve this'.

9. Build faith and surrender. Just trust, hand it over and let it unfold.

10. Revise and re-vision. Read over your vision every day several times a day.

Here's how this amazing manifestation process has worked for me. A few months after my back surgery on a trip to New Zealand, one of my closest friends and one of the most amazing business minds I know inquired as to how I was going. I decided there was nothing to hide. I told my dear friend Alan everything; how I had a constant fear of letting the business, and my team, down. I explained my constraints, my limitations, the increasing number of bills, and how I had felt the passion I held so strongly would always get me through. But the business had grown too big, and it needed more than I envisaged. It was all getting too much. I was drowning in a lonely, entrepreneurial, downward spiral.

This beautiful man said quite calmly, "It sounds like your business just needs more structure and some fuel on the fire." I knew he was meaning better processes and some monetary investment, I also knew we didn't have it. I shared with him my biggest dream, and the reason I had kept going for so long, "To be able to live comfortably, to create a business that gave work and meaning to others, to inspire my family and one of my biggest wishes was to make up the money I felt I had lost, and to earn enough to have my husband home."

Danny has been on the road traveling with his cricket career, firstly as a player, and then a commentator, for over thirty years. He has loved it, but for the past decade has wanted to get off the 'merry-go-round' and be home more. I have really missed Danny not being at my side, let alone not in the same country. He has absolutely loved his job and had forged a remarkable career, following the sport he has loved, it has been amazing. But it has also nearly cost us our marriage and has meant a heck of a lot of time apart. Danny had also missed many of our family's milestones, like our Australian citizenship ceremony, Tayla's dance concerts and competitions, Jakob's rugby games and prize-giving events, scholastic achievements, and of course all the struggles, challenges, and some of the adversities too.

I sat there quietly looking at Alan, on the verge of tears but also with a feeling of serendipity. I know I have always given my best, my absolute most. Maybe this just wasn't meant to be anymore?

Alan looked at me and just quietly said, "It's time he came home. Kimmy."

I have come to realise that when times get tough or challenging, I go still and surrender. I don't mean quit. I just mean I get to a certain point, stop, and just let it go. I let go of all the drama. You could say I withdraw, or even drop out. But I stop worrying about the outcome. There's no other word, I simply surrender.

My business coach, Bruce, taught me that when faced with opportunities or challenges, it is a good time to stop and write it down. Head up three columns on a blank piece of paper with these three questions. What is the upside? What is the downside? Can I live with the downside?

The question front and centre of my mind was 'Should I close the business doors? I knew if I closed the business, I would walk away with debt and a massive journey to finalise it all, as well as huge disappointment for many. I knew if I kept the doors open things had to change. And that too would be a massive journey with lots of capital required.

I also knew that no matter what, I had to be accountable, responsible, and take ownership for all the good and the not so good. So, on the question, "Could I handle the downside of closing the doors?" Then yes, okay, I could handle that. I mean, I wouldn't like it, but yes, I could handle it. So, in that moment, I knew it was time for me to hand it over and let the universe guide me in the right direction. I had to take a breath and let the answer come.

Conversations continued with Alan around my business and my dreams. Then out of the blue, he asked if he could help and become a part of the vision. Alan is someone I have known for 20 years. He has witnessed all I had given for almost two decades. He said he felt this was something worth investing in. He also told me he wanted nothing more than for me to have my dear husband home by my side.

I was gob smacked, and you'll understand why. Here is a part of what was written in my manifestation journal at the end of 2016:

It is the 1st of December 2017 and we are celebrating our new partnership with an extraordinary business partner. We have systems in place, we have a happy healthy team, we have a plan to forecast, direct, budget, evaluate, grow and expand throughout Australia and into New Zealand so that I can now travel between my two most favourite countries on the planet. Our education programs have all been re-evaluated for the better, we have new packaging and brand-new products being released in 2018. I have more time to commit to the things I know I contribute my best, like creating products, speaking and writing programs. We have systems and procedures in place. We stand proud in our messages and behind all of our products. Our team is happy. We are one and in our own lane. There is no competition. And there is ease in my mind. Money flows in and out of our bank account with forecasting for a 10% growth in 2019. I finally believe in myself and all the years I have been working to grow this dream. I have a deep innate knowing that life is grand. The best part is my husband is home more to help me guide this ship. My children are living their dreams and realising more and more their amazing worth. I take their lead and am living and realizing my worth. I say all of this with love, grace and ease.

I pinch myself as I re-write this vision. Alan is a remarkable entrepreneur. He is an amazing husband and father and the kindest, most generous person I know. We signed our partnership contract in October of 2017. Since then, along with some amazing new resources, we launched into New Zealand on the 28th March 2018, which just happened to be my 50th birthday. I still pinch myself that a dream was manifested and came true. To have someone with his skills and coaching in my corner has been a game-changer. At this very moment we are expanding internationally, collaborating with some extraordinary people and businesses, and Danny and I have even been able to buy a gorgeous home, our first home purchased in over twelve years. I've never felt prouder, not just of my business, or my team, but of myself. I dug my heels in, surrendered, held on tight as all the turbulences had to be figured out, and then realised what I needed and set my mind and energy in the direction required to bring about the change. That direction was to surrender, then work on my manifestation.

As my beautiful friend Cyndi always says, 'It doesn't surprise me anymore, this stuff really works!'

I feel so empowered writing this, and as I reflect on this part of my journey, I'm looking back feeling very grateful for the contrast that these limiting beliefs and challenges showed me, but more than that, I know now, that using the self-love circle is the quickest and most efficient way to get back on track when faced with adversity. Throughout my nine years in this business I have had people come into my dream, I have had people lift and support me and I have had people give so much of themselves. I have to remember if I ever question myself again, which I'm sure I will, I just need to dive straight into the first three steps of the Art of Self-Love again. It's like getting back out on the track and not giving up. One foot in front of the other.

Let's look at how this can apply to you. We know that what we believe determines what we achieve, and the results you currently have in your life are a result of the effort you put in, coupled with your belief about where your limit was. I'd like to encourage you to explore every area of your life, including your bank balance, family relationships, career, relation-ship with your partner, relationship with yourself, health and well-being, social life, and examine the experience you have in each of these areas. Are you satisfied, fulfilled, grateful? Or would you prefer improvements in each area? Then ask these three questions:

What's the upside?

What's the downside?

Can I live with the downside?

I can assure you that any part of your life that is lacking in lustre for you is directly a result of your limiting beliefs about what is possible in that area.

The beautiful, late Louise L. Hay said, "We learn our belief systems as very little children, and then we move through life creating experiences to match our beliefs. Look back in your own life and notice how often you have gone through the same experience."

Let's inquire into a step-by-step process to unearth these beliefs and then maybe to give ourselves a bit of relief so that we can stop re-creating the same outcomes in areas we would really like to change. You can quickly read over these or take the time to really do the work and enquire deep within. I was at breaking point when I decided something had to change. I needed to do something different. These next steps were a game-changer for me.

Step 1: Write down any and all limiting beliefs you have

This may take a while but stick with it. Think of everything you say to yourself that holds you back, or stops you taking giant, courageous leaps forward in your life. As you do this, on a scale of one to five, note how strongly you believe this belief and how it makes you feel. These are important steps to take to begin identifying the power of the role they play in your life.

Step 2: Acknowledge that these are beliefs, not necessarily truths

Remember that for something to be a 'truth', it is actually hard to define what truth is. You only have to ask a philosopher to define truth to see that. Is it perspective or is it truth? Everyone's experience of the world is a bit different – we all have different life experiences, background beliefs, personalities and dispositions and even genetics that shape our view of the world. This almost makes it impossible to declare an 'absolute truth'. Truth can be defined as: in accordance with facts or reality. How you view truth will impact how you show up in the work you do and will impact the decisions you make about how you raise your family or choose your partner or settle conflict. Belief can be defined as: an acceptance that something exists or is true, especially one without proof. So, a limiting belief then is a belief, and not a truth. Now it's about choice. Which would you prefer: to defend your limitations or to expand them? You choose.

Step 3: Try replacing the old belief with a new belief that actually works

Use your imagination here, and don't discount what you've learned through the challenges of life. The important part of this step is that you don't just say it because I'm suggesting you do it. You have to really embrace this new thought, so as you experiment with new thoughts about old beliefs, be willing to put your heart into it. Something like, *I've had some big financial lessons and I've learned so much from them, including how to not spend more than I earn, and how to save twenty percent each week before paying my bills. I'm fully prepared to value my money now and I'm great at it.* The aim here is to really loosen your grip on what you think is true about yourself and this process will go a long way towards that outcome.

Step 4: Now it's time to get into action

From our thoughts come our emotions then our actions. Sometimes this can be in different order and back to front but if we can be logical for a minute then ideally it would be great if we just take a breath and:

1. Think
2. Feel
3. Act

So, what have you got to lose? Try it! Act as if your new belief is true. Do it for a week and see if you feel better, as well as begin attracting different experiences into your life.

It's easy to brush past these steps because they take a bit of effort. However, know that these efforts are necessary if you plan to create fresh neurological habit-patterns in your brain. Remember, you can keep doing what you've always done, and keep getting what you've always got. Or you can try something new!

I knew something had to change for me and my business. Many years ago, a good friend Murray said to me, "Kim, there is no way you cannot do anything you set your mind to achieve. All you have to do is go on an 'information gathering' exercise and then see what you are capable of, and willing to do, to get it." I still use his advice.

And so, in my business make-or-break situation, I decided to go on an information gathering exercise and ask a number of successful people how they did it. One of those people was my Cyndi's husband, Howie. I knew this man was a success in his own right. I knew he had helped turn Cyndi's small one-person business 'Changing Habits' into a massive, family run enterprise. He was willing to help, and one of the biggest lessons I took from Howie was that I had to learn to put me and my family first. He told me some cold, hard truths and observations he had made. He then said I might not want to hear what he had to say next. My desire to please everyone was not helping me and it certainly wasn't going to help get my husband home. If I did not learn to put my family front and centre, then I may even drive the business into the ground. For the first time ever, I heard those words for what they were. My people-pleasing days were over.

The exercise of asking for others' opinions was confronting. It set in motion many conversations, sometimes even judgement, and I had to stand up and take it. I had other well-meaning friends and advisors tell me openly that what I was doing was wrong and why I was in this position. I had one person tell me I should shut up shop and just go and work for a much larger aromatherapy company. It was tough, I won't deny it, but in hindsight it was an incredibly important part of accepting my limitations and strengths.

Now, I understand that this can be really challenging for all of us, and to make changes in our mindset and in our life can take a mammoth effort. I am sure you have walked in these self-doubt shoes, and I appreciate that we can all feel exhausted by life and the constant up-hill battle of trying to get everything right or on track. Running a business or having a family is not for the feint-hearted. And if you have kids, then the pressure to succeed is even more intense, because, predictably, you want to be a shining example to your children. You want them to know everything will be okay, even when it's not.

There are some days when you look at that person in the mirror and know the most important thing you could do is acknowledge it and forge ahead.

My dear friend Brett Hill's world fell apart the night his wife told him it was over. He had just returned from winning the grand final with his indoor cricket team, on a complete high, when she broke the news. With two small children, the white picket fence, the family dog, and a winner's trophy under his arm, you can imagine how he felt.

I knew my friend was devastated, he had lost a lot of weight over the ensuing weeks and when we met in Melbourne to present at The Wellness Summit. I was a little shocked. We had breakfast together. He was so down, so broken, so hurt. I just listened. I was hurting with him. I wanted to wrap him up and make it all ok, but I couldn't.

Whilst I completely understand how we can stop believing in ourselves, and can feel completely and utterly lost when our heart is broken, I also know that continual self-sabotaging thoughts do not help us. After some time of listening to my friend repeat the story, I found these words just spilling out of my mouth.

"Look honey, I totally get it, and I am so, so sorry you are going through this. It has happened for some strange reason, and not that you are even wanting to look ahead, who knows who or what could be around the corner. You cannot change what has happened, you cannot make your wife take you back, and you have no idea what the future holds, but I can tell you this. Your kids need you, your family needs you, the people attending this summit need you, and your future partner in life needs you, so the only thing you can do right now is man the fuck up and get on."

Harsh as it was these were the same words I used with Danny when he was in a self-sabotaging world of no respect, no confidence, and no self-belief repeating the same story. And to be honest I have had people who love me give me the same advice in a similar way; it's a real wake up call.

There's a postscript here: Brett has gone on to meet the love of his life in his partner, Steph. They are absolutely besotted, and they have both never stopped believing in the power of love. They are marrying next year. Brett and I still both chuckle about those profound words of wisdom on that cold Melbourne winter morning and has since told me they were a turning point in his life.

And now I ask you. Are you ready to man- or woman-up and start believing in yourself the way people around you need you to?

Essential Oils for Limiting Self-Beliefs:

Cardamom Oil: When you feel like you're in a rut, Cardamom reminds you of all that is possible leaving you feeling content, fulfilled, generous and warm. Leave behind feelings of depression, disheartened, mental fatigue, judgement, lethargy, and tension. This precious oil eliminates fears and worries and helps to restore your appetite for life.

Application: Massage, compress, inhale, diffuse, bathe and spritz this supporting and inspiring oil.

May Also Benefit: Digestion issues, flatulence, monthly feminine balance, immune support, coughs, bronchitis, nausea, circulation, and is even an aphrodisiac!

Cinnamon Oil: This warm, spicy oil is best when you're feeling emotionally separated or fragile. It can help alleviate fears, worries, lethargy, rigidity, feelings of withdrawal, and disheartenment. Reach for this oil to feel connected, energetic, expansive, passionate, vital, and comforted.

Application: Massage, compress, bathe, inhale, diffuse and spritz.

May Also Benefit: Muscle cramps and spasms, fever, headaches, bronchitis, coughs, colds, flu, digestion issues, weight loss, and even as an aphrodisiac!

Immortelle Oil: This oil helps clear the mind, awaken the senses and promote inner peace, bringing the qualities of adaptability, connectivity, forgiveness, positivity, strength, warmth, and wisdom when you're feeling disheartened, sorrowful, heartbroken, hurt, insecure, negative, stressed, or worried.

Application: Compress, massage, bathe, spritz, inhale, diffuse.

May Also Benefit: Bruises, scars, stretch marks, anti-aging, mature skin, sensitive, and dry skin. A great liver detox and terrific for inflammation, muscle aches and pains, bronchitis, coughs, and colds.

Lemon Oil: This fresh and stimulating oil is an instant pick-me-up, leaving you with energy and mental clarity. You'll feel less confused, defeated, disheartened, exhausted, weary, and worried.

Application: Massage, compress, diffuse or spritz. This oil makes a refreshing addition to your bath, opening the heart, alleviating exhaustion, and creating self-confidence.

May Also Benefit: Anti-aging, nausea, cellulite, weight loss, oedema, varicose veins, warts, colds, flu, immune support, and a liver tonic.

Note: Avoid exposure to the sun after using lemon in a massage or bath as it is phototoxic (will cause a sunburn like skin condition when exposed to sun light)

Mandarin Oil: This is your 'lighten up and enjoy life' oil and the one to call on to bring out your softer and more playful side, connecting you with your inner child. Sweet and uplifting, this oil will transition your experience of chaos, depression, fear, grief, rigidity, shock, stress, and worry into calm, inspiration, celebration, and trust.

Application: Massage, compress, inhale, bathe, spritz, diffuse.

May Also Benefit: Digestion issues, indigestion, muscle cramps, stretch marks, scars, insomnia, nausea, muscle tension, acne, oily skin, and wrinkles.

Myrtle Oil: Cleansing, positive, harmonious, and peaceful, kindness and sensuality replace anxiety, chaos, fear, tension, hurt, hopelessness, and feelings of worthlessness. Supporting deep inner wisdom and knowing, calm the busy mind, and feel reassured that we are all supported and connected.

Application: Inhale, diffuse, spritz, massage, sitz bath, bathe, compress, and hair rinse.

May Also Benefit: Bronchitis, catarrh, coughs, urinary tract infections, haemorrhoids, acne, oily skin, open pores, hormone support, and head lice.

Patchouli Oil: This enduring and sensual oil makes for a hypnotic aroma when blended with ylang ylang and orange, increasing intimacy and passion. Attract abundance, confidence, courage, enlightenment, expansion, focus, grounding, peace, and sensuality. When you're feeling anger, anxiety, controlling, disheartened, distant, hopeless, stressed, or tense, keep this harmonising and re-generative oil on hand.

Application: Massage, compress, spritz, bathe, inhale.

May Also Benefit: Cracked and dry skin, stretch marks, fluid retention, cellulite, dermatitis, eczema, inflammation, wounds, and guess what? It's even an aphrodisiac!

~ Negativity and Drama

"Negative people need drama like oxygen.
Stay positive, it will take their breath away."
– Anonymous

I have a dear friend who reached out to me after experiencing a particularly painful breakup. Without going into the sordid details, suffice it to say that no one walked away unscathed, and there was a very long and drawn out process that followed which required legal intervention in the end. It was messy.

My heart was breaking for my friend as she unloaded the pain she was feeling over the phone, at midnight. I tried my best to be supportive of her circumstances, but there really wasn't anything I could do other than listen. After about a month, I found I was getting messages, emails, phone calls, and unannounced drop-ins at all hours of the night, and it became a bit disruptive. I tried to be understanding. After all, she was in pain and I was her confidante.

Three months later, I was still experiencing late night and early morning calls, text messages, frantic requests for help, and repetition of the same story. But each time her narrative became more embellished and intense. At the six-month mark, I began to regret the incessant demands for rescuing and I began to feel a bit resentful.

My friend had no idea how I was feeling. On the outside, I was still expressing a great deal of compassion for the situation she was in. The great challenge, however, began when she started feeling angry and hurt whenever she felt that I wasn't available, or couldn't rescue her right at her time of need. In those moments, she would tell me that I was, "Obviously too busy for her", or tell me how she wouldn't cope if I wasn't there for her. Her attitude became a little possessive and needy.

After nine months, I couldn't hold it in any longer and I had to talk to her about self-responsibility, and self-control. I tried to tell her gently that maybe there was an element of drama and it needed to change. She needed another confidante or a good therapist. I could no longer be that person for her. She was shocked, so I shared some books with her that might help. I offered some amazing TED talks she could watch to comfort herself, and suggested we attend a few conferences with expert teachers on health, wealth, relationships, self-care… anything to redirect her focus on the outer world, to give her inner journey a bit of space.

Although she was shocked, she became apprecia-tive, and while her anguish and demands didn't subside immediately, it became evident that she didn't seem to have the skills to support herself. To her credit, she began reading the recommended books and watching the videos I recommended, like Dr Brian Weiss's book *Only Love Is Real* and Brené Brown's TED talks on vulnerability. She also enrolled in a weekend retreat I was running on self-care and self-love.

After a short while I began to see a new person, with a new outlook on life, and instead of pushing people away with her need for drama and rescue, she was able to draw people in and surround herself with friendships that were beautiful and beneficial for all involved. It was a wonderful experience to witness. Because of her ability to move beyond her need for drama, she has formed spectacular friendships. To this day, we honour the journey we traversed as she moved beyond negative drama and I moved beyond rescuing her.

It appears there is no delicate way to approach this self-sabotaging behaviour, simply because anyone who creates negativity and drama is usually doing it habitually. Research suggests this need to generate drama to achieve more attention is usually established when we are young, and it may be because we weren't given enough attention. Those who tend to live in this negativity-and-drama habitual pattern will experience people pulling away, because their behaviour tends to highjack others' lives around them by drawing them into an endless succession of daily problems. There is anxiety, overreaction, emergencies, exaggeration, over-sensitivity, and a deep fear of insignificance. It's exhausting at best, and manipulative at worst, and sadly, it's not intentional. It's almost subconscious, and even though the negative drama king or queen can see the response they are getting from people around them, they have no idea how to behave differently because it's been their way of expression since childhood.

This constant drama manifests in the form of urgent demands, incessant complaints, boundary violations, endless soap operas, and deep resentment if, in their opinion, the person (or people) they 'trust' let them down. It's a challenging situation, and interestingly, quite common.

On the flipside, our negative drama kings and queens can be very charismatic, attractive, and engaging people, and being drawn to them initially is effortless because they are so compelling. However, being the good-natured friend of a drama king or queen by helping, supporting, coaching, and rescuing can enable the negativity and drama, reinforcing the behaviour and ultimately abusing the friendship. The old proverbial, where you're, 'Damned if you do, damned if you don't' applies here.

If you're seeing some of your own behaviour in this section, or feeling you could be suffering from the effects of negative drama, you may want to investigate some professional support, because while we are working towards understanding ourselves and the slip-ups that can make us fall out of the self-love circle, there are some causes that are beyond the help we can provide here, and it's my most sincere wish that every single one of us can find that warm, loving, and nurturing centre within ourselves. There is nothing wrong with needing a little extra help. Goodness knows my amazing therapist Jacqueline has helped Danny and I more times than I can count. I honestly believe that having a professional in your corner who you can turn to when things get too far out of reach, can help us in our greatest times of need.

Taken from an excerpt on the *Out of the Fog* website (http://outofthefog.website) here are some scenarios that may sound familiar, either about yourself or someone you know:

- A family member starts an emotional argument with relatives while the bride and groom are cutting the cake.

- A parent rushes their child to the hospital with a minor complaint.

- A man habitually calls the police when no one is at risk.

- A person calls or shows up unannounced when they have been politely asked not to, claiming a crisis makes it necessary they ignore your request.

- A person always repeats the most outrageous, salacious, and dramatic gossip in order to get attention.

- A man threatens a lawsuit when a waiter spills his coffee.

- Someone seems to be more often than not in a state of crisis for no apparent or logical reason.

- The person makes a challenging situation all about them instead of the situation at hand

- Constant cries for help, advice, support or rescuing with no change no matter how much support is offered.

Just like a drug addiction, the need for an attention-fix tends to drive the behaviour of a negative drama king or queen, and the people around them become the drug dealers. The more support friends or family provide, the more is needed. It's a vicious cycle, but I'm confident that with a bit of self-awareness, self-care, and self-discipline we can really turn the tides around and flow beautifully into the well of self-love.

If you are ready to step into a new and fresh experience of your life, where you attract people you love, and love you right back, then it's time to really look at what is making you, you! Is it what may have happened to you when you were a child, or is it who you choose to be now?

We are so much more powerful than we give ourselves credit for, and the recipe for peace, calm, bliss, joy, and love all starts here. You don't need to DO anything. All you need is the willingness to change; nothing more, nothing less. You may want to add some beautiful, restorative essential oils to your kit bag though. They have always been my go-to remedy, and if you can surround yourself with gentle reminders like diffusers, vaporisers, and spritzers around your home, car, office, your bathroom or bedroom, you will find the process of change and self-love a much more enriching and lasting experience.

Chapter 2:

THE POWER OF THE SELF-LOVE CIRCLE

You Possess the Power

Human kind, you are the Godforce that walks this plane. You are the controllers of what happens through your free will. You possess the power to have the most beautiful life imaginable. It is up to you to create it. You have this beautiful power of love – use it, develop it. Ensure that it is what you want in your life and spread that love, decide to be that love, and you will have everything you need. You are love, and from that love you will find a wonderful peace that you will radiate out, changing your environment, your world. It is only from love that you will have your true desires fulfilled. Please bring it to be.

– Kay Meade

I am a person who likes to feel she knows what to do. I like to follow a plan, a protocol, or a program. I like to be able to follow a pathway to achieve my goals and dreams because I like some form of structure when creating new ways of being. It's not that I am averse to altering the pathway, or in fact changing it. I just like to know what to do when my heart and soul are set on something. Likewise, when I am hurting or struggling too much to think clearly, I also like to have a plan and know there is a way out.

Maybe it is because of my athlete/coach mentality. You set a goal, your coach gives you the program, then you get on and just follow it. Your coach is there to push you, guide you, support you, and bring out the best in you. I think this is how the self-love circle was created. I see it a bit like my coach. When I am hurt or feel challenged I want to know what to do. How the hell do I pick myself up off the bathroom floor, deal with someone who has hurt me, or fight through self-sabotaging thoughts? I would prefer someone take the pain away or fix it. I want someone to tell me to follow some sort of a plan, so I can work through it as quickly and effectively as possible.

Whilst I am yet to meet anyone lucky enough to escape pain or challenge throughout their life, I also appreciate that neither is it helpful to bury or avoid the agony that comes with it. Put simply, my reason for establishing the self-love circle was to have a step-by-step process so we can all fast track our way out of there with as much courage, grace, strength, and dignity as possible.

I have watched every person I love go through varying degrees of challenging times. Yes, some things may be quite small in the scheme of things, but there are the big, 'hit by a truck' moments in life, too. Yes, you can have empathy, you can feel incredibly sorry for, and stand beside someone you care about. And you can support them with all your heart as they endure what is before them. But an even more powerful thing to do is to support them while they gather the tools to support themselves, and take the necessary steps that enable them to come out the other side whole, and unbroken.

Ultimately, when it is you experiencing struggle, you may have discovered that very few really care about what you are going through. I don't say that lightly. I mean, people may ask how you are, and they can say things like "I'm here if you need", or compliment you with things like, "You're coping so well". But the truth is, they're not being awful, it's just that everyone has their own lives to lead, their own struggles and challenges, and their own personal battles. We're all in our own worlds, just doing the best we can with what we've got.

So, who is there to pick you up when you're down? Who is there to help you breathe through the agonies and challenges of life? Even if you have your best friend, your partner, your mum or your dad right there beside you, no one can live your pain or take that pain away for you. That, my friend, is fundamentally personal. And it's in those darkest moments you realise you are, in fact, all alone. You cannot put a date on when it will be over, you cannot determine what will help you get through such times. And you certainly cannot expect anyone or anything to take that pain away. Things like alcohol, drugs, food, wild behaviour, even turning a blind eye may temporarily subdue the pain, but none of this can ever truly take it away.

Having faith in something greater than you, a belief that a larger force will carry you through is important. But ultimately what gets you through these troubles is you, and time.

At the centre of your whole self is the driving force, the super-power, the all-empowering utopia, and that is self-love. Spiritually, emotionally, physically, mentally; love is the essence. We are reminded to love ourselves. We are told that in order to love someone else we need to love ourselves first. We tell our children, our brothers and sisters, mothers and fathers, and our friends how much love is inside of them, how much they are loved. Love is the answer to all things.

Yet in life we often fall out of that feeling when we are struck by bathroom floor moments, frightening news, health issues, relationship challenges, loss, grief, hurt, self-sabotaging beliefs; things that distract us and pull us away from feeling self-love. In other words, we fall out of the circle of love. But here's the truth again. No one escapes falling out of the circle of self-love. We have all cried, we have all hurt, and we have all endured things we wish we hadn't.

The amazing thing about the power of hindsight is that, in time, we can become grateful for those 'out-of-the-circle' experiences. We know we would not be where we are, or who we are today, had those things not happened. Although it is hard to feel grateful in the moment, we all know that if we choose to grow through what we go through, we usually emerge on the other side much better people.

I have heard the saying, "The meat cleaver comes down on everybody at some time in their life, and no one escapes it."

So, if that's the case, isn't life more about learning how to deal with those tough times, those challenges, and those bathroom floor moments?

The minute you are even slightly aware that you are out of the circle of self-love you are automatically back in it. Self-awareness is the first step of the six-step process back to self-love. In other words, being aware that you are feeling the way you are feeling is the beginning of your healing.

I want to share a story on how the self-love circle has literally helped me and saved me. Throughout my life I have been motivated to be kind. Maybe it is the fact my mum worked so hard and gave so much of herself. Maybe it is the loving genes of both of my grandmothers, Dorothy May, and Myrtle Rose Milllicent, that I admired. I have wanted to treat everyone I meet with care and kindness like they did.

Even when someone is passing judgement, or being mean-spirited and grumpy, I try to think of one of my favourite books, *The 4 Agreements*, mentioned on pages xxix and xxx. I try to remember to:

1. Be impeccable with my word.

2. Ask questions, and not make assumptions.

3. Do not take things personally, and

4. Always give my best.

I try to err on the side of curiosity. What is making them behave in this way? Maybe they have had a bad day? Maybe someone has been awful to them? Maybe they have lived through something I could never understand? Maybe they just haven't had enough sleep? Or maybe their gluten intolerance has caused them to react badly! Whatever it is, I must remember they have their own perspective, their own reality, and most importantly, I have not walked in their shoes; and that's okay. My job is not to react to their behaviour, but to act according to my own values and principles, and for me, the place I am most comfortable with is a place of kindness.

Sometimes, I will decide in that moment that my mission is to try and make them smile. Make them a little more happy. Or help them see another perspective. Or try to see theirs in a more open way. And sometimes that works beautifully. But sometimes, no matter how much I try, or want to make it okay, it just isn't enough.

I have lost what I thought were beautiful friendships, people have come and gone. And I have come to learn this too is part of life. My girlfriend, Maria, said to think of life as being on a train. You typically start out with your parents. Along the ride there could be siblings and other family members. At one stop you might pick up a new friend who rides for a few stops. Some will hop on that train and be with you forever more. Others may be on the train for a shorter period, hop off and then hop back on. The train is always moving forward, and the passengers can change along the way. The same goes with friendships. That is life; and it is all okay.

When I am struck by a broken relationship, or friendship that has been lost, it is true to say it is like having the wind knocked out of my sails. I don't like it, and I'm not very good at feeling like I have let someone down, or someone has let me down. There is a sense of loss, maybe even hurt, and it's not a fun place to be.

When I am aware I have fallen out of the circle with self-doubt, self-judgement or self-sabotaging beliefs, I will remind myself that some things are out of my hands. I then attempt to take extra care for myself. It could be that I put on the diffuser and some music or simply go for a barefoot beach walk. Or take myself for a coffee on my own and write in my journal. I might do a nice self-care bath with calming essential oils like chamomile, rose, lavender and mandarin. I could listen to a new podcast, cook my family a healthy meal or get outdoors and take photos of nature. I just like to do something that is nice and on my own and remind myself this is all part of the train journey. And if I am feeling flat about it I commit to the act of self-care for the next twenty-eight days.

One of the most impactful things I can do whenever I get that horrible feeling in my gut is to ensure I use an aromatic tissue with conscious breathing. One drop of precious rose oil, which is known to help when there is a sense of loss, anger, grief, resentment, hurt or fear onto a tissue and take some nice, long deep breaths. I hold my tummy with my right-hand, so I remember to breathe right down into that area and breathe deeply into the other hand holding the aromatic tissue.   Controlled restorative breathing helps to send a signal to the brain and calm the nervous system. This can help reduce stress and anxiety, calm your heart rate, ease digestion, reduce the release of stress hormones like cortisol and boost your immune system. This simple self-care ritual almost always helps me to come to a gentler place within.

People come into your life for a reason, a season, or a lifetime.

When you figure out which one it is you will know what to do for each person.

When someone is in your life for a REASON it is usually to meet a need you have expressed. They have come to assist you through a difficulty; to provide you with guidance and support; to aid you physically, emotionally or spiritually. They may seem like a godsend, and they are. They are there for the reason you need them to be.

Then without any wrongdoing on your part or at an inconvenient time this person will say or do something to bring the relationship to an end. Sometimes they die. Sometimes they walk away. Sometimes they act up and force you to take a stand. What we must realise is that our need has been met, our desire fulfilled; their work is done. The prayer you sent up has been answered and now it is time to move on.

Some people come into your life for a SEASON because your turn has come to share, grow or learn. They bring you an experience of peace or make you laugh. They may teach you something you have never done. They usually give you an unbelievable amount of joy. Believe it; it is real. But only for a season.

LIFETIME relationships teach you lifetime lessons; things you must build upon in order to have a solid emotional foundation. Your job is to accept the lesson, love the person and put what you have learned to use in all other relationships and areas of your life. It is said that love is blind, but friendship is clairvoyant.

– Unknown

You will know you have found yourself out of the circle of self-love, when you find yourself asking questions or making statements like:

- Why me?
- It's so unfair
- Why am I here?
- How could they do this?
- How dare they do this?
- What's wrong with me?
- What's their problem?

It is times like this when I especially love the serenity quote:

God grant me the serenity to accept
the things I cannot change;
The courage to change the things I can;
And the wisdom to know the difference.
– Dr Reinhold Niebuhr

Working within the framework of the self-love circle above has allowed me to create more calm in my life. It also has given me the courage and the grace to move through hurtful times and to come to a place of acceptance. I know I may not always get it right. I know sometimes I completely and wholeheartedly muck it all up. And that's ok, we all do.

When I seek to exist in a place of love I can appreciate that we're all doing our best, even if that best is not good enough in other people's eyes. With this work I have learned to have more empathy and love for all. And I have also come to appreciate that when anyone is in crisis or going through something really tough, then this is how I can help them best.

My wish is that the self-love circle will become a wonderful go-to for you. I hope it will support you to crawl through those moments of challenge and leap towards a more empowered life that you love, regardless of what it feels like life can throw at you.

One thing I've always known, and I'd love you to try out this mindset, is that we may not always have the answers, but if we have the question and we are willing to look, we may always be surprised and amazed by what we find!

> *"We delight in the beauty of the butterfly,*
> *but rarely admit the changes it has gone*
> *through to achieve that beauty."*
> - Maya Angelou

The next part of this book will break down the 6 steps to embrace so you can always live in the ultimate place of self-love. The first three steps are the DOING. You have to DO something to make it happen and these steps include self-awareness, self-care and self-discipline. When you practice and apply these three steps you will find yourself automatically flow into BEING your best, with more self-control, which leads to enhanced self-respect and true self-acceptance.

Essential Oils Self-Love Kit:

Cedarwood Oil: Release the strains of chaos, mental fatigue, negativity, neglect, sensitivity, stress, and withdrawal and embrace courage, focus, inspiration, purpose, worthiness, and wisdom.

Application: Massage, compress, bathe, inhale, diffuse, spritz, sitz bath.

May Also Benefit: Eczema, dermatitis, respiratory conditions, urinary tract infections, cystitis, acnes, oily skin, greasy hair, cellulite, and oedema.

German Chamomile: A very calming and healing oil to ease anger, irritation, nervous tension, stress, and hopelessness, instead inducing feelings of harmony, joy, and relaxation.

Application: Massage, bathe, compress, spritz and diffuse.

May Also Benefit: Inflammation, arthritis, dermatitis, muscle aches and pains, sensitive skin, dry skin and rashes. Great for bruises, burns, acne, psoriasis, and feminine balance. Dilute to 2.5% to help heal inflamed skin conditions. A high content of the active compound azulene give this oil its deep blue colour.

Roman Chamomile Oil: One of the best oils to use when feeling grumpy, agitated or irritated. Ideal for hormone support and relieving stress. It is a wonderful oil to reinstate a sense of comfort and belonging and one of the safest oils to use on children. You'll experience calm, expansion, peace, relaxation, and a sense of worthiness instead of anger, anxiety, heartbreak, impatience, negativity, sorrow, or worry.

Application: Compress, spritz, massage, diffuse, inhale.

May Also Benefit: Acne, boils, cuts, sensitive skin, dry or red skin, insomnia, muscle tension, nausea, digestion issues, menopause, endometriosis, pre-menstrual syndrome, and infertility.

Clove Oil: You'll feel confidence, courage, creativity, focus, openness, strength and warmth instead of confusion, depression, lethargy, and negativity. When mixed with peppermint oil, clove oil is well known to ward off fatigue.

Application: Diffuse, inhale, spritz, massage, bathe, direct application (for mouth ulcers and dental issues only - dip a cotton bud into the undiluted oil and apply to the surface and surrounding areas of the aching tooth).

May Also Benefit: Colds, flu, arthritis, rheumatic pains, digestion issues, parasites, mouth ulcers, muscle aches and pains, insect repellent, and air freshener.

Note: Use in moderation as considered a potential skin irritant. Be careful with topical application during first trimester in pregnancy.

Fennel Oil: With its cleansing and energising properties, fennel encourages you to be more productive, creative and on-task to meet your highest aspirations. You'll enjoy compassion, courage, fulfilment, and strength in the place of chaos, frustration, insecurity, negativity, and stress.

Application: Massage, compress, bathe, inhale, diffuse, spritz.

May Also Benefit: Constipation, diarrhoea, flatulence, indigestion, nausea, headaches, pre-menstrual syndrome, hormone support, fluid retention, varicose veins, weight loss, and respiratory conditions.

Note: Be careful with topical application during first trimester in pregnancy.

Geranium Oil: Call on this delicate yet potent oil when life feels like a continuous rollercoaster ride. When you're feeling chaotic, deceived, distant, moody, negative, or sensitive, geranium will bring balance, calm, connection, focus, harmony, and protection.

Application: Compress, massage, bathe, spritz, diffuse, inhale.

May Also Benefit: Acne, eczema, dermatitis, congested skin, mature skin, broken capillaries, pre-menstrual syndrome, hormone support, infertility, menopause, wounds, bruising, and oedema.

Note: Be careful with topical application on hypersensitive or overly red and inflamed skin.

Immortelle Oil: This oil helps clear the mind, awaken the senses and promote inner peace, bringing the qualities of adaptability, connectivity, forgiveness, positivity, strength, warmth, and wisdom when you're feeling disheartened, sorrowful, heartbroken, hurt, insecure, negative, stressed, or worried.

Application: Compress, massage, bathe, spritz, inhale, diffuse.

May Also Benefit: Bruises, scars, stretch marks, anti-aging, mature skin, sensitive and dry skin. A great liver detox and terrific for inflammation, muscle aches and pains, bronchitis, coughs, and colds.

Juniper Oil: Helping to clear your mind from negative thoughts and mental clutter, this purifying oil will bring confidence, focus, joy, openness, relaxation, and clarity. Dust off apprehension, chaos, exhaustion, negativity, and weariness.

Application: Massage, bathe, diffuse, spritz, compress, inhale, and sitz bath.

May Also Benefit: Liver detoxification, muscle aches and pains, oedema, inflammation, cellulite, varicose veins, oily skin, pimples, cystitis.

Note: Be careful with topical application during first trimester of pregnancy.

Lemongrass Oil: Bring balance, clarity, endurance, energy, enthusiasm, expansion, motivation, and vitality to your days as you say goodbye to apprehension, depression, mental fatigue, impatience, lethargy, negativity, stress, vulnerability, and feelings of worthlessness.

Application: Massage, compress, bathe, spritz, inhale, diffuse.

May Also Benefit: Muscle aches and pains, bruising, oedema, inflammation, indigestion, fever, headaches, weight loss and cellulite. Works wonderfully as an insect repellent and air freshener and when used in massage, boosts energy and endurance.

Neroli Oil: Considered a wonderful rescue remedy oil, making it an ideal choice if suffering from shock or hysteria. It is one of the best oils to enhance creativity, trust intuition, and to connect to your higher self. Enjoy calm, contentment, courage, joy, nurturing, passion, peace, strength, and trust. Support depression, fear, grief, moodiness, negativity, sadness, shock, sorrow, and worthlessness.

Application: Massage, compress, spritz, diffuse, bathe.

May Also Benefit: Sensitive and dry skin, insomnia, muscle tension, diarrhoea, digestion issues, scars, broken capillaries, stretch marks, and is even an aphrodisiac!

Orange Oil: Just like its flesh, the oil promotes health and vitality. It's uplifting, radiating, relaxing, calming, and soothing properties bring contentment, creativity, ease, joy, kindness, and warmth. Let go of distance, hopelessness, irritation, moodiness, negativity, nervousness, obsessiveness, and sadness.

Application: Massage, bathe, compress, inhale, spritz.

May Also Benefit: Stretch marks, cellulite, arthritis, digestive issues, large open pores, acne, dry skin, liver detoxification, weight loss, insomnia, and muscle tension.

Oregano Oil: A beautifully purifying oil that warms to the skin during massage. Feelings of frustration, hopelessness, lethargy, impatience, negativity, procrastination and rigidity will be replaced with clarity, openness, protection, safety, and strength.

Application: Massage, compress, inhale and spritz this warm and stimulating oil.

May Also Benefit: Staving off colds, flus and sore throats, digestion issues, urinary tract infections, asthma, bronchitis, bacterial, and fungal conditions.

Pine Oil: This cleansing, refreshing, and invigorating oil can have the same effect as if you were standing in a pine forest. A fabulous oil for clearing the air, improving alertness, and increasing inspiration.

Application: Inhale, vaporise, bathe, spritz and compress this motivating and intuitive oil.

May Also Benefit: Coughs, colds, flu, asthma, cystitis, pyelitis, inflammation, muscle aches and pains, headaches, arthritis, rheumatic pain, and liver detoxification.

Sage Oil: An excellent physical detoxifier and emotional cleanser. It is also known to help enhance intuition and develop innate wisdom. This beautifully regulating oil will bring trust, confidence, adaptability, and energy as the antidote to anxiety, depression, grief, hopelessness, and negativity.

Application: Massage, bathe, compress, direct application (for cold sores only), spritz, inhale.

May Also Benefit: Muscle aches and pains, cold sores, loss of appetite, digestion issues, hormone balance, pre-menstrual syndrome, menopause, and excessive perspiration.

Note: Be careful with topical application during first trimester in pregnancy. Use in moderation.

Tea Tree Oil: Highly recommended for those who struggle with their body, depression, victimisation, and a sense of doom and gloom. Feelings of confusion, mental fatigue, irritation, lethargy, negativity, and shock will be soothed instantly. If you're wanting to feel protection, strength, vitality, energy, and wisdom, this is your oil.

Application: Massage, bathe, spritz, compress, diffuse, inhale and sitz bath.

May Also Benefit: Bacterial and fungal conditions, colds, flu, immune support, candida, cystitis, acne, pimples, rashes, burns, wounds, cuts, bites, and stings. The most antiseptic of all oils!

Wintergreen Oil: The sweet and minty scent of wintergreen is a powerful antidote to stressed muscles and head tension. Replace feelings of hurt, negativity, procrastination, and rigidity, with energy, endurance, motivation, positivity, relaxation, and heal those deep-down emotional wounds. As an added bonus, this oil has the ability to act as a natural pain reliever! It is also antiseptic, anti-arthritic, and an astringent.

Application: Massage, compress, diffuse, spritz, and bathe in this relieving and warming oil.

May Also Benefit: Colds, flu, muscle aches and pains, digestion issues, inflammation, bacterial, and fungal conditions.

Note: Avoid topical application during pregnancy. Always use diluted as the methyl salicylate content can cause skin sensitivities.

Chapter 3:

SELF-AWARENESS

"The ability to look within through reflection and insight. It's an inside job."
– Renee England

Now that we are aware of things that pull us from the circle of self-love, we can focus on what to do when we become present to what is. But what is it that has us missing the meaning of this presence, this mindfulness? When life and time passes us by and we feel harassed by the demands of family and work, we may feel that we are constantly making mistakes. We're never present in the moment and there is just never enough time to do everything we 'should'. We're confused more than we are clear, we're rushed, stressed, anxious, and maybe even feeling depressed. We're convinced we're totally alone in a busy world. We could be surrounded by a hundred people and still feel completely disconnected. We beat ourselves up for not being enough for those we love, we're irritable, withdrawn, and apathetic and can't figure out why self-sabotage follows so closely behind everything we attempt to get right!

Phew……. There is a high price to pay for being 'absent' from doing the best WE can, to live the life we've created.

I hear people asking, "Is there an alternative?"

Imagine knowing our own mind, behaviours, and how it feels to truly BE YOU.

Imagine what it would be like to master the inner conversation so that above all, we were kind to ourselves, first and foremost.

Imagine having the tools to be able to stay connected to YOU, no matter what the outside circumstances were presenting you with.

And imagine knowing that the moment we do become aware of our thoughts, actions, and behaviours, we are back in the circle of self-love.

If we've been stuck in the opposite to love, if we are in the throes of challenges and struggles, then we may be in the painful cycle of being 'absent' from ourselves, and we may be wondering how we will ever feel happiness or love again.

We may even recognise ourselves in any of the scenarios I've mentioned above, so this chapter will give us the top five signs of self-awareness and how we can spend more time in flow, and less time in fight or flight!

What I love about this journey is that self-awareness is the very first step in getting ourselves back into the self-love circle. That's why it makes sense that we explore this powerful tool right here and at this point in this guide.

Believe it or not, the minute we acknowledge our behaviour and become aware of what we're doing, we're automatically straight back into the self-love circle. It's that easy!

The minute you notice you are not yourself, feeling down, judging, or beating up on yourself, or using more negative language, you are ready. For when you notice, you are self-reflecting, and back in the circle of self-love. It's that simple. Awareness is the opening, the beginning, the start of the healing.

To say that I am inspired by someone who gets knocked down and then gets up and on with their life is an understatement. I have seen many amazing people demonstrate their ability to get up again, in formidable ways, and it all starts with self-awareness. To arrest their own ego and bring awareness to the way they handle life's events, there seems to be vital steps they all take. I've also added a few additional hints on how to begin assuming the 'observer' role in your own life, so that while you may not always get it right, you can at least be aware of what you can change to do it better next time.

Here are some more insights to support your own self-enquiry and awareness.

Step 1: Be aware of how you behave in all situations. Observe yourself for a week.

Bring your attention to your thoughts, beliefs, and habits. Create a relationship with yourself by listening to everything you say to yourself, how you respond in certain situations and experiences; watch how your habits may limit the choices you have as life unfolds moment by moment. There is no need to do anything about these observations initially; it's enough to just have the awareness.

Step 2: Write down your reactions, behaviours and actions.

If needed, think what you could have done better. Once you have observed yourself for at least a week, take notice of, and journal your thoughts, beliefs, habits, and behaviours. Keep your phone or a notebook close on hand so you can jot down what you observe about yourself. Notice if your behaviours are contributing to the outcomes you are creating. Maybe reflect on what other outcomes could have been achieved if you had been more selective, conscious, and aware of yourself. Start by noting the kind of outcomes you'd prefer, and then work backward to the thoughts, beliefs, and behaviours you will need to develop to bring the new outcomes to life.

Remember that it is important to understand that the life you have created right now, is a result of the YOU that you've been, up until now. In the areas that you are not satisfied, the only way to effect change is to determine what you would prefer to experience in terms of outcomes first, and then to 'build a new version of you' in that area. We do this by working through 'who' we are being while we are doing what we are doing. Our thoughts, beliefs, actions, behaviours, and inner dialogue are the keys to creating change, and I'd like to invite you to spend some time, first in self-reflection and observation, and then, invest some energy into 're-creation'.

Step 3: Check in with your beliefs and perceptions. Do they benefit you?

Do we waste energy judging ourselves and others? Are we expecting the world to be a certain way, and when it does not meet our expectations, do we spiral into resentment, negative self-talk, and exhaustion? That incredible lump of grey matter between our two ears make is where all of our beliefs and perceptions lay. They are not necessarily true, right, or real, but when we relate to them like they are, we're forced to judge the rightness or wrongness of ourselves and the world around us.

I'm not suggesting that we give up everything we believe, because that is not possible, but I am encouraging us to ask, "Does this perception or belief work for me?" And then FEEL how you feel when you act on those beliefs or perceptions. Does it leave you feeling happy and energised, or does it leave you feeling negative, heavy or tired?

Your inner world is completely determined by what, and how, you speak to yourself. When you swap your attention to focus on how you feel inside, rather than reacting to what is happening outside, you can make new decisions and choices that will bring you not only greater self-awareness, but greater self-love. By putting in the effort here, you put yourself back in the driver's seat of your life.

Life has a way of sending you challenges and opportunities in order to continue growing and it is HOW you choose to behave in life that determines the outcomes you attract. Awareness = Attraction.

Step 4: Invest in a great exercise regime that demands your attention.

Choose to participate in activities like running, walking, yoga, or swimming, on a regular basis. It doesn't have to be strenuous, as that is not the objective. The reason I recommend this sort of exercise is because most physical activities require your mindfulness.

Psychologists say that we spend up to ninety percent of our day on autopilot. When this happens, we are effectively not present in the here and now of our lives. When we live this way, it is difficult to be self-aware because we become so distracted with regrets, memories of the past, or anticipation and anxiety of the future. When the mind is so busy with chatter and noise, we forget to stop and breathe in our surroundings; feel the wind on our skin, enjoy the juicy crunch of an apple, or lose ourselves in the laughter of a child.

By giving ourselves physical activities to do daily, we give ourselves the opportunity to go into a mindful state and support our self-awareness at the same time. This mindfulness opportunity brings our focus into our body, mind and spirit, rather than what is going on around us and outside of us.

A great tip after completing the physical activity is to take at least five minutes to breathe slowly and/or meditate. I know this kind of stillness can be challenging for a lot of people, and there have been many times that my life has been so hectic that the thought of having to stop and sit still even for a minute has caused me more frustration than peace. It's not always easy, but making the time to quiet the mind after moving the body will bring benefits you can only understand once you've done the practice.

Personally, I'm a huge fan of transcendental meditation (TM). I've been doing it for many years on and off, depending on the time I have available.

While my busy schedule doesn't always allow me to do the full twenty minutes morning and night in TM, I always try to do something to soothe my mind. That could be a guided meditation by Dr Joe Dispenza, or my podcast co-host Carren Smith, or I will spend a few minutes practicing being mindful; it could be watching the warm flame dancing beneath my vaporizer or paying close attention to everything I am cutting up for a beautiful meal. Restorative breathing using an aromatic tissue has been an incredible tool for me.

You can take control of your life, and your mind, instead of allowing your ego to run the show. Regardless of any frustration or resistance you might have with meditation keep trying. This is you telling your ego mind that you are in control and you will create your life to be the way YOU want it!

Self-love is your birth right, so it's important you claim it. This starts with self-awareness and your willingness to look inside, quiet the mind and the body, and pay attention to how it feels to BE you.

Mindfulness = Self-Awareness.

Step 5: Create a rituals kit

This will remind you to bring your attention and awareness back to yourself as opposed to what is happening outside. Remember, you're working on creating change in your life and it's going to take a bit of effort on your behalf to do things a bit differently. Participating in consistent rituals will ensure that these changes taking place deep inside of you happen more quickly, and their effects last more permanently. My favourite rituals involve essential oils and include things like the daily body boost ritual and using a diffuser. See more on pages 335-337.

And furthermore, your go-to rituals could include:

- Carrying an essential oil like lavender, patchouli, frankincense, sandalwood or lime with you to create an aromatic tissue. Or have a made-up aroma mist spritzer bottle with your favourite blend. To see how to make one go to page 337.

- A small journal and pen that you can carry with you. This may not always work, especially when you're a busy parent or you have an incredibly full-on career, but my dear psychologist friend Jacqueline always says, "It's better to have all the thoughts and feelings out on paper than it is to have them circulating in your head." When your mind is emptied out onto paper, you may find you can see more clearly, and make more practical judgements about your actions or reactions. It's a great way to assess the validity of your perceptions and beliefs.

- Create a daily 'Gratitude' ritual and try to list ten things you are grateful for each day. If you find it challenging, it might be that you have not taken the time. Create a space each day to look for what you can be grateful for, even if it is only one thing. There is always something. My husband and I will often say just as we are going off to sleep, "Tell me three things you were grateful for today." It's a lovely way to end the day.

- A precious bottle of lavender oil can do wonders. Or invest in a blend that you love. I have created precious blends like Instant Calm which is made up of lavender, mandarin, orange, frankincense, roman chamomile and neroli, Peace and Meditation with lavender, frankincense, patchouli, sandalwood and myrrh, and Courage and Confidence which includes grapefruit, bergamot, orange, geranium, clary sage and rose, that you can inhale when the going gets tough. These are easy to carry, perfect rescue remedies and bring you instantly back to the present moment where you have the most potency. To know what is in the synergy blends we created, go to page 344.

- Set up a few diffusers around the house and at work. As you turn on the diffusers each day, take a moment to really appreciate where you are, the work you are doing, the gifts of your brilliant mind, body, and spirit, the children in your life, friends and loved ones, and the challenges you're experiencing that are inspiring you to grow.

- Place a feather or a picture of a feather on your desk or next to your bed to remind you to be gentle with yourself.

- A book of positive affirmations can change your state of mind almost instantly. One of the reasons I created the Aroma Cards pack (available at twenty8.com) was to call on the messages of the fifty plants I chose to research. I carry these cards in my handbag, take photos of the messages written on each of them, and have them on my desk at the office.

- A lavender-filled eye pack that you can use prior to dropping off to sleep. The magical scent of the lavender will bring relaxation and presence of mind to the moment, while the heaviness of the eye pack will be a wonderful invitation to begin the ritual of sleeping.

- Wrap a box in beautiful paper and cut a slit into it so that the box becomes a 'letterbox' to the universe. In the event of life circumstances becoming overwhelming, write a letter to the universe asking for the help you believe you need to create lasting solutions. Once you've 'posted' your letter, leave it alone. Don't open the box, re-read the letters, or keep score on how your request is progressing. Once the letter is posted, consider it done, and your job from there is to trust that the universe has your back.

- Wear a wristband to remind you to be present. When it becomes comfortable on one hand, switch it to the other. The point of the wrist band is that you are aware of its presence, which reminds you to come back to your own sense of self each time you feel it.

- Set a timer on your phone that goes off each morning and afternoon. This timer is specifically to remind you to take one minute of mindfulness in whatever it is that you are doing right at that time. Pay one hundred percent attention to the task you have at hand, and surrender your entire self to the sensations, smells, sounds, tastes, and the emotional connection you have to the experience. Really give yourself to what you're doing and notice how amazing you feel on the inside when you concentrate in this way.

- Download a mindfulness app that has a gong go off every hour. On the hour, with each gong, take it as the cue to do the Four S Ritual – Stand, Stretch, Spritz (with an aroma mist bottle), and most of all, Smile!

- Get up twenty minutes earlier each day and use this time to meditate.

- Create a ritual around your meals so that at least three times a day you are bringing yourself back to the 'awareness' of self. Personally, I set up a vaporiser or the diffuser at meal time, I love fresh flowers on the table, and sometimes I like to place a drop of an essential oil like lemon or rosemary onto the place mat, so when the hot plate hits the table the heat helps to release the aroma beneath it.

- Play beautiful music during meals. This can prompt you to pay close attention to the sounds and the feelings they evoke. The music you choose can be different every day; sometimes it might be a ballad, sometimes classical. Let your mood guide you when it comes to the tunes you play.

- Take a moment to show your gratitude for the food you are about to eat. Turn your attention inward to feel how that gratitude feels inside your soul. Note where it is located and describe the sensation of this gratitude. It really takes mealtime to an entirely new level and as a bonus, it creates the digestive enzymes that allows your body to 'assimilate and eliminate' all that it needs. It's quite a magical process if you can set yourself up with things that are special to you, and recipes that bring light to your body and soul.

- Create a Champion and Challenge ritual at meal time. Eat without the distraction (phones, books, newspapers, TV) and be present with who you are sharing a meal. Meal times can be a sacred ritual, and according to ancient Vedic traditions, the kitchen is the most sacred space in the home because that is where the nourishment of the family begins and is restored. Give this one some close consideration because it's easy to do, you can involve the entire family, and everyone will benefit. Additionally, to each share a Champion and Challenge moment of the day is a wonderful connection ritual. The person sharing has the floor for one or two minutes with no interruptions.

Then whoever is at the table can not only congratulate the person sharing for their champion moment of the day, but everyone can also offer support for the challenging moment if required. This becomes a beautiful way for everyone to talk and be heard.

There are plenty of rituals you could create. In support of your self-discovery journey, there is a guided meditation available in the link below. Feel free to use this as a starting point to begin your exploration of the power that meditation can bring to your self-awareness. I've kept the twenty-minute process simple so that you can revisit the meditation anytime you like as a refresher to your practice.

Set up a special place in your home solely devoted to meditation. Roll up a blanket or yoga mat, or even a pillow, and sit on the edge of it with your legs crossed. It is recorded as an MP3 that you can listen to from your most convenient device. Use earphones and make sure that all potential distractions have been limited including kids, pets, phones, alarms, or calendar reminders. Now, close your eyes and begin the meditation.

Interrupting a meditation is not dangerous, as some have suggested, however it could leave you in an altered state for the day. Some people have reported irritability; others have felt vague and disconnected. Anywhere in-between can be possible so to prevent feeling 'out of sorts' be sure to devote the full twenty minutes to your meditation, without interruption if you can.

LINK TO MEDITATION:

www.twenty8.com/selflovemeditation

Essential Oil Self-Awareness Kit:

Clary Sage Oil: Considered the 'champagne' of essential oils, clary sage calms anger, anxiety, irritation, judgement, nervousness, stress, and feeling overwhelmed. Strengthening and fortifying the mind with clarity, creativity, enthusiasm, inspiration, intuition, and strength, this oil can help you become joyful and intoxicated with life.

Application: Massage, compress, bathe, diffuse, and spritz.

May Also Benefit: Keep this oil on hand for monthly feminine balance, labour, childbirth and infertility, asthma, bronchitis, muscle aches and pains, and even oily hair.

Pine Oil: This cleansing, refreshing and invigorating oil can have the same effect as if you were standing in a pine forest. A fabulous oil for clearing the air, improving alertness, and increasing inspiration.

Application: Inhale, vaporise, bathe, spritz, and compress this motivating and intuitive oil.

May Also Benefit: Coughs, colds, flu, asthma, cystitis, pyelitis, inflammation, muscle aches and pains, headaches, arthritis, rheumatic pain, and liver detoxification.

Rosemary Oil: Known to have a very stimulating effect on the mind, a cleansing effect on the emotions, and is renowned for being the oil for memory. This energising oil improves mental clarity, focus and intuition while calming exhaustion, mental fatigue, neglect, procrastination, and feeling overwhelmed.

Application: Enjoy this delightful oil in a bath, compress, diffuser, spritzer or massage.

May Also Benefit: Liver detoxification, weight loss, cellulite, muscle aches or pains, respiratory conditions, sinusitis, heart palpitations, circulation, and hair growth.

Note: Be careful with topical application during first trimester of pregnancy as the high level of camphor may be neurotoxic.

Sage Oil: An excellent physical detoxifier and emotional cleanser. It is also known to help enhance intuition and develop innate wisdom. This beautifully regulating oil will bring trust, confidence, adaptability, and energy as the antidote to anxiety, depression, grief, hopelessness, and negativity.

Application: Massage, bathe, compress, direct application (for cold sores only), spritz, inhale.

May Also Benefit: Muscle aches and pains, cold sores, loss of appetite, digestion issues, hormone balance, pre-menstrual syndrome, menopause, and excessive perspiration.

Note: Be careful with topical application during first trimester in pregnancy. Use in moderation.

Chapter 4:

SELF-CARE

Your soul is your best friend

Treat it with care

Nurture it with growth

Feed it with love

– Ashourina Ylada

When you have become aware that you have fallen out of the circle of self-love, the most important step next is to take action. You have to DO something. And the best thing to do is to immediately do something to take care of yourself. It's imperative. It doesn't have to take a lot of time or cost a lot of money. It's the action of taking care that matters and makes the difference. It pulls you up and out of where you have been. Taking a little time to do something nice for yourself will help you stop and refocus your energy. It can help ease a difficult moment, support you to get through the next breath, and help create a safe space away from the difficulties of daily life.

I remember a while ago, my son Jakob reminded me of the significance of self-care by acting *for* me when I couldn't do it for myself. A beautiful friend of ours had just passed away. She was young, with a hideous cancer. We all believed in the miracle that she would pull through. If anyone could, it would be her. Nature had other plans. After seven amazing years of her thriving and surviving with this disease, our friend passed away.

I was incredibly privileged to be one of a few in the room with her as she took her final breath. It is hard to watch those left behind, and it's even harder to make sense of something so seriously sad. I don't remember the drive home, but when I walked through the door some hours later, I just fell into my teenage boy's arms, sobbing. All he said was, "It's okay mum, it's okay."

My son hugged me and then gently led me up the hallway, not expecting me to have to talk. This young man had run me a bath, put on the iPod with my favourite music, reached for my favourite and most comforting essential oils, and lit the bathroom vaporiser. I didn't know what to say, I could only mouth the words, "Thank you" with tears running down my cheeks. This is a ritual I do for my babes and my husband when I know the world has had its way with them. In my hour of need he had returned the love.

Some of our bathroom moments along our journey can create huge pain as we struggle to draw a breath or even think straight. While others take us to a place of solace and warmth.

As you face the heart wrenching death of a loved one, or an equally painful loss, try to remember that you're not alone. When you really need it, there will always be people, maybe your partner, your children, family or your friends, to be there for you. And if none of them are present, then you still have YOU! My children and husband have stepped up to support and encourage me, often when I've felt overwhelmed and didn't know where to turn. I have also had to show up for myself, when there has not been anyone present.

If you are someone who always appears to have it together, you may have to find the courage to reach out and ask for that help, and remember, that's okay. People will not necessarily be aware that you're struggling, and that you could use some tender loving care. If you are the type of person who is always strong, it may be even harder for you. Just remember: it's okay to be vulnerable sometimes.

Creating the space and allowing others to help you is a huge part of self-care, and if we can see it, our children—our family—can become our most profound teachers in the toughest of times.

As we know none of us are immune to sadness or struggle; we have all been on the receiving end of life's downs more than once or twice, and if you were attracted to reading this book for that reason then you are no doubt looking for ways to create balance and harmony, maybe even sense in your world. It is for YOU that I've written this book, because I know that when we return to home base, to self-love, we can get through tough times and, in fact, move mountains.

The challenge is that when you've been thrown out of the self-love circle by self-sabotage, self-guilt, self-loathing, self-doubt, negativity, judgement, or even things like loss, grief, procrastination, and gossiping, you're often left feeling depleted and flat. After all, these things can sap your energy. You may find yourself in a space of feeling over yourself, overwhelmed, or maybe even sick and tired, or sick and tired of being sick and tired! You know these feelings, and in some instances, may even feel desperate. You may have been spun out of the circle of self-love because you have been abusing yourself and resent what you see in the mirror, or you may have been abusing others with vicious thoughts or verbal exchanges. Whatever your weapon of self-destruction is, when it strikes, you know it.

It makes sense, then, that we would have a set of strategies or steps we can take to bring us back to a state of equilibrium and inner peace, and most importantly, when times are really tough, we want to know that we can coax ourselves back to a place of calm in the most gentle, loving, and caring way.

I proudly co-wrote *Like Chocolate for Women* with my dearest friend and beauty therapist, Fleur Davis. We captured the phrase "Self-care, is not selfish, it's essential." and from that day on, I continue to see many people making time for almost everything BUT self-care.

Life is so busy these days and can be so distracting, that we forget the little things that make a big difference in the way we feel about ourselves. As a pivotal piece to the self-love circle, no matter who you are, how old you are, where you live, what you do, when you do it, or whom you do it with, it's an absolute game-changer to place self-care at the top of your priority list each day.

As we've discovered, it's expected that we will be spun out of the circle of self-love. We have all been there and we will continue to go there. Those niggling, negative thoughts instantly take us out. That inner dialogue that is self-sabotaging may rear its ugly head from time to time, and has the power to take us out, if we allow it. So, once you are aware that you are there, or conscious of those thoughts, you have effectively spun yourself back into the circle. And the best way to *stay* in that circle is to practice the art of self-care.

Self-care is the number one strategy that will always bring you back to self-love. If you take nothing else from this book, then this is what I would love for you to receive. Self-care is one of the most important, critical things we can do to keep that inner spark alight. It is the number one thing we can do for our health. And considering health is our greatest asset, it makes sense to give it the time it deserves.

> *'The foundation of health comes*
> *when we connect in with our soul.'*
> – Dr Sherrill Sellman

I love Dr Sherrill Selman. Her work is pivotal in understanding cycles and rhythms. It is through the daily act of self-care that you find that you can improve your health and connect within. You can find a way to help keep that inner light shining bright.

I've always been one to create a set of rituals for myself each day. Some of these are just micro-moments— like a three second aromatherapy spritz—where I take the time to be grateful for the gifts I have in my world. It may also be lighting my vaporiser with a favourite essential oil or lighting unscented candles around the house in the evening to soften the ambience after a hectic day. These rituals are my 'go-to' self-care strategies to remind me to stay connected to the self-love circle, and I've been doing them for so long now, they've become habits in my husband and kids' lives, too.

It warms my heart to see my daughter, Tayla, in her own apartment with her own rituals, celebrating, and showing gratitude for the life she is creating. It's amazing how family traditions can create stability in our children's lives, that bring them a sense of wholeness and connectedness to their own roots.

There are different kinds of rituals you can create around your physical, spiritual, psychological, social, and emotional states. The power of these rituals allows self-guilt to disappear, and brings a real, holistic approach to your health and well-being. Honouring yourself this way can unlock an intimacy in your relationship with life; everyone and everything in it, and most importantly, with yourself. Through self-care, self-love can blossom.

In my heart of hearts, I truly believe this is where the power of essential oils can work their magic. Smell is so closely linked to our emotions, and emotions govern behaviour, so it makes sense to use these powerful plant extracts to support us not only with our emotional welfare, but with our personal care as well.

Ultimately, self-care is not selfish – it's essential!

Self-care is unique for everyone, and it can be a real challenge if you've never considered it as a 'vital' key to your happiness and fulfilment before now. It doesn't have to take a lot of time, and to help you start, this chapter offers strategies you can easily embrace and implement as rituals into your life, and that of your family.

Firstly though, let's remember how you will recognise when you're not taking great care of yourself, and in turn, these things have spun you out of the circle of self-love.

- Feeling stressed and overwhelmed.
- Arguing with people or work colleagues.
- Fighting with your partner or children.
- Worried and feeling anxious about events.
- Bags under your eyes from lack of sleep.
- Experiencing weight gain or weight loss.
- Struggling with loss of libido.
- Feeling constant irritability.
- Experiencing lack of muscle tone and fitness.
- Feeling depleted of energy.
- Skipping meals or overeating.
- Eating too much sugar.
- Drinking too much alcohol.
- Feeling constantly bloated.
- Drinking caffeinated drinks to keep you going.
- Withdrawing from areas of your life that feel too hard.

If any of these signs are present in your life, then you know for sure that the time has come for you to truly invest in self-care.

If you are interested in getting a bird's eye view of where your self-care status is right now, you can quickly answer these questions below, or better still, create a ritual. It might even be one of your first rituals that you can check in with on a regular basis. Quickly scan if time is a challenge, or better still, grab a pen and notebook, a cup of your favourite tea and a quiet spot, and write down your answers to these questions:

1. What do I enjoy doing with my time?

2. When do I feel most alive?

3. Which people provide me with strength and hope, rather than drain me?

4. What activities make my heart feel peaceful and at rest?

5. When do I feel the fullest of life and well-being?

6. When do I feel the tension release from my neck, shoulders, and jaw?

7. What makes me feel guilty and negative?

8. When do I feel my life is full of purpose and meaning?

9. How do I look after my own emotional well-being?

10. How often do I check-in with myself to see how I feel?

These insights will form the motivation to overcome any guilt or fear you may feel about not deserving self-care. From now on, instead of waiting to get sick or injured to give yourself permission to stop, honour your well-being and give yourself permission to take time out. Use your answers here as permission to start looking after yourself; your whole self.

Our immune system is an excellent gauge for self-care. Illness or disease could provide us with an insight into our lack of self-care. You may not be exercising enough or eating the right types of foods to nourish your body and meet the needs of your busy life, or, you may need to look at the environment you're in and begin to question the chemicals that are around you daily. Pay close attention to the signals and signs that your body is providing for you and determine what self-care actions you need to take.

Dr Libby Weaver is someone I look up to immensely when it comes to understanding the body. With a PhD in bio-chemistry, she talks proudly of the fifty trillion cells that make up your body, and the value of good, whole-food nutrition as an extremely important element of self-care. She also focuses a lot of her work on understanding the nervous system and how it impacts the fuel you burn, your sleep, skin, and sex hormones. The central nervous system (CNS) is the control centre for the whole system via the brain and spinal column. The autonomic nervous system (ANS) controls the internal organs and supports functions you don't ever have to think about, like your hair growing, food digesting, and the female menstrual cycle. The ANS breaks down further into the sympathetic nervous system (SNS) and the parasympathetic nervous system (PNS). The SNS is your fight, flight or freeze zone, also known as the red zone. It is extremely important for when you are threatened or need energy to react and respond quickly. The PNS is the rest, repair, digest, and repro-duction zone, also known as the green zone.

Sadly, in today's word, we spend a lot more time in the red zone than is deemed good for our health. Factors such as caffeine, adrenalin, stress, and anxiety activate our red zone response. But here's the interesting thing Dr Libby talks about in her Beautiful You Weekend events. Look at your perception of what is required of you and your relationship to stress. Notice the word *perception*. After all, it is the lenses with which we see the world that is 'our truth' not necessarily the truth of others. To down-regulate the SNS look at your caffeine intake if you are a coffee drinker and of course look a little closer at your stress levels and the pressure you have put on yourself.

To up-regulate the green zone there are a couple of quick simple things you can do straight up. By simply extending the length of your external breath and practicing diaphragmatic breathing you will activate this calming zone. Restorative practices like yoga, qi gong and tai chi are also magical. If you can incorporate regular self-care practices with kindness it has an incredible ripple effect. Not only does this impact our own health but it can impact the wellbeing of others too. It's quite extraordinary; the ripple effect.

Another way you have control to support self-care and improve your state of health is to eliminate toxins that could be around you. Here are some main culprits that you may find in your home in both the bathroom and kitchen that can be causing you to feel depleted or lacklustre. When you begin to replace or remove these chemicals or additives, you'll be so surprised by how quickly you will bounce back to feeling energised and vital again.

QUESTIONABLE ADDITIVES TO AVOID IN FOOD

BAD FATS	COLOURS	FLAVOUR ENHANCERS
Vegetable Oil	102, 107, 110, 120, 122–129, 132, 142, 150, 151, 155, 160b (annatto)	620-625, (621–MSG), 627, 631, 635
Hydrogenated & Partially Hydrogenated Oil	**PRESERVATIVES**	**SWEETENERS**
Trans Fat	Sorbates 200–203	Aspartame 951
PROCESSED PROTEINS	Benzoates 210–213	Sucralose 955
Hydrolysed Vegetable Protein (HVP)	Sulphites 220–228	High Fructose Corn Syrup
	Nitrates, Nitrites 249–252	**HOW TO CALCULATE THE AMOUNT OF SUGAR IN FOOD**
Textured Vegetable Protein (TVP)	Proprionates 280–283	Take Total Sugars (listed under Carbohydrates per serving) and divide by 4. This equals approx number of teaspoons per serve.
Hydrolysed Soy Protein (HSP)	**ANTIOXIDANTS**	
Soy Protein Isolate (SPI)	Gallates 310–312	
	TBHQ, BHA, BHT 319–321	

QUESTIONABLE INGREDIENTS IN SKIN CARE

EMULSIFIERS & SOLVENTS	PRESERVATIVES	PETROLATUM PRODUCTS
Diethanolamine (DEA) and Tiethanolamine (TEA)	Paraben Preservatives including Methyl, Ethyl, Butyl & Polyparaben	Mineral Oils
PEGs (Polyethylene Glycol) Isopropyl Alcohol	Parahydroxybenzoate Imadazolidinyl Urea	Petroleum Jelly
LATHERING AGENTS	Phenoxyethanol	**ARTIFICIAL COLOURS**
Sodium Lauryl Sulphate (or Laureth)	**ARTIFICIAL PERFUME & FRAGRANCES**	D&C Reds, Yellows & Blues
All solid Soaps	Avoid all as they are often made up of over 200 ingredients, mostly chemical	Amines
MOISTURE CARRYING AGENTS		**ANIMAL PRODUCTS**
Propylene Glycol		Collagen Amino Acids
		Elastin Amino Acids
		Epiderm Oil R.

www.twenty8.com

TWENTY·8

Recently I was speaking for an audience of men and women who were interested to enhance their health and well-being journey and I posed the following question:

"What are the two biggest reasons why we don't pay attention to self-care?"

I have reflected on the number of times I've asked my audiences this question, and it struck me that just about every time I ask, I get the same response. The reason we don't look after ourselves usually comes down to time and/or money. These are the reasons we use to justify putting ourselves last. Especially women, and even more so, mums.

I know how tough it can be to juggle kids, a home, throw in your work or running a business, add in a relationship, family and friends, all the have-to's, money issues, and sometimes it can feel downright overwhelming. Some days it can feel as though everyone wants a piece of you. But what if we could get curious here and consider a slightly different perspective?

What if we replaced time and money with the word priority? When we know that self-care is the foundation for good health, doesn't it make sense for this approach to be one of your top priorities? After all, you cannot keep withdrawing from a cup that is empty. At some point your body will say, "Enough!"

If you still believe that time and money would stop you from making self-care a top priority in your life, then think about the following: What if someone you really loved, someone you'd be devastated to lose, had their health dependent on you having a massage every week for a whole year? What if their life depended on it? Would you find the time and money to do it? The answer would almost certainly be yes, of course.

Now, that we've added the extra incentive—a strong WHY—suddenly, getting the massage has become a priority, and the time and money has been relegated to merely 'incidental'. It might still be important, but it is not the main focus anymore; getting the massage is.

What would you say if I suggested you join me in doing a marathon tomorrow? Most people to whom I ask this question shake their heads immediately. I get a resounding, "Ahhh… no thanks". I can assure you that not many raise their hands in the air with excitement or confidence. Many respond with comments like, "I have bad knees", or "I'm not fit enough", or "I can't even run".

Before I move on, a quick acknowledgement if you said, "Yes". Congratulations!

So, let me rephrase the question if you said no. I'd like to suggest that perhaps we are not looking from a broad enough perspective. I dare say, most people reading this book COULD, in fact, do a marathon. Now, I didn't say, "You must run one", and I didn't say, "You must *run it in four hours*", and I definitely didn't say, "You must *run with the perfect running style*".

Let's reach for that bigger perspective.

If, at the end of the 42 kilometres, your child, or that particular person you would be desperately sad to lose, was sitting on the edge of a cliff, and you had to save them from dying: I promise you that you'd do that marathon. You would walk it, you would crawl it, you would do it in twelve hours or twenty hours, you would do whatever it took. Why? Because your "Why?" just became your main motivator; your reason to do it.

When your "Why?" drives the decisions and the priorities in your life, the game changes, and so does your perspective. This new lens reaches beyond just time or money, and it surpasses reasons and excuses, while placing you in a position of clarity and motivation. The trick is to develop a powerful "Why?" for anything you do. And watch as it trumps sacrificing self-care every time. So, when it comes to your self-care, you may have not given it the consideration it deserves in the past because you simply didn't give yourself enough reason, or a powerful enough "Why?" to do it.

One of my favourite writings that always reminds me of the importance of self-care is this beautiful Chinese proverb. I have repeated it so many times I know it off by heart now and say it as I put on my diffuser or light a vaporiser:

If there is light in the soul, there is beauty in the person.
If there is beauty in the person, there is harmony in the home.
If there is harmony in the home, there is order in the nation.
If there is order in the nation, there is peace in this world.

This process of self-care and transformation starts with you. Let's bring some light to your soul with the rituals I have created below. This is to get you started on creating your own list so feel free to expand and add to your heart's content. I have done twenty-eight, so you have four weeks' worth. And the reason for this? We know it takes twenty-eight days to create a habit.

1. Take micro-moments of mindfulness. Would you believe three seconds is enough time for self-care? Taking a deep breath whilst using an aroma mist spritz is self-care. Taking a deep breath focusing on the air coming into your

lungs and then the air leaving your body is mindfulness. Repeat three times and *voila!* You've just adopted a gentle yet powerful self-care ritual.

2. Up your greens. This simple self-care ritual has massive impact. For the next twenty-eight days make sure you have greens with at least two meals a day. It could be a handful of spinach with your eggs and mushrooms. You could roast a bunch of green vegetables like zucchini, asparagus, broccoli, and kale in some coconut oil, sea salt, and spices, and then add a cup full of these to your plate for dinner. It could be adding a handful of spinach or kale into your morning smoothie. Or even making the base of your meal a big serve of greens then building from there with your choice of protein and maybe some sweet potato chips.

3. Move functionally. Our bodies are designed to move in its most natural state. Gardening, house cleaning, climbing a steep hill, walking or running bare foot, carrying supermarket bags or lifting heavy boxes are amazing examples of incidental exercise and how the body naturally moves. Instead of thinking it is difficult or taking an easier option be grateful and mindful of the way in you can actively implement movement into your every day. This is one of the quickest daily self-care rituals.

4. Create rituals for the family. We light vaporisers and set up diffusers around the house every morning and evening to help set the mood. We have done things like A4 paper signs to the walls saying, 'Speak Softly' to remind us to speak to each other with more care.

When the children were little they would point to the sign whenever we, as their parents, forgot to live by that ethos! Each meal, we hold hands and say grace to give thanks for our meal. It is often something like, – *"Earth who gives to us this food. Sun who makes it ripe and good. Dear Earth, dear Sun by you we live. Our loving thanks to you we give. Amen. Blessings on this food."*

5. Develop an essential oil Self-Love Kit that you can reach for when the occasion strikes. You could use these in a bath, aroma mist bottle, compress, massage or diffuser. See pages 335-337 for methods of use and number of drops required. A few of my favourites would include lavender, orange, geranium, marjoram, sandalwood, frankincense, black pepper, and grapefruit and even though they carry a high price tag, I absolutely adore immortelle, jasmine, and rose.

6. Set your pantry and fridge up with wholesome and single ingredient essentials that can quickly be made into a nutritious meal. For me, these include organic ghee, coconut oil, tamari, olive oil, herbs and spices, balsamic vinegar, almond butter, Inca inchi powder, and oil, honey, nuts and seeds, dates, coconut, chia and basil seeds, cacao, sauerkraut, kimchi, butter, eggs, coconut kefir yoghurt, home-made almond milk, chicken, beef and vegetable broth in powdered form, coconut water, apple cider vinegar, maple syrup, coconut aminos, super green powder, colloidal minerals, and of course loads of fresh vegetables and fruit. Whenever I open my pantry or fridge I must admit I feel such gratitude for how lucky

I am to have foods like this in my life. The bounty Mother Nature provides is extraordinary. If you want to know what I do with these foods, the recipe books and people I love to follow are on pages 229 and 357.

7. Clean your house! I know, I hear you! But you might be surprised at how good you feel when your home is tidy. There are health benefits too when we clean with natural cleaning products, remove dust and tidy spaces.

8. Share yourself. One of the greatest ways to be a better person is to share a piece of you. You have no idea what an open heart and how sharing your vulnerabilities will do for another. Often this gives space for another to share and ultimately this is when deeper soul connections happen.

9. Carry a poem or quote with you. My beautiful friend Fouad Kassab writes amazing poems. Here is one I carry in my phone and recite whenever I need a lift or when walking in nature.

Wild Again

A mountain peak is beneath your feet. A soft wind blows in the valley. Can you sense who you are?

Birds fly and sing, insects rave. What do you do?

Why are you here and not on a bus somewhere. Stuck in traffic?

Tune in to your nature. For the first time. And find out what's been hidden behind the walls of a cubicle.

Find your strength. Touch your sadness. Your anger and your grief. They belong. No need to push. They brought you here.

To the place. Where you can find yourself.

10. Walk barefoot on Mother Earth. According to the Journal of Environmental Health,

Environmental medicine generally addresses environmental factors with a negative impact on human health. However, emerging scientific research has revealed a surprisingly positive and overlooked environmental factor on health: direct physical contact with the vast supply of electrons on the surface of the Earth. Modern lifestyle separates humans from such contact. The research suggests that this disconnect may be a major contributor to physiological dysfunction and unwellness. Reconnection with the Earth's electrons has been found to promote intriguing physiological changes and subjective reports of well-being. Earthing (or grounding) refers to the discovery of benefits— including better sleep and reduced pain—from walking barefoot outside or sitting, working, or sleeping indoors connected to conductive systems that transfer the Earth's electrons from the ground into the body. This paper reviews the earthing research and the potential of earthing as a simple and easily accessed global modality of significant clinical importance.

It makes you appreciate that just a few minutes barefoot on the ground or sand discharges the electricity in the body that causes us to feel fragile, unstable, inflamed, irritable, melancholy, and unwell. Earthing is an important part of self-care, especially when you feel a little out of sorts.

11. Take on the two-minute 'body boost' ritual. You can do this morning and night. Take your favourite carrier oil like sweet almond, coconut, or avocado mixed with three drops of your favourite essential oils or blend, and vigorously rub yourself from toe to head, waking up the cells and the systems in the body by smothering yourself in love, gratitude, and appreciation for the spectacular body you have. This is especially beautiful to do when you are going through a challenging time. Check out page 331 for more information on the body boost ritual.

12. Have an aromatic bath or shower. No matter how short on time, or when you least feel like it, use essential oils like peppermint and lavender in a bath with magnesium salts. You can also place 2 drops each, onto a face washer and place over the drain to create an aromatic steam shower too.

13. Roll out your mat and join A Live Yogi where you can do yoga in the comfort of your own home with a live class at https://www.aliveyogi.com. Founder Lauren Verona created this so you can run a full and busy life and enjoy the benefits of this amazing practice.

14. Pay it forward. Every day pick someone you will send a text to or make a comment on their social media page. Let someone you like know what they mean to you. This simple act creates a strong connection to yourself and can uplift the person like you wouldn't believe. So often

we think those we admire are doing well and holding it all together. But they too have their hard days and your text or message could be just the medicine they needed to keep going. Sometimes it's nice to pay for a coffee for the person behind you, or go up to a complete stranger and tell them something you noticed that was nice about them! Pay that love forward!

15. Create a Group Chat. One of the nicest rituals you could embrace is creating a special group chat on Facebook or Whatsapp. I have group chats with my family, my kids, work mates and girlfriends. They are such a great way to use technology at its best. And they provide a wonderful place to connect, share photos, quotes and ideas as well as check in with those you love. Be warned they may be addictive!

16. Photo A Day Challenge. I have followed an app called Fat Mum Slim for 5 years and have never missed a day of sharing a photo a day on Instagram. This small but fun ritual gives me a chance to think of the theme of that day and capture an image that means something to me. The fact that you share it is optional.

17. Meet with friends that lift you. We can be our own worst enemy when we are left to fester with our own troubles, and being around others who are energising will always leave you feeling recharged and able to deal with yourself much better. My girlfriend Cyndi and I will call each other and say we are having a 'level 1 soul moment' when we are not behaving as well as we could! In other

words, we are asking to let it all out and then please be coached to be a better human! Call a friend who knows how to lift you when you are not at your best!

18. Eat SLOW foods. Create something delicious and healthy following the SLOW approach (Seasonal, Local, Organic, Whole) Following your favourite foodies (some of mine are mentioned on page 229) make something they suggest with a loving intent. Dr Natasha Campbell-Mc-Bride author of Gut And Psychology Syndrome says, 'There is nothing more powerful to affect your health than the food you eat! Every morsel of food that we swallow changes everything in the body.'

19. Treat your face and hair. It could be a professional facial or hair treatment that you commit to at least once a week. If you can't afford a professional facial, mix one tablespoon oatmeal and one tablespoon yoghurt together, or one quarter of an avocado with one tablespoon manuka honey, and massage into clean skin. Leave on the face for ten to fifteen minutes and remove with warm water and a cloth. Make a hair mask by using three tablespoons of olive oil or coconut oil, two drops of rosemary oil, and two drops of lemon oil, place onto dry hair at the roots and then comb through to the ends then wrap your head in a towel to infuse the oil mask into the hair follicles for at least thirty minutes. To remove the mask, use a natural shampoo without adding water and massage into the scalp and hair. Your hair will feel clean, nourished, and shiny.

20. Get to the beach, river or lake. If you live within half an hour of the beach, make an effort to get into the ocean for a dip once a week, even in winter. I'll be honest, this is not my favourite thing to do, but when I do take the plunge I feel amazing. It's exhilarating and will prepare your body for a magical day without much more effort. Sea salt is loaded with amazing skin-friendly minerals like magnesium, sodium, chloride, calcium, and potassium. An ocean swim can help cleanse the pores of your skin, flush the nasal cavity and help heal skin conditions such as acne and psoriasis. I am committing to doing this one more! A lake can be just as rejuvenating.

21. Engage in chiropractic care. Having a weekly check in with your chiropractor can help reduce stress, pain, muscle and nervous tension, stimulate your circulation, improve your sleep and boost your immune system. It may be seen as a luxury at first, but when you experience for yourself the long-term benefits of weekly care you can quickly see why it can become an essential part of self-care.

22. Do an online challenge. One step you can take on to improve your health is to eat whole foods and increase your vegetable intake. I love doing programs like the Helen Padarin's 9V9 Vege Challenge, Cyndi O'Meara's Hunter Gatherer Protocol, or Kirsty Wirth's Kickstarter Program. You can find the links to these on page 355. You can support your gut and immune

system better with food-based supplements like live cultures, prebiotics and probiotics, camu camu powder (extracted from the camu camu fruit and rich in vitamin C), turmeric, green powder, and colloidal minerals. Look into food-based supplements or other whole foods that will complement your meals and put you back in the driver's seat of your own health.

23. Fold a blank A4 piece of paper in half and repeat four more times until you have an open page with 32 squares on each side. Now spend some time filling each of those squares with all the things you would love to achieve, fulfil or do over the next month or it could be the next quarter or even the next year. This is a beautiful record to see all the things you do actually achieve. And for the things that you don't, you simply add them to the next time you fill this sheet out. Keep all of these in a special place.

24. Create date nights. If you have a partner great make this a special ritual together, however date nights are just important for you. It could be a self-care pamper night, you might eat out, make a delicious meal for one, watch a movie or documentary, meal prep, go for a walk at sunset, read a book or like me treat your date nights as a chance to write a book just as I did here!

25. Have sex! Be spontaneous and surprise your partner with an invitation to the bedroom where you will be waiting wrapped in a bow. Ha! Bring some fun and playfulness to

the bedroom and find ways that make you giggle instead of sex being a chore to be 'done'. Dr Christiane Northrup author of Women's Bodies Women's Wisdom talks about the release of nitric oxide and oxytocin during orgasm. This triggers more positive emotions including resilience, hope and joy and she recommends getting regular doses of this healthy pleasure!

26. Get your hands deep and dirty in your garden. Nothing relieves stress better than Mother Earth, and by creating a ritual of kneeling gently onto the grass, gently removing the weeds (even the stubborn ones) while sending love to your plants and flowers as you turn the soil, you will not only witness your garden flourish in a way you've never seen before, you will feel remarkably connected to yourself and the earth that sustains you and your family. According to 'Gardening Know How' soil microbes and human health are positively linked. *Mycobacterium vaccae* is the substance under study and has indeed been found to mirror the effect on neurons that drugs like Prozac provide.

27. Select a room in your home to de-clutter, rearrange, or redecorate. Simplify what you have in the room, throw out what you haven't used in the last twelve months and minimise or organise everything that is within sight. Add some fresh flowers, a vaporiser, or a spritzer with a lovely essential oil blend of lavender and mandarin to bring a sense of calm to the air. It's amazing how a new pillow, bookshelf, or beanbag can brighten up a room and make you feel fresh and new each time you look at the room.

28. Unplug from technology each week. Turn your phone off, walk away from the computer or TV. Preferably go outside for some earthing or grounding, but if you can't do that, at least give your brain and your eyes a technology break without the wi-fi or blue light from the screens. Perhaps you can pick up a book (not a digital book; an actual book) and enjoy reading words that are not sent to you via artificial light. Read a light magazine and cut out the colourful pictures to go in your manifestation journal. Take a moment to observe your breath and notice the tempo slowing down and your feeling of being 'wired' subsiding.

These are just some suggestions that I've worked on implementing into my life, and my family's lives, over the years. They are simply rituals that celebrate life, and each other. They cause us to pause and pay attention to what we are feeling inside and allow us to catch our breath in a very busy and fast-paced world. For all the methods of use on how to use essential oils safely and effectively go to page 335 so you can start to create some of your own personal and family rituals for self-care.

I'd like to encourage you to add to this list, or even create your own, and then share it with me; I would love to hear from you on my social media platforms. When you place self-care on the top of your priority list each day, even if it is just for a few minutes at a time, you will find that you have much more to give to those you love. Please don't neglect yourself, thinking you do not have time, or that you are not worth it, because you most certainly are. I love the saying, 'Your health is an investment not an expense. Although it will become an expense if you don't take time to invest in it.'

I always dreamed of having a business with the focus on self-care. Personally I believe that is what Twenty8 is all about - using beautiful essential oils and pure natural products in daily loving rituals. This, to me, is the most effective and productive way to take care of yourself. And without doubt is the pathway back to YOU, always.

I named my company Twenty8 because we know it takes 28 days to create a habit, we are governed by 28 day cycles including the moon, tides, even the women's cycle is 28 days. We know skin cells take 28 days to replace themselves and you might be interested to know about your energy levels around bio-rhythms, especially the 28 day cycle emotionally.

Biorhythm curves describe very well the energy levels and the capacity for performance on 3 Primary levels: physical, emotional and intellectual. The intellectual biorhythm lasts for 33 days and relates to your mental capabilities, creativity, aptitude to solve problems. The physical biorhythm lasts for 23 days and is related to your physical energy, strength, health, stamina. And the emotional biorhythm last for 28 days (just like the moon's cycle) and relates to your emotional stability or stress.

I find this fascinating because smell is closely linked to emotions and essential oils are predominantly known for their smell and their effect on our mood. My dream of creating a self-care business is a reality. I teach people how to DO self-care! And I can assure you the people I have had the privilege to connect with have shown a deep appreciation for the reminder.

Remember, you cannot rely on others to do self-care for you. Self-care is not selfish, it's ESSENTIAL and it's your ultimate and divine responsibility.

Essential Oil for Self-Care:

Bergamot Oil: Helping you release suppressed feelings of sadness, sensitivity, shock, and self-deception, which can often lead to anxiety, nervousness, and depression. This is the oil that will lift your mood, bring you balance, clarity, ease, fulfilment, joy, and motivation.

Application: Spritz, compress, bathe, massage, inhale, sitz bath.

May Also Benefit: Wounds, fever, digestion issues, acne, eczema, dermatitis, hormone support, urinary tract infection, and cystitis.

Note: Avoid exposure to the sun after using bergamot in a massage or bath as it's considered phototoxic.

Cardamom Oil: When you feel like you're in a rut, Cardamom reminds you of all that is possible, leaving you feeling content, fulfilled, generous, and warm. Leave behind feelings of depression, disheartened, mental fatigue, judgement, lethargy, and tension. This precious oil eliminates fears and worries and helps to restore your appetite for life.

Application: Massage, compress, inhale, diffuse, bathe, and spritz this supporting and inspiring oil.

May Also Benefit: Digestion issues, flatulence, monthly feminine balance, immune support, coughs, bronchitis, nausea, circulation, and is even an aphrodisiac!

Fennel Oil: With its cleansing and energising properties, fennel encourages you to be more productive, creative, and on-task to meet your highest aspirations. You'll enjoy compassion, courage, fulfilment and strength in the place of chaos, frustration, insecurity, negativity, and stress.

Application: Massage, compress, bathe, inhale, diffuse, spritz.

May Also Benefit: Constipation, diarrhoea, flatulence, indigestion, nausea, headaches, pre-menstrual syndrome, hormone support, fluid retention, varicose veins, weight loss, and respiratory conditions.

Note: Be careful with topical application during first trimester in pregnancy.

Jasmine Oil: Considered to be the 'King of Flowers', you can draw on its strength to let go of the past and adapt to what is present. Become confident, content, fulfilled, grateful, passionate, positive, sensual, uplifted, and trusting. Release deception, depression, distance, disconnection, fear, rigidity, sorrow, and worthlessness.

Application: Massage, bathe, spritz, compress, inhale, and diffuse.

May Also Benefit: Muscular cramps and spasms, coughs, colds, and flus. Relieve insomnia, muscle tension, dry skin, eczema, dermatitis, infertility, and pre-menstrual syndrome. Can also be used as an aphrodisiac!

Chapter 5:

SELF-DISCIPLINE

"You cannot achieve anything in life without discipline. No skill, art, craft, work or goal can be truly achieved without it."
– Dr Sherrill Selman

I often think back on my original goal of playing netball for New Zealand, as a teenage girl. I got to age group State level, but I never made it to International level like I had dreamed. Who would have thought that I would end up running for Australia and setting a world record and eight Australian indoor records? Now that is an alternative route if ever I saw one! I'll never forget my ultra-running days. They formed the foundations I hold very dear to my heart, including self-discipline, tenacity, persistence, and determination. The formidable Cliff Young was, and still is, a beautiful mentor of mine. I often look back to my time with him as a major contributor to my desire and appreciation of self-discipline.

He taught me that sometimes, it's not until we are really, really challenged that we are even aware of our own capability.

Cliffy's parting words to me as I accepted the first-place medal at a world record pace, as well as accepting a place on the Australian team for the World Indoor 24 Hour Championships in Milton Keynes the following year, were along the lines of, "Nobody knows their true potential. You just have to keep trying to aim for it."

Something that I still carry with me all these years later, thanks to my ultra-marathon days, is that I met the darker side of me. The part of me that was full of excuses, reasons, justifications, judgement, and poor habits. This helped me to discover the resilient and very persistent, strong-willed side of me, and once this aspect of myself was revealed, I knew that nothing would ever be out of my reach again. I just had to keep aiming for my potential, and who knows what or where that limit is.

I also came to appreciate that in order to have that bright side we HAVE to see the dark side; we have to experience the bad to love the joy. We need to appreciate heavy to understand light; we cannot have one without the other.

If that is the case and self-sabotage, hard times, challenges, and fear are all a part of falling out of the circle of love, then maybe these times, these moments in life, are a requirement for human evolvement. We must experience hardship and challenges for the soul to grow and the heart to expand. We need to hurt to understand love. Bad dreams make the mundane ones seem great.

The question is: how long do we need to stay out of the circle, in that pain? My experience has shown me time and time again that the sooner I have awareness, the sooner I am back in the self-love circle. The pain or challenge is still there, but I am now working through it, not being buried by it. The sooner I take better care of myself and apply some discipline to stay there, the longer I stay in focused, the better I love myself. My mantra for this is:

"God give me the courage, grace, strength, and dignity to get through this."

So, when you are aware that you have fallen out of the circle of self-love and you do something nice for yourself, now what? This is where the art of self-discipline really comes into play. As my dear friend Sherrill states, "You cannot have the things you want without self-discipline". There is no question that discipline lies at the root of all change and success.

You want that car, that house, that relationship, that job, that dress, that waistline, that chest, that goal, and that great level of healthy vitality. You know it's within your reach if you put your mind to it and all the signs around you are pointing to your success and readiness. It's an exciting time. You have clarity, energy, direction, and even desire, and you're ready to go for it. *Let's do this*, you think.

After what you would consider a decent effort of daily focus, changes in habits or thought patterns, new actions, and even some little wins, you realise it's not quite as easy as you had initially expected. Later, after a couple of setbacks or hiccups in your plan, it becomes less and less likely that your vision will find fruition as you had imagined it would. You become despondent, disappointed, and disillusioned, and finally find a reason to let the vision fade off into the sunset.

You justify the cause of your exit as 'bad timing', or you tell yourself that you had to let it go because 'something better came along'. The truth is that deep down inside, you've put another 'failure' notch on your belt, you've fallen out of love with—or don't even like—yourself, and you've just confirmed once again that you're a flake and can't make what you want to happen, happen. Your self-sabotage, old habits, procrastination, and subconscious behaviours have trumped your willpower yet again! This battle is frustrating at best and self-destructive at worst.

I honestly think we've all done it, and this is the number one reason we fall out of the self-love circle. No matter how hard we try, we just cannot seem to find another way that works. Sadly, many of us spend our lives experiencing more 'wishful thinking' than experiencing the joy of realizing and living our dream.

Wouldn't it be great to learn how to stick it out? What if it were possible to get yourself back on the wagon when you fall off, instead of giving up altogether, and then having to find a reason or excuse to justify it to yourself and others?

Imagine for a moment that you are bringing to life everything you set your mind on. What would *that* feel like? Now, take one step further and imagine what it would be like if your kids and family were all able to create plans for themselves and be willing to step up and take responsibility for everything that goes right and goes wrong. What if they knew how to adjust, manoeuvre and re-plan when needed, rather than give up, give it away, or give in?

I truly believe that the example we set for our children, by being the best role models we can be, is the most powerful way to parent. The up-side for parents is that it takes very little talking, nagging, begging, or pleading, it just takes our own self-discipline. It's the same in relationships, partnerships, and anywhere else in life.

The dictionary states that self-discipline is the ability to control one's feelings and overcome one's weaknesses; the ability to pursue what one thinks is right, despite temptations to abandon it.

Self-discipline is a combination of applying new routines where old habits lurk and using consequences to encourage you to stay on track. It is also self-realisation; not letting yourself off the hook easily and using a bit of tough love when it's appropriate. One of the best ways to create better self-discipline is through the power of education. Listening to podcasts, taking on something like a new eight-week body transformation program, doing a diploma or degree, enlisting in a new course, going to public talks, seminars, attending online summits, reading books, taking on ac-countability coaching, or joining groups that interest you. Subscribing to channels like Food Matters TV (www.fmtv. com) where you can watch health documentaries and learn as much as you can about your own personal health and welfare. My friends James and Laurentine, who founded this remarkable online platform, are such a strong force. I look up to them hugely as trailblazers in the field of taking personal responsibility for your own wellbeing. Your new discipline could be watching one documentary from their website per week. Listening to one new podcast a week could be hugely beneficial too.

It might be joining the gym, committing to yoga three times a week, or walking, swimming, or cycling every second day for twelve weeks. What about running a marathon? You might have a family discipline that there are no phones at the dining table. No swearing for one month. It could be a six-month gut health protocol. Cooking all meals from scratch from this moment on, or not eating any sugar for eight weeks. It could also be attending your local farmer's market every weekend.

Whatever you decide to do, it could be as simple as accepting what is, letting go of what was and believing in what will be. You could commit to using this phrase, "up until now," when you notice you're being self-deprecating. It was my good friend, Steve Johns, who taught me that phrase, and it is remarkable how it works and defuses that negative self-talk.

Let's look at how using "up until now" can change the whole emphasis of a self-defeating narrative. If I say (and believe), "I am so useless at public speaking," and then add "up until now" it completely diffuses the negative impact of this narrative. Or again, "I can't cook... up until now." And "I have never found the right partner... up until now."

The point is, you need something that is going to keep you accountable, connected, and pull you in when every reason and excuse is there to pull you away from sticking to it. It is often through pain, suffering, or a big challenge that we become really committed to our true core. It is during those moments when we have been lost outside the circle of love that we HAVE to do something in order to change or else we end up on the road to self-destruction. These painful moments can take the form of alcohol abuse, overeating, under-eating, a health crisis, illness. This can be caused by the loss of a loved one, losing your home, business, or job, a tragedy, shock, a relationship breakdown, an operation, injury, an accident. Anything that knocks the wind out of your sails and lands you flat on your back, metaphorically speaking.

I know these situations won't feel good while you're in them. And yes, the last thing you want to hear is, "This has happened for a reason", or, "Good will come of it". And of course, there are plenty of things that occur in life that we could simply do without, thank you very much. The point is: these things DO happen—life does suck sometimes—and there are times it is so out of our control, that the only thing we can do is scramble, crawl, and navigate our way through it, in the best way that we can.

As you make your way through the hardships in life, just remind yourself how amazing you are. Don't forget that you have survived one hundred per cent of your worst days, so far. And that is a genuine accomplishment. It is important to remember that part of self-discipline is training yourself to always see another perspective.

I'll never forget the day that I was with my dear grandmother in the car. She was in her nineties at the time and, as we were driving down the freeway, another driver cut across in front of us, causing me to brake suddenly and slow right down to avoid an accident. I gathered my wits and reached for the window, trying to get it wound down enough to shout at him and give some expletive gesture for being such a bloody fool. It was then that my dear Grandma said, "Oh dear, I hope he's alright". Her words stunned me. "What do you mean, 'Is he alright'? He just about killed us!" I said.

"Oh yes," said Grandma, "but he may have just had a phone call saying that his wife is in trouble, or that his child has fallen and hurt themselves, sweetheart. You just never know do you?"

Oh my, did that stop me in my tracks. Have I ever driven erratically when I was worried about one of my kids? Did I have a perfect driving record? Was I the world's best, under pressure?

Absolutely not.

Now, let's be real, it could be that this guy was just a plain fool, driving like a maniac with no thought or consideration for the other drivers on the road. But what if he was distraught or upset? The point is I'll never know. And there is always another side; there is always another perspective.

How many times have you been misread or taken the wrong way? How many times have you judged someone based on what you 'think' is real only to discover it is not true at all?

As humans, we judge all the time. We assess others with our eyes, our own truths and perception, our emotions, and our energy. And guess what? Others are doing exactly the same thing to us.

I was asked to grace the cover of a wonderful magazine called *Profile*, here on the Sunshine Coast. When the creator and editor at the time, Genine Howard asked me to be the cover girl, I was beside myself, I was flattered, so touched, and so excited. Wow! A cover girl!

Then she asked for me to be naked on the cover. You what? Naked? Are you kidding me? She had decided that seeing how my message was all about loving the skin you're in, and loving your body no matter what, it would be amazing to show me bare; tastefully and beautifully exposed, and vulnerable. She said we would leave my running shoes on and she wanted to title it, *The Marathon of Life*.

So many thoughts raced through my head. How could I say no, when I teach women all the time about loving the skin they're in, appreciating the beauty of who they are; exactly as they are? How could I be naked on the cover of a magazine when my kids were in high-school? What would they think? What would my husband think?

Genine told me to sleep on it and check in with the family. To my surprise, they were all incredibly supportive and said to go for it. They were proud that I had even been asked.

On the day of the photo shoot I was made to feel incredibly relaxed. The photographer and Genine were amazing. It was beautiful; almost a soulful, spiritual experience. My awkwardness and slight embarrassment disappeared quickly through Genine's care. It was quite humbling and liberating too. We were all quite teary, feeling and watching the magic unfold.

On the day the magazine was launched, I was excited to see it. But I must admit, there was a part of me that questioned it too. Had I done the right thing? How would it be received? Did they cover all my bits? The million and one self-doubt thoughts raced through my mind endlessly.

Texts started to come through. My girlfriends were so sweet, so incredibly beautiful. All of them sent messages of love and support. They loved the cover and they loved the story.

And then some messages came through on my social media pages. I started to receive lovely comments from women saying how proud they felt. When I finally got to see the magazine, I was so touched by the images and the story it brought quite a few tears to my eyes.

It received the tick of approval by my husband and kids. They were so proud. There were literally hundreds of positive comments and amazing feedback.

And then it happened. A hurtful, nasty one. And another. There were three I remember very clearly.

How disgusting, how embarrassing. What a joke. Kim Morrison sold her soul. I will not be reading your magazine ever again.

You have let women down everywhere, this is just another self-defacing woman who thinks sex sells.

There is absolutely NO NEED for her to not have her clothes on. Shame on you.

I was devastated. In that moment I felt I had stuffed up. I should never have done this story. I was so upset.

Like a lioness defending a cub Cyndi O'Meara appeared. She arrived at my place knowing these ugly comments would affect me deeply. As she hugged me she tried to make me laugh, saying she had stalked them all on Facebook. "You are not to worry sweetie," she said, "they're just NOT our people. They're keyboard warriors who have no bloody idea." Bless our girlfriends!

It took a few days for me to come up for air and to get a grip on myself. Genine had phoned to make sure I was okay and told me to just ignore those couple of meaningless comments and opinions. The feedback she had received was extraordinary. The cover–the story–had the impact she wanted. Still to this day she says it is one of her favourites. Women like Genine teach us all to champion one another, lift each other up. And this is something I learnt from her and will never, ever forget.

My husband has been in the public eyes for many years. He has been loved, put on a pedestal, and he has been hurt, put down, and beaten up in the media too. He lived by the ethos (and told me to remember), "Opinions are like arseholes, everybody's got one!"

He is right. Genine and Cyndi were right. How could I let these three comments override the hundreds of incredibly amazing ones? How sad and pointless is that. My biggest lesson through all of this was: do what feels right and know you will never please everyone. My friend Claire shared this quote with me recently:

"You could be the ripest, juiciest peach in the world, and there are still going to be people who don't like peaches."

How many times have you ever found it is that one comment, that one piece of feedback or casual remark that cuts to the core? How many times do we dwell on the negatives and not on the positives? The naked cover experience taught me so much, and even showed me the importance of standing up for myself and being the woman that the people who cared about me expected me to be.

"When things are bad, remember:

It won't always be this way.

Take one day at a time.

When things are good, remember:

It won't always be this way.

Enjoy every great moment."

Remember, as the famous proverb goes, "This too, shall pass." In hindsight, and in time, you will come to see that even in the greatest of challenges, tragedies, and adversaries, there is an opportunity to regroup, recalibrate, and one day, see and feel the good. Even the devastation of grief and loss can one day appear in your world as love and gratification for what was.

When Danny's sister died tragically after a suicidal, psychotic episode, it was, and still is, very hard to imagine any good, or a silver lining. But for me, watching Danny's mum has been a huge lesson in loving what 'is'. If you ask Sandi about her daughter she will always say, "I am so grateful for the thirty-six years I had with my beautiful daughter". I know her heart still aches, I know she misses her immeasurably, and I am so in awe of her ability to appreciate the gift her daughter was, for the time she was on this Earth.

Cyndi lost her mum a number of years ago, and her dad always says he is so grateful to have been married to the woman of his dreams for forty-eight years. I know he misses her every day, but it is such a beautiful way to honour the beauty in what was. He doesn't concentrate on what he doesn't have, just what he did have.

I've heard people say how grateful they are for their first marriage and the children that their spouse gave them, even though they have separated, regardless of the state of their ongoing relationship. I know people who are eternally grateful for their business not working, and even though it might have cost them a sweet fortune, or they lost more than you would ever want, they are now in a much better position, or in a better space, thanks to that happening.

I recently had the privilege of spending a week at an organic health retreat. During seven blissful days, I was immersed in the beauty of nature, exquisite food, functional movement, lectures, massages, facials, colonic hydrotherapy, live blood analysis, iridology, horse whispering, meditation… you name it, it was heaven. Every single person who worked there had a story about how they came to be working there. For almost all of them it was their own health challenge or personal tragedy that had led them into the area they were now working in or researching. And every one of them LOVED where they worked.

I have come to learn that if we accept what is, and be as gentle as we can with ourselves as we work through our pain and challenges, we will somehow find the courage and dignity to pull through and rise above it and then arrive in a new place. Maybe that new place is acceptance. We find a way to give thanks and appreciate the experience, the growth, the new opportunities, and most of all, the power of the heart and soul, to expand with greater compassion, empathy, and love.

One day, you may even look back and be grateful for what has occurred, as it forced you on to another path. It gave you a whole new perspective and meaning. I have said it myself, and heard it many times from others, that I would not be who I am today had experiences that rocked my world not happened.

"You have to feel it to heal it."
– Jacqueline Trost

Self-discipline is a practice. Feeling your way through pain is a continual work-in-progress. When we find ourselves out of kilt, drifting this way and that, a mantra like the Serenity Prayer (on page 133) can help us to catch our breath, hit the reset button, and get back on track, acknowledging that sometimes even the best laid plans need an alternate route.

True self-discipline is an expression of inner strength and staying power. One of the most powerful by-products of self-discipline is control, confidence, self-esteem, and happiness. These are some of the beautiful gifts of being human; these qualities provide us with the ability to overcome adversity and challenges. Through perseverance, we can work through our hurdles or setbacks with methodology, courage, and grace.

If we stay in self-sabotage for too long we start to believe this is our new normal, our new belief, or even our new truth. If we want to create new neurochemical pathways to change the wiring in our brain for better thoughts and behaviours, then we must initiate self-discipline.

Now, it might be that you are keen to commit to a new food and exercise protocol, maybe you'd like to create a plan for your family where everyone contributes to the household chores, or maybe you'd like to save some money for that holiday. Regardless of what you'd like to achieve for yourself, you may experience resistance or discomfort at some stage, and old habits or self-sabotage could creep in and lead you astray.

To enable you to determine new strategies and identify the areas of your life that you'd like to work on, here is a very simple quiz for you to take. Also outlined are some basic areas you can focus on, as well as tools that you can lean on to support you through the times when that little voice inside tries to convince you to give up!

Levels of Satisfaction Quiz:

On a scale of 1 to 10 rate how satisfied you are with your experience in each of the following areas:

	Very Unsatisfied						Extremely Satisfied			
Money	1	2	3	4	5	6	7	8	9	10
Health and Vitality	1	2	3	4	5	6	7	8	9	10
Family	1	2	3	4	5	6	7	8	9	10
Spiritual	1	2	3	4	5	6	7	8	9	10
Social	1	2	3	4	5	6	7	8	9	10
Relationships	1	2	3	4	5	6	7	8	9	10
Time	1	2	3	4	5	6	7	8	9	10

Now add up the number in each line for a maximum possible score of 70.

If your total is 65-70: You are on the right path. You are taking life with both hands and you are living the life you dreamed, with skills to support you if challenged. Well done! This book will help you to support others who could be struggling or going through a challenging time.

If your total is 35-65: You might like a stronger structure in place to help shift any limiting beliefs. Taking on a coach, a course, or program could do you well. You may be easily distracted so it is important you have a plan in place or good accountability to support you to complete whatever new goals or directions you choose.

7-35: It is easy for you to put yourself at the bottom of the list for self-care and quite possibly at the top of the list to be taken advantage of. Self-discipline would be your greatest ally. It's time to take charge of your life and create a whole new version of you. A strong, focused, more happy, healthy you.

Any areas that you've scored yourself under five are areas that you could improve and with some well thought out planning, some changes in routines and some self-discipline, you could find yourself enjoying an entirely new version of you in no time!

Here are some ways in which you can find support to prevent self-sabotage from threatening to trump your willpower:

- If exercise and fitness are on your list of new routines, try this discipline for the next 28 days. Download my Workout of the Day (WOD) sheet at www.twenty8.com/selflovewod. This is a series of exercises you can do in your own home in under ten minutes. Doing a WOD each day will certainly be one of the greatest ways you would create self-discipline that will carry on over into other areas of your life.

- A top international athlete would not be without a coach. If you can engage a life or business coach to run beside you as you create new changes in your life, then trust yourself and get one. They don't carry your negative self-beliefs and are not as emotionally involved, so they will help by offering an outside perspective and help you achieve the results you want.

- Jump into online programs and protocols that include instructional videos, communities, feedback, interaction, and accountability. Don't let yourself off the hook by thinking you can do it on your own. You've tried that before and it's time to set yourself up for success. There are other people out there who have blazed the trail, so follow in their footsteps until you can do it alone, not the other way around. A dear friend Nikki Parkinson has a wonderful online community called Styling You. Nikki was named Australian Blogger of the Year for 2011 as online blogging took off. Her loyal supporters show so much love and respect for each other and have created a safe haven where they each feel they can be themselves with no harsh criticisms or judgements. I think this is what we all crave; a place where we belong.

- Set up your home and workplace with reminders of what you are trying to achieve. Create rituals and use essential oils to support you in the work you are doing. Basil, rosemary, and lemon are wonderful for concentration, so each time you set about doing some tasks on your plan, inhale or diffuse some essential oil and use the same one each time, so that your brain knows when it smells that aroma, it knows it's about to do some work.

- Be willing to create new neurological pathways with the way you think. Habits are just thoughts coupled with actions that have been repeated over and over until they form a new habit. If you created them, you can un-create them and create new ones! YOU are in the driver's seat of your brain.

I completely love the feeling that self-discipline brings when you win or achieve something. When you have stuck it out, ridden through the highs and lows, and truly walked the path, there is no greater feeling when you can sit there, reflect, and marvel at what you once thought may have been impossible. Self-discipline is where all great outcomes are achieved.

Dare Your Genius

Dare your genius to walk the wildest, unknown way. Go where you've never been before. Dream up a destination, a path to follow, a wildest unknown way, over rocks and scrag, across hills where the winds bite cold with malice, through deep mysterious valleys where the wild things roar and echo and rumble and stamp and hiss great clouds of steam from their terrible huffing ways.

Dream the impossible dream and start walking towards it. On the way you'll be beaten up, chewed, spat out, mauled, ripped apart, given up for lost. Quite soon you'll learn what it feels like to be beaten up, chewed, spat out, mauled, ripped apart and given up for lost.

This is called 'experience' and it's very, very valuable
in life, because what you mostly learn from it is that
you were more afraid of what might happen than
what did happen. Most successful outcomes are
achieved by calling a series of conventional bluffs.

One bright sunny morning you'll discover that the
wild and unknown way you took is carpeted with
moss and strewn with tiny flowers. It has become a
familiar path, a well-trodden direction which has put
you miles ahead of anyone else and much, much
closer to achieving your once impossible dream.
– Bryce Courtenay

Essential Oils for Self-Discipline:

Black Pepper Oil: This revered, spicy oil helps to activate and excite the body! Think energy, endurance, enthusiasm, focus, vitality, warmth, and stimulation as you wash away feelings of defeat, fatigue, mental lethargy, nervousness, sensitivity, and worthlessness. This oil has a powerful kick so only small amounts are needed for great results!

Application: Inhale, massage, diffuse, spritz, massage, bathe, and compress.

May Also Benefit: Colds, flu, rheumatic pain, muscle aches and pains, bruises, oedema, circulation, liver detoxification, and digestion issues.

Cedarwood Oil: Release the strains of chaos, mental fatigue, negativity, neglect, sensitivity, stress, and withdrawal and embrace courage, focus, inspiration, purpose, worthiness, and wisdom.

Application: Massage, compress, bathe, inhale, diffuse, spritz, sitz bath.

May Also Benefit: Eczema, dermatitis, respiratory conditions, urinary tract infections, cystitis, acnes, oily skin, greasy hair, cellulite, and oedema.

Clove Oil: You'll feel confidence, courage, creativity, focus, openness, strength and warmth instead of confusion, depression, lethargy, and negativity. When mixed with peppermint oil, clove oil is well known to ward off fatigue.

Application: Diffuse, inhale, spritz, massage, bathe, direct application (for mouth ulcers and dental issues only – dip a cotton bud into the undiluted oil and apply to the surface and surrounding areas of the aching tooth).

May Also Benefit: Colds, flu, arthritis, rheumatica pains, digestion issues, parasites, mouth ulcers, muscle aches and pains, insect repellent, and air freshener.

Note: Use in moderation as considered a potential skin irritant. Be careful with topical application during first trimester in pregnancy.

Eucalyptus Oil: Renowned for reviving the spirits and restoring vitality, this refreshing oil will bring you clarity, expansion, focus, strength, and vision, where previously you grappled with anger, distance, exhaustion, lethargy, and sadness.

Application: Inhale, massage, diffuse, spritz, bath, compress.

May Also Benefit: Asthma, colds, flu, catarrh, immune support, sinusitis, headaches, muscle tension, burns, cuts, wounds, insect repellent, air freshener. Blend with lavender and tea tree when colds and flus are prevalent, as a potent chest rub. Combine one drop of each into a teaspoon of carrier oil and rub on the back and chest.

Frankincense Oil: Your personal coat of armour! This oil protects you and keeps you safe. Powerful to use when life gets too busy and emotional and physical reserves are low. It is the oil for personal growth and expansion especially when the past is holding you back. Enjoy feelings of acceptance, clarity, enlightenment, focus, forgiveness, love, peace, and wisdom.

Application: Massage, spritz, diffuse, bathe, inhale, compress.

May Also Benefit: Anti-aging, circulation, arthritis, respiratory conditions, digestion issues, wounds, inflammation, acne, large open pores, dry and mature skin, and wrinkles.

Geranium Oil: Call on this delicate yet potent oil when life feels like a continuous rollercoaster ride. When you're feeling chaotic, deceived, distant, moody, negative, or sensitive, Geranium will bring balance, calm, connection, focus, harmony, and protection.

Application: Compress, massage, bathe, spritz, diffuse, inhale.

May Also Benefit: Acne, eczema, dermatitis, congested skin, mature skin, broken capillaries, pre-menstrual syndrome, hormone support, infertility, menopause, wounds, bruising, and oedema.

Note: Be careful with topical application on hypersensitive or overly red and inflamed skin.

Grapefruit Oil: Call on this oil with euphoric properties when you're feeling tense, overwhelmed, under pressure, defeated, depressed, overwhelmed, weary, or frustrated. Enjoy the feelings of focus, clarity, joy, positivity, trust, and strength, as you're gently uplifted by the delightful citrus scent.

Application: Compress, inhale, massage or spritz this zesty, uplifting, and revitalising oil.

May Also Benefit: Oily, congested skin, acne, weight loss, cellulite, muscle aches and pains, headaches, insomnia, and muscle tension.

Juniper Oil: Helping to clear your mind from negative thoughts and mental clutter, this purifying oil will bring confidence, focus, joy, openness, relaxation, and clarity. Dust off apprehension, chaos, exhaustion, negativity, and weariness.

Application: Massage, bathe, diffuse, spritz, compress, inhale, and sitz bath.

May Also Benefit: Liver detoxification, muscle aches and pains, oedema, inflammation, cellulite, varicose veins, oily skin, pimples, cystitis, pyelitis.

Note: Be careful with topical application during first trimester of pregnancy.

Lemon Oil: This fresh and stimulating oil is an instant pick-me-up, leaving you with energy and mental clarity. You'll feel less confused, defeated, disheartened, exhausted, weary, and worried.

Application: Massage, compress, diffuse or spritz. This oil makes a refreshing addition to your bath, opening the heart, alleviating exhaustion, and creating self-confidence.

May Also Benefit: Anti-aging, nausea, cellulite, weight loss, oedema, varicose veins, warts, colds, flu, immune support, and a liver tonic.

Note: Avoid exposure to the sun after using lemon in a massage or bath as it is phototoxic (will cause a sunburn like skin condition when exposed to sunlight).

Patchouli Oil: This enduring and sensual oil makes for a hypnotic aroma when blended with ylang ylang and orange, increasing intimacy and passion. Attract abundance, confidence, courage, enlightenment, expansion, focus, grounding, peace, and sensuality. When you're feeling anger, anxiety, controlling, disheartened, distant, hopeless, stressed, or tense, keep this harmonising and regenerative oil on hand.

Application: Massage, compress, spritz, bathe, inhale.

May Also Benefit: Cracked and dry skin, stretch marks, fluid retention, cellulite, dermatitis, eczema, inflammation, wounds, and guess what? It's even an aphrodisiac!

Pine Oil: This cleansing, refreshing and invigorating oil can have the same effect as if you were standing in a pine forest. A fabulous oil for clearing the air, improving alertness, and increasing inspiration.

Application: Inhale, vaporise, bathe, spritz and compress this motivating and intuitive oil.

May Also Benefit: Coughs, colds, flu, asthma, cystitis, pyelitis, inflammation, muscle aches and pains, headaches, arthritis, rheumatic pain, and liver detoxification.

Rosemary Oil: Known to have a very stimulating effect on the mind, a cleansing effect on the emotions, and is renowned for being the oil for memory. This energising oil improves mental clarity, focus and intuition while calming exhaustion, mental fatigue, neglect, procrastination, and feeling overwhelmed.

Application: Enjoy this delightful oil in a bath, compress, diffuser, spritzer or massage.

May Also Benefit: Liver detoxification, weight loss, cellulite, muscle aches or pains, respiratory conditions, sinusitis, heart palpitations, circulation, and hair growth.

Note: Be careful with topical application during first trimester of pregnancy.

Spearmint Oil: Brings comfort to the mind and a sense of relief to the body as it calms mental fatigue and exhaustion, confusion, forgetfulness, lethargy, and weariness. Enjoy clarity, energy, enthusiasm, focus, motivation, and a feeling of being uplifted.

Application: Compress, massage, inhale, spritz, direct application (for wounds, cuts, and mouth ulcers only), and bathe.

May Also Benefit: Digestive issues, indigestion, wounds, cuts, mouth ulcers, sinusitis, catarrh, asthma, acne, dermatitis, psoriasis, nausea, and travel sickness. Spearmint shares similar properties to peppermint, with only trace amounts of menthol, making it gentler on the skin. Ideal for children with digestive upsets.

Thyme Oil: This cleansing oil helps to generate strength and enthusiasm, adaptability, focus, vitality, and warmth. Eliminate exhaustion, mental fatigue, stress, vulnerability, and feelings of withdrawal.

Application: Massage, diffuse, spritz, inhale and bathe.

May Also Benefit: Immune support, bacterial and fungal conditions, acne, oily skin, eczema, dermatitis, digestion issues, parasites, and respiratory conditions.

Chapter 6:

SELF-CONTROL

"Self-control is the chief element in self-respect, and, self-respect is the chief element in courage!"
– Thucydides

I had a three-year-old and a two-year-old. I was desperate to get back into training and focus on my fitness. I kept saying, "One day, one day". I finally joined the local gym to see if that could motivate me. Each time I went in, and I do not think this was an accident, I saw a book sitting there by Bill Phillips called *Body for Life*. I was particularly intrigued by all the before and after photos throughout the book. I picked it up each time I went in, wondering if it really would be possible to see me as an 'after' photo. I have always been happy with my body and accepting of the fact that as a young mum my body certainly changed. I am also incredibly mindful that body image is different for everyone. But after looking at this book numerous times, I decided I wanted a goal. I would go to the gym early, before my family woke up—it was the only time I could fit it in— and each morning the 4 a.m. alarm would go off.

It was hard at the beginning, but it gradually became precious 'me-time'. I loved going there and returning to the family home before everyone had even woken. My energy levels would be high; I felt amazing and excited to get into my day. Early morning training is good for me.

One morning, the receptionist said she had a gift for me. She handed over a brand-new copy of *Body for Life*. I was so touched. She said she had been really impressed with my commitment over the past few weeks and thought I would appreciate the gift. I certainly did.

I printed off the Success Chart where you could log your eating and exercise progress each day. I had it on the fridge, easy to see. I loved the 'twelve-week plan', it worked for me and gave me focus.

At the end of the twelve weeks I had lost weight, but more importantly, I had changed my shape; more svelte and lean. I felt so much better energy-wise, too.

One day, a trainer at the gym, Rachel, approached me and said there was a body sculpting competition coming up in seven weeks, and she wondered if I would like to participate. I was flattered as she said she had watched me train and admired my commitment. She felt I would do well, but I did not have her same confidence. I mean, me? Stand on stage? In a G-string bikini? Posing in front of an audience? It seemed way too far-fetched and scary. But there was another voice inside of me reminding me of my desire to attempt such a goal. So, dumbfounded I said yes.

I took it very seriously. I mean this woman had asked to train me. I did exactly as she said. I thought I had trained hard over the previous twelve weeks, but it was taking on a personal trainer that once again I realised we have no idea of our own inner power and ability. My previous level ten in effort was in fact just a six with Rachel. She knew how to push me, and I loved it. I got stronger and leaner still.

It was during this sculpting training I also got to appreciate the power of food. Every single thing that goes through your lips and into your belly has an effect. I mean everything. We would do body fat pinch tests every second day, given the aim was to get down to about 10% body fat. A healthy, active, athletic woman ranges between 18% and 20%. Rachel could tell if I had eaten something with more sugar overnight. It was insane what she knew I had done! I couldn't actually believe it. I became so disciplined with my eating. I did not sway. No matter what anyone offered, I was true to my cause. I was determined to give this my best and see what it was like with 100% commitment. Whatever you think of this crazy sport, what I loved the most about it was the training and the discipline. I also loved being held accountable.

Seven weeks later I did indeed stand on that stage painted in a sticky tanning solution in a black, glittering, G-string bikini. I still to this day cannot believe I stood in front of hundreds of people, flexing my muscles. It was a goal, and I achieved amazing results. I was placed runner up, much to my disappointment, as I really thought I could have won. That's the competitive side in me! Regardless of the result, I have to say this training was a real eye-opener for me, particularly with my understanding of food. I did this competition the traditional way. Using commercial protein bars and powders. I may have looked amazing but was I actually healthy?

Fast track fifteen years, and looking for another fitness challenge, two dear friends of mine, Sharny and Julius Keiser, inspired me to do their eight-week bikini-body program. For eight weeks I trained from my own home and did not eat a smidgeon of sugar; not even lemon juice. One day I did actually lick an apple cut in half just because I wanted to! Sticking to this program I felt better than ever. The program was based on real food and exercises a busy mum could do from her own home. And eight weeks later it was amazing to stand there in a bikini at forty-six years of age, fit, lean, and fabulous.

I remember being out on a boat trip with them both one day. Julius looked at me straight and asked outright, "So what is it that you truly want in life?" I wasn't sure how to respond to that question, but he kept pushing. I actually didn't know how to answer the question. And his response was alarming, "Well then it's no wonder your husband has to work away, and you don't have him home with you." He was right. How on earth could I achieve something like having a successful business and my husband home if I don't even know what that 'something' was?

The *Body for Life* program, the body sculpting competition, the Sharny and Julius 8-week bikini body programs were all very specific in achieving the outcomes I desired. My life, my business, the answer to, 'What is it you truly want?' needed the same intent; the same purpose and focus.

By instigating the power of self-discipline and taking on something different that can potentially change your behaviour, will lead you to more self-awareness and more self-control. It begins to feel easy the longer we stick it out. It's like you get better and then become unshakable in that stand. It is now your new normal.

An example of this is diet. If you are someone who chooses not to eat takeaway fast food or processed foods and you do this for some time, it will become such a part of you that you could even call it a 'non-negotiable'. There is absolutely no way it will ever be put in your body again. The power those foods may have had on you in the past no longer grip you. They no longer have control over you.

I have come to appreciate there are some who choose to do health related programs as a 'detox', only to continue eating and drinking unhealthily when they come off it. I worked in a gymnasium and was a personal trainer for three years. The number of people who joined the gym with the hope that they could just 'buy' the toned biceps and abs was incredible. It was only after a few weeks the realisation that it would take work and commitment sunk in.

I applaud the person who is truly disciplined, someone who has to give it everything they can to instigate change. The person who has educated themselves to become a better person, not just while on a program. They work hard to feel empowered to make new life-long decisions that will benefit their health and well-being. This is self-discipline and self-control at play.

But here's the thing: just as you think you have self-control under your belt you realise there are times that you can be catapulted straight back out of the circle of love.

Are you an emotional type? Impulsive? Are you a daydreamer? Do you resist routine? Does the next 'bright and shiny' object tempt you? Are you ruled by your habits? Do you want what you want NOW? Do you over-eat? Do you _____ (insert any habit that holds you back right in here)?

We could make this list a mile long and still not cover all the areas of our lives that could be resolved by better self-control!

Before we dive into the deep, dark places where we lack self-control, let's take a good look into the mechanics of self-control and its sidekick; willpower.

Interestingly, research suggests that willpower is a resource that depletes the more you use it. Can you believe that? The very gift we have that helps us control our urges is a consumable! Somehow it seems so unfair, but unfortunately, it's true. The more you draw on your willpower to resist the cupcake, get up at 5 a.m. to go to the gym, stop swearing, or not raise your voice at the kids, the more you're depleting the well of willpower.

I honestly believe that when we know better, we do better. We all have the intentions of controlling our eating habits, exercising regularly, cutting back on the alcohol, or finishing work early. We each have an aspect of our lives that can be improved, and no doubt, if we knew we could initiate the change and have it stick, we wouldn't hesitate to embark on the journey. The tragedy though, is that over the years, we have embarked on many journeys of transformation, only to be met with failure or just boredom. These clear setbacks have made us reticent to set ourselves up with yet another chance to fail and fall out of the self-love circle.

You see, you might decide to be disciplined and resist the urge to devour a block of chocolate after dinner on Friday and Saturday nights, and then on Sunday you give in to two or three squares, and then Monday, you inhale the entire block, putting you right back to square one! You're in a worse position than before you started, because now you are feeling like a failure again, yet you were doing so well!

What's happened here?

There was only enough willpower for two days! The stores had not been replenished and you were set up to fail from the outset and didn't even know it!

Do you want the good news or the bad news first?

OK, well the good news is that willpower is not depleted permanently. You're not going to be trapped in the grip of fluffy cupcakes forever! There is a way to replenish the stores, which means you can control yourself while contemplating the chocolate face plant!

Now for the 'bad news'. One of the methods to replenish the willpower stores is to refrain from drawing on it! So, in other words, the thing you need the most is the thing you can't draw on when you need it the most! What a system, hey?

Don't panic, all is not lost. In fact, it's perfect because this part of our biochemistry almost 'demands' that we care for ourselves, so much so that our success in just about everything we initiate is tied to it. So technically, it's an effective system, because without it we feel 'out of control' and with it, we feel accomplished and fulfilled. So, we can choose if we would like to feel 'incapable' or 'accomplished'. In the end, it is all within our control!

Additionally, to give yourself a little more leeway, our brain burns through stores of glucose when we exert our self-control, so if we are physically run-down or tired, we are going to find it challenging to engage in what we know will make us better but is contrary to an existing habit.

Here are some steps you can take that have been scientifically proven to replenish the willpower resources along with some strategies that will support you in becoming a better version of yourself as you expand and grow using this self-love circle.

When I researched the meaning of self-control, I found the American Psychological Association suggest that willpower and self-control are one and the same, and are defined as, "The ability to delay gratification, resisting short-term temptations in order to meet long term goals."

If we bring this definition back to day-to-day living, and explore what it means, I see that it, for example, allows us to choose a beautiful green drink in the morning, over a strong coffee with processed sugar and milk. This simple decision will leave us feeling incredibly virtuous. Instead of seeking out the instant gratification of a sugar-hit, we've asserted ourselves through choice and found another, healthier option, which made us feel fulfilled. It's doing a ten-minute workout in our bedroom before the whole family wakes up, rather than missing out on doing anything at all. It's getting up twenty minutes earlier to make time to meditate or watch the sun rise. When we take control, and make the time, we feel better, and we feel better because there has been an increase in our 'feel good' hormones like dopamine and serotonin. It's that simple. Self-fulfilment trumps short-term gratification every time.

Let's take a look at some of the challenges where willpower and self-control can benefit us:

1. Addictions
2. Excessive spending
3. Self-deprecation and criticism
4. Over indulging
5. Creating new self-serving habits
6. Transforming mindsets
7. Adopting healthy lifestyles

8. Trading instant gratification for fulfilment

9. Developing patience

10. Changing habitual behaviours

I'm sure that there are many more, and I'd encourage you to give this some thought as you reference your own life and where you'd feel more 'in control' if you had more self-control! Think of what you would change if you could control yourself when it comes to your work, your partner, your kids. How about when it comes to your bank account? Are you spending more than you earn? How about your diet and exercise? Is there room for self-reflection so you can reconnect with the ways in which you know how to tame the little voice inside your head, telling you that you can't?

Self-discipline is the fast step to self-control. If we can discipline ourselves with a new habit or choice, and use self-control to keep ourselves in check, we can really learn to master our minds, and master our lives, behaviours, and our achievements

Traits of the Self-Controlled:

Self-preservation.

They understand that to preserve the best life they can live, they will need to exercise self-control from time to time. Sometimes we can't trust our own impulses or initial desires, so delaying our action or gratification can be a method of self-preservation, because there may be a better or alternative opportunity waiting right around the corner.

They have a healthy attitude.

This healthy attitude extends towards 'things' and what they 'need' to live, rather than what they impulsively think they want to consume for the sake of consuming, or to keep up with societal expectations.

They know their own value.

They don't rely on the world outside of themselves to determine self-worth or value. They are able to discern this for themselves. By constantly reflecting on their own thoughts, habits, behaviours, and results, and initiating corrections and exercising self-control or willpower, they see life and challenges as an opportunity to expand and grow.

They are resilient.

They understand the importance of perseverance and can bounce back when things don't always go their way. Self-control helps them to focus on the solution rather than the problem.

They are aware of what serves them and what doesn't.

Because of their ability to be introspective, they can quickly assess situations that are not aligned with their own best interests, and they have the self-control to remove themselves or change the situation.

They extend the same courtesy of worth, value and resilience to others.

Because they have self-control and can evaluate and assess themselves, they are less likely to try to control others. It's only when we are feeling out of control of ourselves that we become outwardly controlling.

Here are some steps that you can take that could put your self-control to the test:

1. When it comes to buying things, ask, "Is this feeding me or eating me?" Is it fulfilling me or depleting me? For example, if you see a lamp that would look amazing in your home, ask yourself, *Do I really need to have another lamp in the house? (Is that feeding me?) Or, Is buying a new lamp depleting me of my wealth because I don't really need it?" (Is it eating me?).* A comparison to this scenario would be, for example, dressing your house to sell it, then this investment in the lamp could be *feeding* you to help you achieve a higher sell price.

2. When it comes to adopting a minimalist approach, especially to reduce the wastage that we all perpetuate, ask yourself, Do I really need it, or do I want this for instant gratification? *(And probably won't want or need it in a month's time).* Do we really need all these gadgets and 'things'? I think of it like essential oils; the fewer drops you use, the more effective they are.

3. When it comes to purchasing new cars (or other big-ticket items), my brother Aaron said to me one day, "It is all very good and well to save up to buy a brand-new car,

but in six months' time, it's not a new car anymore. It is just another car. It has likely cost you an extra $15,000 (at least) to drive it off the yard, but you will tire of it because it's not a new car anymore." My brother's analogy is an interesting one as it represents people's desire to have the biggest, the best, the fastest, the 'whatever...' and that is a form of control—materialistic control—as opposed to self-control. You could spend $20,000 or less on a different car, and still get what you need, as opposed to what we think we want. Unless, of course, getting a new car is something you have saved for, dreamed of, and for which you have worked hard, then of course you most likely have already applied many of the aspects of self-discipline and self-control in order to achieve it. And I am not denying the beautiful sense of accomplishment, pride and joy in owning a new car.

4. When it comes to the language you use when you are irritated, ask why? What is the reason you go there? If you delve deeper, there is always a reason behind your trigger. Why do you get hooked into a drama or story where something, or someone, irritates you?

Here are some possible reasons why your reactions may not be serving you in a positive manner:

a) There could be an element of truth.

b) It causes you to revisit an emotional situation from a previous experience when you were younger, that is now subconscious.

c) You are not feeling that good about yourself and maybe creating a story in your head that blames your boss for those feelings.

d) You're staying in a job that you really don't enjoy.

These are always opportunities to delve deeper into yourself for analysis and reflection rather than being caught in the cycle of judgement.

> *Willpower and desire,*
> *When properly combined,*
> *Make an irresistible pair.*
> – Napoleon Hill

Below is a list of steps that you can take today, to replenish your willpower and support yourself as you transform your relationship with self-control. I do have one caveat before we get to these steps, and that is to manage your addictions first. If or when we are dealing with food addictions, drug or alcohol addictions, shopping addictions, or any other kind of addictions, we are constantly drawing on our willpower stores to overcome them. My suggestion is to manage these addictions first, and then reach for expansion and growth in other areas of your life. Don't try to do it all at once, as the brain and the body are more likely to respond to these one at a time. Addictions can take time. You and your source of willpower and self-control will need all the resources you possess in order to kick these habits. So, when you dive into the suggestions below, be sure you're ticking off any addictions first.

If you've struggled to kick a smoking habit or sugar addiction, or any habit that has you trapped, and you'd prefer a way out, you'll be pleasantly surprised by the difference these steps below can make to your ability to feel like you can win.

NOTE: You may have tried other avenues in the past and for some, you may even be on medication to support yourself. I want to stress here that this is not medical advice and I do not recommend you disengage any psychological or medicinal help you may be currently using. These suggestions should be considered complementary only.

Meditation

Evidence has shown that the process of meditation releases neuro-transmitters that calm and soothe the brain. We also know that through the simple practice of mindfulness, we can enhance our own emotional intelligence, which means we are more likely to maintain self-control in situations that would otherwise cause a stressed response.

If you've never meditated before, I'm a huge fan of transcendental meditation (TM), which is taught by certified teachers through a standard course of instruction. The practice involves the use of a personal mantra. You're encouraged to meditate for twenty minutes in the morning, and twenty minutes in the evening. It's an easy calming technique and wonderful for beginners.

There are many other styles of meditation that you can explore, including guided, mindfulness, kundalini, Zen, Tibetan, the use of mala beads, as well as many others. I recommend that you begin your search for the meditation style that works for you and begin a practice that is just five to ten minutes each day. If you can manage more, go for it, of course! No matter what your schedule allows, you will reap the rewards over time, in more ways than just replenishing your willpower. Calm, bliss, and clarity are all waiting for you on the other side of a regular meditation practice.

Food

You brain needs food to exert self-control, and if you haven't eaten wisely, or your blood sugar level is low, you will find yourself more and more likely to fall back into habituated responses rather than feeling in control. Eating sugary foods causes the blood sugars to spike and crash, which causes mood swings, lethargy and craving more sugary, quick-fix foods. To the contrary, eating a meal high in protein and full of health-giving foods like green vegetables, and good fats like butter or coconut oil will sustain your blood sugars for much longer periods of time, sustaining your energy and self-control.

If you're not sure how to manage your diet, I strongly recommend you look at following certain people–nutrition experts–whose philosophy you believe in, and you have an affinity with. You could look at our 5 Day Feel Fit & Fabulous by the Weekend kickstart of the 28-day Aroma Living program that supports you with recipes, essential oils, rituals, exercises, and tips. You can find this program on our website at www. twenty8.com . Some of my favourite food experts I love following on Instagram with healthy and simple recipes include; Cyndi O'Meara, Helen Padarin, Pete Evans, Kirsty Wirth, Jordan Pie, Sheridan Austin, Charlotte Carr, Luke Hines, Ashley Jubinville, Tania Hubbard, Jo Whitton, Fouad Kassab, the Merrymaker Sisters and Marnie Perkinson to name a few. You will find their websites on page 357

Exercise

Moderate exercise has been proven to release endorphins that make us feel good, and with these endorphins in the blood stream, we are more likely to make empowered and better controlled choices for ourselves. Dopamine, serotonin, and norepinephrine are the neurotransmitters that control our moods and, as a result of exercise, the body is bathed in this wonderful chemistry. The opposite is cortisol, which, if there is too much, is the stress chemical that makes us feel bad, and is released into the blood stream under stress, which often happens when we do not feel we are in control anymore and the pressure is on.

You could try creating a routine in your week where you select what you want to do for at least four days of the week. You could walk, run, ride a bike, or swim. It doesn't matter what you select, the key is to get started without delay. If you can work up a bit of a sweat, and still hold a conversation, you're in the right zone for achieving better fitness. Remember the Workout of the Day option on page 203.

Sleep

It may sound strange to link sleep with self-control, but when we are tired the brain begins calling for more glucose as its uptake is inhibited. We can tend to crave more sugar-rich foods, looking for that burst of energy, only to find that we've compromised our own decision-making ability with a spike in energy, followed by a crash. It's also harder to feel motivated to initiate self-control when we are tired, and while you may be tempted to think you're just being lazy, it's typical and a sign there hasn't been enough sleep! Interesting, isn't it?

Sleep is one of the most important parts of recovery and good health. It helps with mental clarity, it is our immune booster, libido booster, fat and sugar burner, and it is our happy pill. Good sleep reduces our risk of chronic illness and determines our performance for each day. Our sleep can also switch our genes on and off; genes that affect our circadian rhythms, metabolism, immune system, and stress. You could then expand to incorporate antioxidants, anti-aging, hormone production and motivation within these main categories. Let's face it, without good sleep nothing works properly, and we are more likely to feel overwhelmed and emotional. And as Carren Smith says, "When emotions are high, intelligence is low."

Road blocks that inhibit good sleep include alcohol, caffeine, a lack of nutrients (particularly zinc, magnesium and the B vitamins), poor blood sugar balance, dehydration, late nights, travel, babies, and even breathing issues. Of course, one of the biggest inhibitors of them all is stress. Remember stress in the red zone (as discussed on Page 167) creates a sympathetic, fight or flight, nervous response, making us less productive. And although we might think that we have it all together, we have less self-control than any other time.

If we can learn to master spending more time in the green zone–and stimulate the parasympathetic nervous system– we find it is here that we get to truly rest and digest. Our body starts to connect from within a lot more; we are able to respond to all of life's occurrences in a much more relaxed and controlled way. It is imperative that we build strong neurological connections to a more peaceful way of living, so we can support the sympathetic system and the daily stressors. Here are a few things that might help you sleep better and restore effectively.

1. Respect your sleep time: Don't compromise; get in at least seven or eight hours a day.

2. Learn how to rest: Wind down in the evenings with sleep rituals.

3. Do more softer exercise: Gentle walking, yoga, tai chi, qi gong, or yoga, for example.

4. Reduce screen time: Switch off technology, reduce electromagnetic exposure.

5. Meditate: And if you wake in the night, listen to a meditation to stay feeling rested.

6. Look at what you are eating: Avoid sugar, caffeine, and alcohol.

7. Breathe: Consciously slow down your breathing to decrease anxiety.

8. Energise yourself: Exercising regularly helps your physiology and ability to rest.

Reflection

Regardless of whether you've effectively managed your self-control or not, allow yourself time at the end of each day to reflect on what you did, how you could improve, and what you were pleased about. Allow yourself to attribute a specific feeling, and location in the body of that feeling, and congratulate yourself on your self-awareness.

Reflection time does not have to take forever. It can just be a simple acknowledgement. Or you could grab a journal from your favourite stationery store and use it specifically for self-reflection each day. Consider looking for evidence each day that you are one step closer to full self-control and find opportunities to congratulate yourself. Make this journal a positive and encouraging log of events on how you handled yourself. Your inspiration for tomorrow starts today, so make sure you're setting yourself up with the incentive to succeed.

Another question that we ask in our family around the dinner table is, "What was your greatest lesson today?" It gives us each a chance to reflect on the day, what we did well or maybe what we didn't do so well. It's a really nice way to share your vulnerabilities with those you love. You can implement this into the work environment or friendship circles too. It's powerful.

Forgiveness

"Forgiveness does not change the past,
but it does enlarge the future."
– Paul Boese

In the event that things didn't quite go to plan that day, be willing to forgive yourself. We are all a work in progress and if we can make it easy on ourselves to change and improve, we will be more likely to continue on the journey. If we beat ourselves up, we will be less likely to persevere when things get a bit tricky, because we have become our own worst enemy instead of our own best friend and supporter!

You may like to place some positive affirmations around your home, in your car, and at work, to keep you on track, and provide encouragement to stay on track. Create your own essential oil ritual with uplifting oils such as bergamot, orange, and grapefruit. Add a splash of frankincense or lavender and you have a sensational potion for potency right there!

I've included here a short list of my favourite books that have been invaluable in my own personal journey over the years and I hope that you're able to draw inspiration for yourself from some of the messages offered by these incredible authors:

- The Journey – Brandon Bays
- Changing Habits Changing Lives – Cyndi O'Meara
- The Four Agreements – Don Miguel Ruiz
- Manifesting Matisse – Dr. Michelle Nielsen

- The Five Love Languages – Gary Chapman

- Soul Survivor – Carren Smith

- Anam Cara: A book of Celtic Wisdom – John O'Donohue

- E-Squared – Pam Grout

- The Secret Life of Plants – Peter Tompkins and Christopher Bird

- A Course in Miracles – Helen Schucman

- Personality Plus – Florence Littauer

- Broken Open: How Difficult Time Can Help Us Grow – Elizabeth Lesser

- The Invitation: Oriah Mountain Dreamer – Oriah

- Rising Strong, Daring Greatly and The Power Of Vulnerablity – Brene Brown

- To Bless the Space Between Us – John O'Donohue

- Beauty from the Inside Out – Dr Libby Weaver

- Shine from Within – Amanda Rootsey

- Loving What Is: Four Questions That Can Change Your Life – Byron Katie

- Healing with Essential Oils – Dr Eric Zielinski

- The Complete Guide to Aromatherapy – Salvatore Battaglia

- Low Tox Life – Alexx Stuart

There is a saying that books are a uniquely portable magic, and for many they can be liberating, even life-changing. I have gained many pearls of wisdom and wonderful quotes from the books I love.

Along with any of your own favourite quotes, here are some powerful affirmations that can be used on a daily basis to keep you grounded on your self-control journey. You might like to take a photo in nature and attribute one of these quotes to that image. This could be something you choose to share on social media or in your journal.

I love and accept myself no matter what happens.

My life is a series of lessons and I am the student.

I learn and love with ease and flow.

I am a work in progress.

I am never wrong, I am learning.

When I forgive myself I release the pain.

I am willing to see this differently.

I am the creator of my destiny.

I am whole and complete. Nothing is missing.

I feed my soul with love, kindness and forgiveness.

I sleep to replenish my willpower.

I eat to replenish my willpower.

I meditate to replenish my willpower.

I reflect to replenish my willpower.

I am my own cheerleader.

I am my best friend.

A superhero lives in here.

I have the power to change.

What I believe I achieve.

I was made to succeed.

When I'm in control, everyone is safe!

I was born to be brilliant.

I was born to expand.

I was born for this!

I can do anything and everything.

I LOVE myself.

I am great with money.

I love and honour myself.

Journal Page

Date:

What I am grateful for today:

1

2

3

4

5

Where did I lose control today?

How can I do this better tomorrow?

What will inspire me tomorrow?

Who can I share this with now?

What leap am I willing to take?

What have I learned about myself that is empowering today?

Essential Oils for Self-Control:

Black Pepper Oil: This revered, spicy oil helps to activate and excite the body! Think energy, endurance, enthusiasm, focus, vitality, warmth, and stimulation as you wash away feelings of defeat, fatigue, mental lethargy, nervousness, sensitivity and worthlessness. This oil has a powerful kick so only small amounts are needed for great results!

Application: Inhale, massage, diffuse, spritz, massage, bathe and compress.

May Also Benefit: Colds, flu, rheumatic pain, muscle aches and pains, bruises, oedema, circulation, liver detoxification and digestion issues.

Cardamom Oil: When you feel like you're in a rut, Cardamom reminds you of all that is possible leaving you feeling content, fulfilled, generous and warm. Leave behind feelings of depression, disheartened, mental fatigue, judgement, lethargy, and tension. This precious oil eliminates fears and worries and helps to restore your appetite for life.

Application: Massage, compress, inhale, diffuse, bathe and spritz this supporting and inspiring oil.

May Also Benefit: Digestion issues, flatulence, monthly feminine balance, immune support, coughs, bronchitis, nausea, circulation, and is even an aphrodisiac!

Ginger Oil: Brings clarity, confidence, courage, endurance, motivation, and strength to situations when you're feeling trapped by mental fatigue, forgetfulness, grief, lethargy, and worthlessness.

Application: Inhale, massage, bathe, compress, foot-bath, spritz and diffuse.

May Also Benefit: Digestion issues, indigestion, bruising, muscle aches and pains, cold hands and feet, arthritis, nausea, travel sickness, catarrh, coughs, and sinusitis.

Lemongrass Oil: Bring balance, clarity, endurance, energy, enthusiasm, expansion, motivation, and vitality to your days as you say goodbye to apprehension, depression, mental fatigue, impatience, lethargy, negativity, stress, vulnerability, and feelings of worthlessness.

Application: Massage, compress, bathe, spritz, inhale, diffuse.

May Also Benefit: Muscle aches and pains, bruising, oedema, inflammation, indigestion, fever, headaches, weight loss and cellulite. Works wonderfully as an insect repellent and air freshener and when used in massage, boosts energy and endurance.

Wintergreen Oil: The sweet and minty scent of Wintergreen is a powerful antidote to stressed muscles and head tension. Replace feelings of hurt, negativity, procrastination, and rigidity, with energy, endurance, motivation, positivity, relaxation, and heal those deep-down emotional wounds. As an added bonus, this oil has the ability to act as a natural pain reliever! It is also antiseptic, anti-arthritic, and an astringent.

Application: Massage, compress, diffuse, spritz, and bathe in this relieving and warming oil.

May Also Benefit: Colds, flu, muscle aches and pains, digestion issues, inflammation, bacterial and fungal conditions.

Note: Avoid topical application during pregnancy. Always use diluted as the methyl salicylate content can cause skin sensitivities.

Chapter 7
SELF-RESPECT

"Self-respect comes from within. It should not be reliant upon outside influences like physical appearance, public image, wealth, social status, praise, accomplishments awards, or achievements."
– Kim Morrison

I was nineteen years of age when my girlfriend Lizzie and I won a trip to Perth. We both worked for the same travel agent and the first-class tickets were a dream come true for two excitable teens. I had broken up with my boyfriend of five years a few months beforehand, so this was a just what I needed, and Lizzie's sister lived there so it would be a week of fun.

On the flight over we consumed a good amount of Bailey's Irish Cream, an alcoholic liqueur that, I must admit, I have not really been able to stomach since! These were the days where we could sit in the cockpit and watch the pilots do their thing and sip on our favourite beverage the whole time. Lizzie told me she had a mate playing in the New Zealand cricket team, that it would be great if I could meet him; she thought I would fancy him. I was not really that keen. Neither was I that interested in watching a day/night cricket match at the WACA (West Australian Cricket Association) grounds, but the following night we went along with our black and white New Zealand colours on.

Cricket fans are crazy. They clearly love the game and their favourite players. They yelled, screamed, and seemed to watch every single ball that was delivered and played (and there're a lot!). I was intrigued and interested, but slightly bored if I am honest. That was until half time of the match. Lizzie took me down into the tunnel where she asked a staunch man in a white coat for Danny Morrison. The white coat disappeared, and I felt like we were just two blonde groupies standing there. People in the stand were staring down at us, clearly waiting to see who would appear from the players' dressing rooms.

And when Danny finally walked out, I must admit I was a bit stunned. He hugged dear Lizzie and, as you do, I noticed his incredibly muscly arms and tanned face. As she introduced him, he surprisingly turned, smiled, and then embraced me too. I will never forget that moment. I loved how he smelt and how he hugged. As corny as it sounds I really did go weak at the knees, and I suddenly became very interested in cricket!

We caught up on two occasions while we were in Perth, once at a barbeque and another time at Lizzie's sister's place. It's fair to say I was totally smitten. And on our return flight to New Zealand I told Lizzie I wanted his babies! Okay, maybe in hindsight that was a little over the top, but I knew I had just met the man I wanted to marry.

Danny sent me a fax (yes, we faxed back then!) and invited me to Melbourne for the Boxing Day Test Match between Australia and New Zealand in 1987, as all the other wives and girlfriends were coming. The fact he put me in the same sentence just confirmed I HAD to go!

I quit my job, sold my car, and booked a one-way ticket to Melbourne.

As I write this, I seriously do wonder how I managed to make this all happen. I arrived in Melbourne on Boxing Day and when my twenty-one-year-old fast bowling great hunk of a cricketer arrived back at our hotel, I knew I had made the right decision. He instantly dropped his cricket sports bag and whisked me up in his arms turning us both around in a number of circles. Yes, I was gone.

I sat in the Members Stand of the Melbourne Cricket Ground in my running shorts and a singlet each day, listening to the radio commentary on my Walkman, trying to get a grasp of this crazy, long game. I had no idea of the protocol—that I should have been more appropriately dressed—and it was on day five of the Test Match that security told me I needed to cover up! I was just nineteen years of age. Can you imagine it? What I did learn is that NZ should have won this Test match.

Australian umpire Dick French gave a decision, that on television replay was clearly incorrect. Now, I am not an expert in the game, but it was—in cricket terms—an absolutely plumb LBW (leg-before-wicket) decision. An LBW is one of the ways in which a batsman can be dismissed in the sport of cricket. Following an appeal by the fielding side, the umpire may rule a batsman out LBW if the ball would have struck the wicket but was instead intercepted by any part of the batsman's body (except the hand holding the bat).

Danny had bowled that infamous ball to Australian batsman Craig McDermott and had the correct decision been given New Zealand would have won that Test match and squared the Series. Sadly, it did not go his way and Australia won the Series 1-0. It's fair to say the NZ team were not in high spirits back at the hotel that evening.

I travelled with the New Zealand cricket team across to Perth for a day/night game, and then to Sydney for another one-day game. It was at this point Danny had succumbed to a muscle injury and was forced to return to New Zealand. Our whirlwind three-week romance had come to an end.

I remember that day like it was yesterday. My heart felt like it was being ripped out of my chest. When would I see him again? What if this was it? How come I knew he was the love of my life, yet he didn't know I was his, at that point? Danny gave me a big hug, he told me he'd see me again real soon and wished me all the best on my travels, as I had intended to continue the adventure and meet Lizzie in the United Kingdom.

He smiled a cheeky grin, blew me a kiss from down the hallway… and that was it, he entered the lift and was gone.

I couldn't breathe. I sobbed so hard into the hotel pillow and just didn't know what to do with myself. He was my world, my life, he was my soul mate, and the sad thing was, he didn't even know it! I instantly rang my mum, and as she heard the agony in my voice, she just told me I would be okay and to remember the old proverb: "If you love something, set it free, if it comes back, it is yours, if it doesn't, it never was." I had to let him go, I had to find a way to create a life for myself and make him want to come back.

I did not end up going to the UK. Instead, I ended up in Melbourne and started working in a gymnasium. Right next door was a Natural Therapies College, and so began my love affair with essential oils and ultra-marathon running.

Danny and I stayed in touch over the next three years, the old-fashioned way; with hand-written letters. Every letter Danny wrote started with the lyrics of his favourite song. The one that made my heart skip a thousand beats was one he wrote from Pakistan in October 1990. The letter started with the lyrics from the Police song, *Every Little Thing She Does is Magic*, and he declared how much he missed me. He said he was looking forward to the upcoming New Zealand cricket tour of Australia and was hoping to see me. I was in the middle of my running training and Aromatherapy Diploma. I couldn't believe it.

It was Monday the 17th December when he walked through the doors of the clinic I was working in. He invited me downstairs into the shopping centre for a hokey-pokey ice-cream from my favourite, New Zealand Natural ice cream stand. Danny took my hand, curious to know where I was at, and if there was any chance I would return to New Zealand. I told him if I was to come home it would be for keeps. I think he was a little taken aback by my forthrightness, but he could see I was not prepared to give up everything I had built over the past three years if he wasn't serious.

My world was in a spin. It sounds so cliché, but it was like my knight in shining armour had returned! I told Danny I needed to complete my Diploma in Aromatherapy and was to graduate on Valentine's Day 1991. He left and took a taxi back to Melbourne city. My heart was in my throat, but I was still unsure if it was right to drop everything for this man.

Margaret Smalley is a beautiful woman who became like an adopted mum to me during my time in Australia. She took me aside at one of our College events as she noticed I was not myself. She said she was there for me if I needed someone to talk to. I nearly burst into tears there and then. I had not told anyone in Australia about my love for a New Zealand cricketer. I poured my heart out to Margy. I didn't know what to do. Leave the School I was now a Director of, the relationship I was in, and my running? But what if I did go back to New Zealand and it didn't work out with Danny? Margy asked me to take a breath.

She then asked me to tell me how I would feel if Danny walked in through the door in that moment? I looked at the door. Oh gosh, I stared back at her, my breathing changed and then grinning from ear to ear I felt my throat and cheeks blush. Margy held my hand and looked deeply into my eyes. She said, "Sweetheart, if you don't go back home, you will spend the rest of your life wondering, *What if?*"

She was more than right. I had to go back. I booked my flight back to Auckland and was on that plane a few days later. It was not easy, but I knew when my feet touched down in the city I was born, it was the right thing. Danny was waiting for me at the airport with my beautiful family, my mother Anne, my brother Aaron, and my sister Keri. It was a vision that will never leave me. I was so relieved and excited to be home. I had missed them all terribly.

Danny proposed to me on Christmas Day 1991. We were married on the 4th April in 1993. It was a profoundly romantic day and a celebrity affair. We were on the covers of magazines; television news channels were there, and many members of the public had turned up to see Danny Morrison marry. Danny was a well-known, regarded, and respected athlete who had been named New Zealand's bowler of the year the night before. I was, and still am, so proud of him.

My husband is the kindest and most caring soul you will ever meet. He is charming, witty, naughty, and cheeky. He has been a top international athlete and television commentator, a pin-up boy, and a celebrity. He is also an incredible dad, husband, son, and friend. Danny is fiercely loyal and wonderfully calm. He is my rock. I admire him wholeheartedly.

Danny was told he would not make it as a fast-bowler because he was too short. But Danny had other plans. He not only made it, he stayed there for ten years. He's had tens of thousands of people chant his name as he ran in to bowl in an international cricket match at the MCG (Melbourne Cricket

Ground). And at the other end of the spectrum, he has passed out on the floor as I gave birth to our son! But the fact he forged a career doing what he loves is quite incredible. The fact he has constantly reinvented himself within the game of cricket, despite all the challenges and heartache he has endured, is truly remarkable.

I invite you to look around you. Think about the people you admire and look up to and ask yourself, what are the attributes they possess that you are inspired by? Is it how they talk or hold themselves? Is it the way they look? Is it their success or ability to overcome challenge? Their incredible spirit? Their kind heart?

If you are willing to identify what you find attractive in those you admire, you will see a common thread among each of these people that runs deeper than appearances and any achievements. There is often a subtle energy, an essence that you love. It's a profound deep sense of self-respect that you can feel when you're in their presence, and you find that you are drawn into it with ease and with love.

But what does someone with self-respect look like?

When we look to others with admiration for who they are and what they represent, it's often because we feel uplifted by them, or we seem to feel better reading about them, watching them, or listening to them.

Conversely, if we find ourselves competing with people, comparing ourselves to others, feeling inadequate, not measuring up, and not feeling good enough, we may not necessarily bring out the best in ourselves. Sadly, the real fallout from this often sends us down a slippery slope of self-loathing and at worst, self-destruction.

In this chapter, I'd like us to explore the little voice inside and begin to pay attention to what we want and what serves us so that we can build our self-esteem and self-confidence. This, in turn leads us to the ultimate experience of self-respect and self-love.

I asked my twenty-year-old daughter, Tayla, to explain to me what someone with self-respect looked like to her. She said, "They know who they are and never apologise for it. They won't settle for relationships that do not serve them. They don't seem to concern themselves with what other people think of them, and they won't compromise their own values to fit in, they don't gossip or judge, they look after themselves, and they care for themselves, for others, and the planet!"

Tayla nailed it. In my mind she seemed to encapsulate self-respect beautifully. Interestingly, when I ask people in my workshops to answer this question they are not as forthcoming in their response. People tend to have to really think about it.

'Self-respect can be defined as a feeling of confidence and pride in your own ability and worth.'

As I investigated communities that have a powerful relationship with self-respect, I found myself drawn back to my roots of growing up in New Zealand, where the Maori culture is founded on the respect for family, including respect for self, elders, the land, and of course, their culture.

The Maori word *mana* means *power*, in the literal translation. The Maori dictionary defines mana as prestige, authority, control, power, influence, status, spiritual power, charisma - *mana* is a supernatural force in a person, place or object. *Mana* is the enduring, indestructible power of the *atua* (God).

Maori who grow up with the belief in *mana* since birth automatically have the notion of respect, which, generally speaking, seems to be missing in our European-based modern culture. Tribal cultures are blessed with an innate knowing that they have a force inside each of them that is akin to the power of God, or Source, or Spirit, which leaves them free to honour themselves, each other, and the world around them as a natural expression of being alive. It's beautiful, and while there are many ways our modern progress has added enormous value, when it comes to the greatest expression of ourselves, I believe we have a lot to learn from our Maori and Aboriginal traditions, and cultural history.

I was once told, "A mother is only as happy as her saddest child." It's so true! If either of my kids are in a world of pain or struggling to navigate their way through challenges, my instinct is to do all I can to get them out of it. I want to wrap them up and protect them from the big, bad world. I want their lives to be truly amazing and happy and perfect and right and I don't want anyone to ever hurt them. But we know this is a ridiculous fallacy, and haven't I said in this book already that our greatest growth comes through our greatest adversities? And that we often find that 'supernatural force within' can come to the fore through such times. As hard as it is to say this, why would I want to rob them of that?

I remember one time when Danny and I were seeing our counsellor, and asking dear Jacqueline how on earth do we behave with our kids if we ourselves are struggling. She told us both, "It's not your job to hide your troubles and neither is it your job to lump your troubles on your children. All you have to do is show your children how to get through tough times, and challenges with strength and grace. Show them that it is possible to overcome problems and that you can always find a way."

Tayla had been going through a bit of a tough time with herself around love and relationships recently. I, of course, wanted to just hug her and tell her to never stop believing in the power of love. That one day she will truly experience something extraordinary. And that she will just 'know' when it is right.

Tayla is an incredibly deep thinker, she is wise beyond her years, and I admire her in the way she processes things. I decided to ask for an insight into her world and what she had learned about relationships and love in her twenty years, so far. This is what she wrote:

When the word 'love' comes to mind we don't think hurt or pain or destruction... we think warmth, passion, tenderness, togetherness... so why is it that we often self-sabotage in order to settle for a less-than-loving relationship?

I am the first person to take responsibility for allowing myself to settle when it comes to love. But in many ways, and after deeper reflection, I realise that I'm grateful for the lessons and the heartache too.

Sometimes, when I think about the situations I have allowed myself to be in, it brings tears to my eyes. I remember allowing myself to be treated so poorly and to be taken advantage of. I now realise that to respect oneself means to love oneself. I was at a time in my life where I was seeking love in someone else and not in myself. And the worst part is that I knew this. I didn't want to look in the mirror and love myself, so I looked for it in the wrong places, and it ended up causing more pain than beauty. This so-called 'relationship' felt restricting, like pulling teeth, instead of making me feel wanted and loved. The hardest part wasn't letting him go but forgiving myself for falling in love with his potential, all the while knowing that I had seen the warning signs all along. I've learned that you'll break your own heart if you allow yourself to fall in love with ideas instead of people.

As time has passed and I have let go of the toxicity, I chose to look in the mirror instead. I found beauty, dignity, and self-love. I look back on what was, and I don't regret a single moment because it taught me so much. I wanted to experience emotions—good and bad—and that's what I got. I got a life lesson. Be thankful for the struggles you go through. They make you strong, wise, and humble. Don't let them break you. Let them make you. All you can do is learn your lesson. There's no point in wishing you had done it differently. The past is the past. Blossom, to be the beautiful soul in the now and for tomorrow. The best deed we can do in this world is to love and be loved... yourself and others.

Don't settle for a relationship. Why should a relationship mean settling down? Wait out for someone who won't let life escape you, who'll challenge you, and drive you towards your dreams. Someone spontaneous you can get lost in the world with. A relationship with the right person is a release not a restriction.

Through all of this I have found me. My self.

The Power of Finding your Essence, your True Self, your Mana.

Since the age of nineteen, I have practiced the ritual of giving myself a full-body massage every morning and most evenings. I call it my *Daily Body Boost*. Coupled with three drops of my chosen essential oils into a carrier oil like sweet almond, coconut, or jojoba.

I mindfully and quickly massage every part of my body from my toes to my head, honouring the gift of my legs that get me around every day, my tummy and chest that housed and fed two babies, my strong back, my arms, and my face.

It is a one- or two-minute ritual and as I stand there for a few seconds longer, thinking about my intention for the day, and those that I love, I am brought to tears often by the love that flows through me in this simple act. What a privilege it is to take the time to do it, a treat to get to know myself, choose essential oils according to my needs that day, and respect the role that self-care has in my world.

When you have such love for yourself, and all that your body does, you come to appreciate yourself in a way that deserves all the love, care, devotion, and attention you can give it.

But if you are feeling the opposite to this, then it's time to explore what it looks like when we LACK self-respect:

- Lack of attention to self-care.
- Don't care what we're doing and certainly don't care what we are putting into our bodies.
- Fail to realise what we (individually) want.
- Become miserable and more likely to take dangerous risks. An attitude of, "Who cares, anyway?"
- Unable to stand up for ourselves.
- Life is not that worth the effort; lack responsibility.
- Often don't think of the consequences.
- No regard for the outcome or any people involved.,

On the flip side now, again let's explore what it looks like when someone oozes self-respect and how you can recognise it:

- Know who they are and never apologise for it.
- Like being who they are.
- Not reliant on things outside of us (a level of wealth, social status, praise, physical appearance, accomplishments, rewards, or achievements).
- Won't settle for situations that don't serve them.
- Don't concern themselves with how others perceive them.
- Can say no to things that don't suit them rather than compromise their values just to fit in.

- Take responsibility for themselves and their actions.
- They can still feel down and have the full experience of human emotion but, they are honest with themselves.
- Will never give up on themselves. Even in their low points they will find a way through or they will always try to see the lesson, or the opportunity.
- Pick themselves up in a graceful and dignified way. They keep going.
- Have a great respect for others.
- Are not swayed by fads or other people's opinions.
- They are driven to know more; curious, questioning, investigating and enquiring.
- Pleasing others is not their motivation.
- Not driven by 'keeping up appearances' with other people (appearing successful).
- Honour their own uniqueness and exude the feeling that they know they are enough.
- They are comfortable in their own skin.

Sometimes we just need to take a breath and surrender. Trust the path that is already mapped out for us and build a relationship with the *mana* inside as it grows to be a present and powerful force in every aspect of our lives! I am so grateful I let Danny go and build a life for myself in those three years we were apart. I am sure that was one of my greatest lessons in self-respect; knowing that my happiness and success was not determined by needing someone else to be present to experience it.

Ultimately we know that self-respect is earned and not demanded or bought. I truly believe taking on just a simple beautiful Body Boost ritual (like on Page 331) is a sure way to earn a deeper more loving respect and connection with yourself. As well as giving huge thanks and appreciation to the most important person on this planet.

Essential Oils for Self-Respect:

Clove Oil: You'll feel confidence, courage, creativity, focus, openness, strength and warmth instead of confusion, depression, lethargy, and negativity. When mixed with peppermint oil, clove oil is well known to ward off fatigue.

Application: Diffuse, inhale, spritz, massage, bathe, direct application (for mouth ulcers and dental issues only – dip a cotton bud into the undiluted oil and apply to the surface and surrounding areas of the aching tooth).

May Also Benefit: Colds, flu, arthritis, rheumatism pains, digestion issues, parasites, mouth ulcers, muscle aches and pains, insect repellent and air freshener.

Note: Use in moderation as considered a potential skin irritant. Be careful with topical application during first trimester in pregnancy.

Ginger Oil: Brings clarity, confidence, courage, endurance, motivation, and strength to situations when you're feeling trapped by mental fatigue, forgetfulness, grief, lethargy, and worthlessness.

Application: Inhale, massage, bathe, compress, foot bath, spritz, and diffuse.

May Also Benefit: Digestion issues, indigestion, bruising, muscle aches and pains, cold hands and feet, arthritis, nausea, travel sickness, catarrh, coughs, and sinusitis.

Jasmine Oil: Considered to be the 'King of Flowers', you can draw on its strength to let go of the past and adapt to what is present. Become confident, content, fulfilled, grateful, passionate, positive, sensual, uplifted, and trusting. Release deception, depression, distance, disconnection, fear, rigidity, sorrow, and worthlessness.

Application: Massage, bathe, spritz, compress, inhale, and diffuse.

May Also Benefit: Muscular cramps and spasms, coughs, colds, and flus. Relieve insomnia, muscle tension, dry skin, eczema, dermatitis, infertility, and pre-menstrual syndrome. Can also be used as an aphrodisiac!

Juniper Oil: Helping to clear your mind from negative thoughts and mental clutter, this purifying oil will bring confidence, focus, joy, openness, relaxation, and clarity. Dust off apprehension, chaos, exhaustion, negativity, and weariness.

Application: Massage, bathe, diffuse, spritz, compress, inhale, and sitz bath.

May Also Benefit: Liver detoxification, muscle aches and pains, oedema, inflammation, cellulite, varicose veins, oily skin, pimples, cystitis, pyelitis.

Note: Be careful with topical application during first trimester of pregnancy

Palmarosa Oil: Encouraging a sense of balance, security, compassion, confidence, creativity, forgiveness, and generosity, this oil melts away anxiety, deception, hurts, hopelessness, insecurity, obsessiveness, and vulnerability.

Application: Massage, compress, spritz, inhale, bathe.

May Also Benefit: Oily or dry skin, broken capillaries, rashes, eczema, dermatitis, pre-menstrual syndrome, hormone support, scars, wrinkles, anti-aging, and digestive issues.

Patchouli Oil: This enduring and sensual oil makes for a hypnotic aroma when blended with ylang ylang and orange, increasing intimacy and passion. Attract abundance, confidence, courage, enlightenment, expansion, focus, grounding, peace, and sensuality. When you're feeling anger, anxiety, controlling, disheartened, distant, hopeless, stressed, or tense, keep this harmonising and regenerative oil on hand.

Application: Massage, compress, spritz, bathe, inhale.

May Also Benefit: Cracked and dry skin, stretch marks, fluid retention, cellulite, dermatitis, eczema, inflammation, wounds, and guess what? It's even an aphrodisiac!

Pine Oil: This cleansing, refreshing and invigorating oil can have the same effect as if you were standing in a pine forest. A fabulous oil for clearing the air, improving alertness, and increasing inspiration.

Application: Inhale, vaporize, bathe, spritz and compress this motivating and intuitive oil.

May Also Benefit: Coughs, colds, flu, asthma, cystitis, pyelitis, inflammation, muscle aches and pains, headaches, arthritis, rheumatic pain, and liver detoxification.

Rosewood Oil: Uplifting and enlivening, this oil is wonderful for meditation and can help restore emotional balance and enhance spiritual healing. Trade your depression, insecurity, procrastination and moodiness for balance, confidence, courage, energy, peace, and joy.

Application: Massage, diffuse, inhales, compress, bath or spritz this regenerating and balancing oil.

May Also Benefit: Acne, dermatitis, sensitive skin, dry mature skin, bronchitis, respiratory conditions, headaches, nausea, and inflammation.

Sage Oil: An excellent physical detoxifier and emotional cleanser. It is also known to help enhance intuition and develop innate wisdom. This beautifully regulating oil will bring trust, confidence, adaptability, and energy as the antidote to anxiety, depression, grief, hopelessness, and negativity.

Application: Massage, bathe, compress, direct application (for cold sores only), spritz, inhale.

May Also Benefit: Muscle aches and pains, cold sores, loss of appetite, digestion issues, hormone balance, pre-menstrual syndrome, menopause, and excessive perspiration.

Note: Be careful with topical application during first trimester in pregnancy. Use in moderation.

Sandalwood Oil: This wonderful oil is best on those long busy days when you want to feel grounded and centred without feeling sedated! A popular choice for meditation as It's renowned for bringing quiet to a busy mind, along with balance, acceptance, compassion, and confidence. Wash away anger, depression, grief, nervousness, rigidity, and feelings of being unattractive.

Application: Massage, sitz bath, compress, spritz, inhale.

May Also Benefit: Cystitis, urinary tract infections, dry skin, eczema, dermatitis, acne, oily skin, inflammation, respiratory conditions, sore throats, and can even act as an aphrodisiac!

Chapter 8:

SELF-ACCEPTANCE

"Self-Acceptance comes from meeting life's challenges vigorously. Don't numb yourself to your trials and difficulties. Nor, build mental walls to exclude pain from your life."
– J. Donald Walters

I t is said that knowing yourself is the beginning of all wisdom. Respect for who you are and what you are about is a gift to all of those who know you. It is time to honour your strengths, constraints, and everything in-between. To love, embrace and accept yourself, and everything about you. Embrace a delicate and divine relationship with yourself knowing that the only opinion in this world about you that truly matters is yours.

As I write this I picture you now knowing what it means to trust yourself, back your decisions and choices, surrender your self-judgement and self-sabotage to a higher force that always has your back. More importantly, what a gift it is to accept you are safe in the knowledge that we are all imperfectly perfect.

I know this navigation through the circle of self-love is asking you to pay attention to some new, and maybe some old, concepts and ideas, and it's tempting to be caught by our old habits and thought patterns. The brain can become conditioned with belief systems that cripple our ability to create new responses to old triggers. We can find ourselves trapped by defensiveness, self-loathing, and sabotage. We trade self-acceptance for inadequacy, which compromises our vision and creates a minefield of doubt. Questioning our judgement and missing the clues our authentic self has been eluding to means that we've misunderstood our highest intentions, and it's time now to set a new intention for our life.

Once you become well acquainted with the 'truth' or rather, beliefs about who you really are, you'll never want to leave yourself again! There is an inherent softness and a beauty to the concept of self-acceptance, and it is in this soft place that you can rest when inner turmoil strikes. When you view your experiences from above, and see them as powerful contributors to your journey, as opposed to reasons why your life isn't as perfect as you'd thought it would be, this is the moment that self-acceptance begins to take hold of your life. You will see that through self-acceptance, your perfectly imperfect life can be everything you've ever dreamed of, and so much more.

Self-acceptance is an individual's satisfaction and happiness with themselves. It involves understanding and embracing who you really are, including your strengths and constraints. Self-acceptance can de defined as; the awareness of one's strengths and weaknesses, the realistic (yet subjective) appraisal of one's talents, capabilities, and general worth, and, feelings of satisfaction with one's self despite deficiencies and regardless of past behaviours and choices.

One way you can learn to know and accept yourself more is through understanding our different personalities. Have you ever noticed how different people can be? Have you noticed that some people you meet are instant friends? And then there are others who can rub you up the wrong way even before they have said anything?

It is natural that we tend to see the world through our eyes, our viewpoints and our beliefs only. But one of the most powerful things you can do is learn to see the world through someone else's eyes and viewpoint. You might not agree with it, but you can learn to appreciate we are different, not wrong.

Hippocrates noted some 2500 years ago that each of his patients displayed one of four common areas of vulnerability in these health concerns:

- Choleric types – yellow bile conditions
- Phlegmatic types – phlegm conditions
- Sanguine types – blood conditions
- Melancholic types – black bile conditions

Each of these conditions represented certain personality traits and behaviours.

Florence Littauer wrote a book in 1983 called *Personality PLUS – How to Understand Others by Understanding Yourself.* She reinforced Hippocrates work, saying that we are born with a certain personality, and then according to our upbringing, circumstances, teachers, parents, experiences, and beliefs this can either be enhanced, masked (covered up), or blended. She gave the four personalities more commonly accepted names, which I now share as Powerful, Playful, Precise, and Peaceful.

Littauer says this work teaches us how to use our God-given personality to be more effective in the work place, at home, in relationships, and how to communicate more effectively with those who may appear different to us. This 4 Temperament model is the foundation that many personality profiling approaches use, including the more commonly known Myers-Briggs and DISC models.

The idea of any personality profiling is that you come to know you, and why you behave the way you do. It's not that you use it as an excuse, but more as a tool. I can proudly say this work has saved marriages, changed the state of business culture, and helped people understand that we are all different, not wrong. I think about all four types of personality when I write, present, parent, and even when I create any new products.

To give you an idea, here is a brief overview of all four types and how they behave, react, and what they do. I invite you to look over them and see which one you relate to the most and if it helps you to understand yourself just a little more. I am introducing this, so you can see people are not out to get you or that they annoy you on purpose. And also, to see that maybe your personality has a part to play in the way you take care of your mind, body and soul.

Self-acceptance is an amazing by-product of understanding ourselves with more love, empathy, and power.

Choleric Powerful	Sanguine Playful
DOER	**TALKER**

Melancholic Precise	Phlegmatic Peaceful
THINKER	**WATCHER**

Choleric Powerful - The Doer

Key Statement - Let's do it MY way!

Key Strengths - Ability to take charge of anything almost instantly, they make correct, quick judgements, get stuff done, and have high achievement drive.

Key Weaknesses - Can be too bossy, domineering, autocratic, insensitive, impatient, and unwilling to delegate or give credit to others

Emotional Needs - Sense of control, credit for accomplishments, and loyalty in the ranks.

Reaction to Stress - Tightens control, works harder, and exercises more

Recognised By - Fast moving approach, quick grab for control, self-confidence, restless, and a more overpowering attitude.

Main desire - is to have control

Gets upset when - life feels like it is out of control and people do not do things they ask or the way they want it done.

Is afraid of - losing control of anything, it could be losing a job or not being promoted, they are afraid of becoming seriously ill, having children that do not do as they ask, or a partner who is unsupportive.

Likes people who - are supportive and submissive, see things their way, cooperate quickly and get things done.

Dislikes people who - are lazy and not interested in working constantly, who buck authority, challenge them, or are not loyal.

Is valuable in work - because they can accomplish more than most in a shorter time and are usually right but may stir up trouble.

Could improve if - they became a little more patient and didn't expect everyone to produce as they do.

As a leader they - have a natural feel of taking charge, a quick sense of what will work, and a sincere belief in their ability to achieve, even though this can overwhelm more passive people.

Tends to marry - Phlegmatic Peacefuls, who tend to go with what they want, do not challenge authority, and love to support their desire to achieve.

Blends I created for Powerfuls - Courage & Confidence, Detox & Strengthen, and Immune Boost.

Phlegmatic Peaceful - The Watcher

Key Statement - Let's do it the EASY way!

Key Strengths - Balance, even disposition, great listener, dry sense of humor, and a pleasing personality.

Key Weaknesses – Lack of decisiveness, enthusiasm and energy, procrastinates, hidden will of iron, stubborn.

Emotional Needs – Peace and quiet, sense of respect, valued for who they are.

Reaction to Stress – Hides from it, watches television, eats.

Recognised By – Calm approach, relaxed posture, sitting or leaning when possible.

Main desire – is to have no conflict and keep the peace.

Gets upset when - life is full of conflict, hurt and pain, having to face confrontation, no one wants to help, when the pressure is on them.

Is afraid of – having to deal with a major personal problem, being left holding responsibility, making major changes.

Likes people who – will make decisions for them, will recognize their strengths and not ignore them.

Dislikes people who – are too pushy or expect too much of them.

Is valuable in work – because they co-operate and have a calming influence, they keep the peace, mediate well, objectively solve problems.

Could improve if – they set goals and became more self-motivated, was willing to do tasks faster than expected, and could face their own problems as well as they manage everyone else's.

As a leader they – keep cool, calm and collected, don't make impulsive decisions, is well liked and inoffensive, won't cause trouble but does not often initiate ideas or change.

Tends to marry - Choleric Powerfuls because they respect their strength and decisiveness, however they can get tired of being pushed around and looked down upon.

Blends I created for Peacefuls - Destress & Revive, Instant Calm, and Peace & Meditation.

Sanguine Playful - The Talker

Key Statement - Let's do it the FUN way!

Key Strengths - Can talk about anything, at any time, at any place, with or without information, a bubbling personality, optimism, sense of humor, can tell good stories, likes people.

Key Weaknesses - Disorganized, doesn't always remember details or names, exaggerates, not overly serious about anything, trusts others to do the work, is often gullible and naïve.

Emotional Needs - Attention, affection, acceptance, and approval.

Reaction to Stress - Leave the scene, go shopping, find a fun group, create excuses, blame others.

Recognised By - Constant talking, fairly loud volume, bright eyes, moving hands, colourful expressions, enthusiasm, ability to mix with others easily.

Main desire - is to have fun.

Gets upset when - life is no fun, out of favor with people and when no one seems to like them.

Is afraid of - being unpopular or bored, having to live by the clock or keep a record of where money and time is spent.

Likes people who - have high energy, listen, laugh, praise, and approve.

Dislikes people who - criticize, don't respond to their humor, don't think they are fun, put people down.

Is valuable in work - for their creativity, optimism, light touch, cheering others up, entertaining, thoughtful.

Could improve if - they got more organized, didn't talk so much, and learned to tell the time.

As a leader they - inspire, have fun, trust others to do their work, charm, and are positive.

Tends to marry - Melancholic Precise who are sensitive and serious, however they can tire of having to cheer them up all the time and being made to feel inadequate or stupid.

Blends I created for Playfuls - Celebrate & Uplift, Romance & Intimacy, and Vigour & Spice

Melancholic Precise - The Thinker

Key Statement - Let's do it the RIGHT way!

Key Strengths - Ability to organize, set long range goals, have high standards and ideals, analyses deeply.

Key Weaknesses - Easily depressed, too much time on preparation, too focused on details, remembers the negatives, suspicious of others, can be nit-picky.

Emotional Needs - Space, silence, sensitivity, and support.

Reaction to Stress - Become more depressed, withdraws, gets lost in a book or television, can seem like they give up, recounts the problems.

Recognised By - Serious, sensitive nature, well-mannered approach, meticulous and well-groomed (with the exception of the more eccentric, hippy type), intellectuals, musicians, poets whose attention to clothes and looks detracts from their inner strengths.

Main desire - is to have it right.

Gets upset when - life is out of order, standards are not met, and no one seems to care.

Is afraid of - no one understanding how they really feel, making a mistake, having to compromise standards.

Likes people who - are serious, caring, intellectual, deep, and will carry on a sensible conversation.

Dislikes people who - are lightweights, forgetful, late, disorganized, superficial, prevaricating, and unpredictable.

Is valuable in work - for their sense of detail, love of analysis, follow-through, high standards of performance, compassion for the hurting.

Could improve if - they didn't take life so seriously and didn't insist on perfection.

As a leader they - organize well, is sensitive to people's feelings, has deep creativity, wants quality performance.

Tends to marry - Sanguine Playfuls for their uplifting personality and social skills but soon tire of them talking too much and being late.

Blends I created for Precise types - Balance & Harmony, Energy & Vitality, and Focus & Clarity.

This is not about boxing people into categories, or for it to be used as a weapon or excuse for certain behaviours. It is a wonderful tool to help you to seek before you understand. In other words, it can help you to try to see the world through other people's eyes and not just through yours.

We know we are not the same as everyone else. We know we each have personality and spiritual beliefs that are different. Honouring the way we each do self-sabotage—and self-love—is the most helpful path to self-acceptance.

If we are curious enough to look inside ourselves and explore the journey of self-sabotage and self-love, and look at it from our individual perspective, we may indeed find these polar opposites are what allows us to understand there is a magnificent life waiting for each and every one of us.

If you would like to know more about the personalities I have written an eBook called 'Why Can't You Be Normal Like Me?' which is available here at www.twenty8.com under Books and eBooks.

A dear friend Trevor Hendy speaks beautifully of the power of self-acceptance through challenge, negativity and hardship. He says that,

"It is there to help us each connect to our consciousness. From darkness there is an invitation to find the light. It is from the shadows there is an invitation to step out."

Trevor believes this work is around empowering the sacred feminine, the yin as opposed to the yang energy, the softness. And he believes this is more important than ever for both men and women.

~

Self-sabotage and fear is the opposing force of love. It is darkness showing up, and perhaps now we can see it is a gift after all. You could think of it as an opportunity not to succumb to the pain but to choose to work through it and ask, "What is the direct opposite of this? What is the opposing direction I need to be heading in? Where can I go after here?"

Authenticity is the daily practice of
letting go of who we think we're supposed to be
and embracing who we are.
- Brené Brown

I was fortunate enough to hear the late author and speaker, Wayne Dyer, speak live. I will never forget his analogy on the outcomes in life. My understanding was that he believed they were already pre-determined, that they were always going to happen, but depending on the decisions and choices we made, the way in which we got there, and how it happens could be different. He called them doors of opportunity.

Let's say at sixteen years of age you had three 'opportunity doors' in front of you. One said you were offered a job and should leave school. The next one said stay at school and finish your school years. And the third one said you were offered a scholarship to attend a different school. Let's say you chose door two. A few years later you were given four doors of opportunity that included doing a degree at university, the opportunity to travel, settle down with the partner of your dreams, or take on a job that allowed you to study and work. You chose door three. And, so it continues. Let's say at age thirty-five you had two doors; behind door one you stay in the comfortable job you have, behind door two you extend yourself and take an overseas posting. And you chose door two. Now, let's say whilst you were on that overseas posting you were walking to work one day and there was a terrorist attack and you were badly injured. Was it chance? Was it bad luck? Is it shocking? Of course, it is all of these and more. The point is, it happened, whether we like it or not. According to Wayne, you were always going to be injured at thirty-five years of age. If it was meant to be different there would have been other doors of opportunity that you chose.

Opportunities arise, and decisions are made throughout your life, and at the time these are the best for you, or else you would have made a different choice. It took me some time to come to understand, or even comprehend what Wayne was saying, but whether you agree with him or not, it brought me a sense of comfort and trust.

It also has helped me to look at the tragedies in life with a more spiritual lens. I mean, how else can we make sense of someone living well into their nineties, yet they have drunk and smoked all their life, compared to a two-year-old who dies from something hideous like cancer? It just does not make sense. And that poses the question: Is there any point in trying to make sense of it? After all, it seems senseless. It is what it is. And if it was meant to be different then it would be, right?

I'm not sure if this is a spiritual lesson in acceptance or an emotional reasoning for all the wrongs in our world. But like

I said, it has brought some sense of comfort into my world when sadness and tragedy strike. I truly admire people who get up, get on with it, and get through tough times. I admire people who, through their own ups and downs, can still see and feel love. I love this quote:

There is nothing more beautiful than a person whose heart has been broken but still believes in love.
– Anonymous

There are certain traits that people who are accomplished in the 'art' of acceptance and self-acceptance exhibit, and I think it's important that we explore these, so you know what to look for in your own self-acceptance journey.

- Trust that life is imperfectly perfect.

- Don't judge themselves and others for mistakes. They understand that we're all a work in progress.

- Accept that life comes with highs and lows, challenges, and celebrations.

- Understand that we are all different rather than right and wrong.

- Refuse to make excuses and justifications. Instead, accept that 'it is what it is'.

- Refrain from beating themselves up if things don't turn out as planned.

- Understand we all have different personalities and viewpoints of the world with an appreciation we are different, not wrong.

- Give up the belief of 'I'm not good enough'.

- Live with the mantra 'this too shall pass'.

- Tenaciously celebrate their strengths and wins.

- Set powerful intentions for the outcomes they'd like to experience.

- Quiet the inner critic and discover that it's never the voice of reason.

- Even though they make take detours, they can accept that there are no accidents.

- Learn to allow the universe to support them while they invest their energy into what they DO want rather than what they DON'T want

- Feel compassion for themselves and others and accept that we are all doing the best we can with what we have.

- Look for evidence that their self-acceptance journey is working. Make a point of looking for ways that life is supporting them and the experiences they like to enjoy. They may even write them down along with their intentions each day so that they can reflect and adjust where necessary.

Your commitment to your own self-acceptance journey will mean the difference between being in sync with your purpose or spending your time wishing things were different. Don't you think you deserve better than worrying?

In my darkest hours I've written myself love notes, or I have really focused my mind hard, outlining the experiences I'd rather have, and then taken ten minutes to meditate on how it feels to experience what I want, rather than the sadness I may be feeling in the moment. My sister, Keri, gave me a painting that I have on my wall that says:

It is what it is.

Every time I feel life is unfair I look at that picture. I cannot wish for it to be different and I may not ever be able to change what is. Not only does this quote help me to accept the situation for what it is but it takes my mind to a more creative place that leaves me feeling inspired. Couple this mindful exercise with essential oils and I'm anchored into the precious state of peace and self-acceptance.

I met a lady at a workshop once and, the minute I met her, I could tell she was not only good at worrying; she had mastered it. Her angst and stressful demeanour led me to ask if she was okay. As she was ushering her guests into the workshop room she admitted that she was worried about her husband, as he had not texted that he had arrived in Gympie (approximately an hour north of the Sunshine Coast) for work. Apparently, his job was up there, and he always texted when he was leaving and when he arrived to let his wife know he was safe. It made her worry sick whenever he didn't text as she expected.

I asked how long he had been working in Gympie, thinking it must have not been long, and was shocked to learn it had been two years. I thought, *Wow, you get that worked up each time he doesn't text you?* She admitted she wasn't great at hiding her fears, but she couldn't help it. She then mentioned that a certain stretch of road on the highway was treacherous, and that it had claimed more people's lives than many other roads in Australia.

I asked her if he had ever had an accident on that road yet? She said no. I said, "What if every time you had that worrying thought, it was your guardian angels asking you to send white light and loads of love to your husband, to help keep him safe?" She looked calmer, she was quiet. I then told her the story about my grandma's wisdom and how much peace it had bought me. "I would much rather put that energy into a positive experience than a dark one," I told her.

She loved the idea. Just as her husband texted she looked up at me and smiled. She was going to give it a try. She had spent two years worrying pretty much each day. I could not help but think how much we all worry over little things, or things we have no control over anyway.

Now my disclaimer here is that sad things do happen. Awful tragedies occur daily, and some of us will be struck down as if we were hit by a bolt of lightning, changing our lives forever. And my dear reader, if that is the case, we have most likely been ejected from the circle of self-love, and as our emotions calm we become more present, and more aware, and then we go through the process, with self-care being the most important next step. It is only through self-care and self-discipline that we find the energy to keep our heads and hearts buoyant to some degree.

Remember that the first half of the circle is the *doing*. The second half of the circle is the *being*. Everything takes time and we are all different, depending on our circumstance, of course. The point is that you can use the circle of self-love to get you through anything. You now have a map, a guide, a pathway to keep you focused.

My beautiful friend Deb has endured a hideous ride losing her gorgeous husband Laurie who battled courageously for 18months with bowel cancer leaving Deb and their three young children. To watch her step up, over and through her agony is remarkable, it's inspiring. And to be there with her as she agonises is a privilege too. I asked her recently how does she do it? What would be her advice to someone in a similar position be?

She said, 'Breathe. Take one step at a time, hour by hour, day by day. Trust in yourself. Understand it's ok to have bad days. Believe that you will get through and whilst the hole is always there gradually it feels less painful. Believe in the good. Love even when you feel broken. Surround yourself with good people, best friends and family, including professionals. Take the time to heal and rebuild. Be kind to yourself. And most of all take care of yourself.'

To help you take the next step towards your own self-acceptance, I've included a downloadable meditation that you can use to support yourself when life throws you a curve ball. You can go to the website www.twenty8.com/selflovemeditation for more details.

Essential Oils for Self-Acceptance:

German Chamomile: A very calming and healing oil to ease anger, irritation, nervous tension, stress, and hopelessness, instead inducing feelings of harmony, joy, and relaxation.

Application: Massage, bathe, compress, spritz, and diffuse.

May Also Benefit: Inflammation, arthritis, dermatitis, muscle aches and pains, sensitive skin, dry skin and rashes. Great for bruises, burns, acne, psoriasis, and feminine balance. Dilute to 2.5% to help heal inflamed skin conditions. A high content of the active compound azulene give this oil its deep blue colour.

Geranium Oil: Call on this delicate yet potent oil when life feels like a continuous rollercoaster ride. When you're feeling chaotic, deceived, distant, moody, negative, or sensitive, Geranium will bring balance, calm, connection, focus, harmony, and protection.

Application: Compress, massage, bathe, spritz, diffuse, inhale.

May Also Benefit: Acne, eczema, dermatitis, congested skin, mature skin, broken capillaries, pre-menstrual syndrome, hormone support, infertility, menopause, wounds, bruising, and oedema.

Note: Be careful with topical application on hypersensitive or overly red and inflamed skin.

Myrtle Oil: Cleansing, positive, harmonious, and peaceful, kindness and sensuality replace anxiety, chaos, fear, tension, hurt, hopelessness, and feelings of worthlessness. Supporting deep inner wisdom and knowing, calm the busy mind, and feel reassured that we are all supported and connected.

Application: Inhale, diffuse, spritz, massage, sitz bath, bathe, compress, and hair rinse.

May Also Benefit: Bronchitis, catarrh, coughs, urinary tract infections, haemorrhoids, acne, oily skin, open pores, hormone support, and head lice.

Petitgrain Oil: The orange tree produces three essential oils. Orange from the fruit of the tree, neroli from the flower and petitgrain from the leaves. Hence why so many of their qualities overlap. Petitgrain is uplifting, refreshing, and an emotional comforter in times of anger, exhaustion, mental fatigue, and frustration. Be nourished with balance, calm, creativity, and gratitude.

Application: Compress, spritz, massage, inhale, diffuse, and bathe.

May Also Benefit: Acne, boils, pimples, digestive issues, dry skin, mature skin, insomnia, muscle tension, inflammation, and arthritis.

Ylang Ylang Oil: Meaning 'flower of flowers' and often referred to as the Perfume Tree. This oil creates a sense of peace, harmony, and passion as it dispels anger, anxiety, and shock. Along with rose, orange, and patchouli, it is an exquisite aphrodisiac! And is a beautiful love-making oil!

Application: Inhale, spritz, massage, diffuse, compress, bathe

May Also Benefit: Heart palpitations, circulation, dry skin, oily skin, anti-aging, pre-menstrual syndrome, menopause, hormone support and of course, an aphrodisiac!

Chapter 9:

SELF-LOVE

"Every choice you make is either an expression of love or an expression of fear. There is no other choice."
- A Course in Miracles

I did a training run down in Wilson's Promontory in Victoria, Australia when I had been selected to run for Australia. It was a fifty-kilometre training run leading up to the race in England, and I must admit that the last ten kilometres really hurt. There were a lot of hills and it was a tough run, on an incredibly hot day.

The next day, I had my regular Monday morning client named Brett who came to see me. He was in a wheelchair. Brett had been a rising star in the AFL (Australian Football League), with a promising career ahead of him, but had his legs taken out from underneath him in one particular game. He landed smack on his back and became instantly paralysed from the waist down. Not only did he never get to play AFL again, but he also never walked again. It was devastating to see. Imagine someone so young, and so great, in a wheelchair for the rest of his life. He came to see me every Monday morning for a remedial massage, as he was training for the Seoul Paralympics in 1988.

In his usual positive, upbeat way, Brett asked, "Hey Kimmy, how was your run on the weekend?"

I replied without even thinking, "Oh my gosh, Brett, my legs are killing me." And right then, in that moment, I realised what I had said. But it was too late, those words were out there, and I couldn't take them back.

My girlfriend Fleur often says to me, "Kim, a closed mouth gathers no feet." Brett shook his head, knowing I was feeling terrible. The shock on my face said it all! He graciously said, "Don't worry about it. I know you didn't mean it!" I couldn't apologise enough and then the reality hit me as he proceeded to say, "Just know I would love to know that feeling again," he continued, "I would love to know I could have a pulled muscle, blisters on my feet, or a calf muscle that was sore from running. I would give anything for the chafing between my thighs!"

He let me off the hook, but I was so damn conscious of such limiting thoughts and words. I've never forgotten that moment. I now refer to those types of slip-ups as a 'Brettism'.

We can all take a leaf from Brett's book by never complaining about our bodies, our circumstances, and our lives, because we are in fact lucky enough to BE here. Most of us are fortunate to have our health, our sense of well-being, education, food, water, shelter, air, support services, and the awareness to know how blessed we really are. There are many who don't have the same luxury and it's vital that we appreciate the power that comes from accepting what is and the power to change it if we really want to!

You know there is always more to life than what you think.

You may have tried everything to fill the void inside and no matter what you try, where you go, how distracted you are or how much you depend on others to make you feel 'full', none of it may actually seem like it works. At least not long-term anyway.

You might be terrified of getting 'life' wrong and you can't shake the suspicious feeling that maybe it's all empty and meaningless and in the end, it doesn't matter how hard you try. You might trip over yourself by attempting to make the 'right' choices and create the best outcomes but you doubt your ability to even know what's 'right' much less *get* it right!

I *get* it!

The sad thing is so many of us live this way with a more limited mind set and so few have discovered the path beyond it. Today is YOUR day.

Today we are going to leap to a new level of life, especially now we understand that love is all there is. Nothing can fill that void inside us but love. And not just any love, it must be self-love!

As a natural by-product of the self-love circle, we are dancing to the beautiful tune of nature's greatest gift to us, which comes wrapped in the parcel of contrast - which includes both love and fear. As we dive into, and experience the fullness of all that the self-love circle offers us inside it and out, we are given the opportunity to fill the love tank, open our heart and expand our consciousness more and more. And every new belief, act, thought, or habit we form, leaves little room for fear to take a hold and trap us in old patterns.

On stage, I've often referred to self-love as a practice, an art, rather than a journey or destination, simply because the nature of a journey implies that we are progressing, and the nature of a destination implies that we have arrived. In the case of self-love, there is nowhere to go and nowhere to arrive.

> *Love is patient, love is kind. It does not envy, it does not boast, it is not proud. It does not dishonor others, it is not self-seeking, it is not easily angered, it keeps no record of wrongs. Love does not delight in evil but rejoices with the truth. It always protects, always trusts, always hopes, always perseveres. Love never fails.*
> –Corinthians 13:4-8

It's the power of love that beats our heart and brings life to our spirit and colour to our creativity. It creates deeper connection to all things and brings hope to our challenges. Without it, we can find ourselves wracked with fear and anxiety, self-judgement, judgement of others, self-destruction, self-abuse, and sabotage. We've spoken about each of these in the earlier chapters and it's important to recognise that these 'fear-based' behaviours and responses are the very attributes that will keep us disconnected from self-love.

This matters most when times are tough because it is self-love that will have us triumph even in the darkest and most challenging of times. To confidently reach deep within ourselves when the outside circumstances feel insurmountable, and to find everything you need to calm the storm residing lovingly in your heart, means that you can restore peace within, instead of crumbling or feeling incapable in the face of adversity.

As mentioned at the beginning of this book, self-love is the regard for one's own well-being and happiness. This meaning implies that it is up to each one of us to be responsible for our own 'love tank' and how we fill, maintain, and share it!

If you had to measure your own love tank right now, out of ten, with ten being full and zero being empty, how would you rate your love tank level? Most of us pay very little attention to the up-keep of our love tank or even realise that it is the number-one most important aspect of self-care until we feel depleted, alone, sad, empty, and disconnected. Sometimes, we don't even realise the reason why we are feeling this way, as nothing on the outside seems to be particularly wrong. Inside however, is an entirely different story and because we haven't been paying attention, we are now paying with pain.

Loving ourselves means accepting every aspect of ourselves. This includes our physical bodies, our mental capacities, spiritual evolvement, level of self-confidence, emotional intensity, and personal development. Of course, there are times we would like to be further along the path in some areas of our lives, and the key to transformation, is first accepting where we are, without any judgement or resistance.

Fear is to love what resistance is to acceptance. In order to learn one, we must experience the other. It's the law of opposites and necessary for our own growth and expansion. The question is which would we prefer to dance with longer?

I visited a naturopath and iridologist recently. He said my eyes were incredible, and that I have obviously had some traumas throughout my life, but I have bounced back from all of them remarkably. He picked up on my back pain and noted different times in my life when stress levels were high. He asked me if I had taken something throughout my life or had done anything special to reduce my stress.

It was in that moment I truly got to appreciate just how much my essential oils have done for me. When I speak about the Body Boost ritual (mentioned on page 331) which I have done every day since I was nineteen years of age, and have never ever missed a day, I truly believed in that moment that it has been my secret weapon, the key to my healthy constitution, my open-hearted beliefs, and positive attitude.

It is a beautiful ritual when you are feeling great with life, even more so when challenged. The most important thing I can say is you MUST commit to doing the body boost ritual especially on these days. You might not find positive words to say to end the ritual, but on those days, stay real; be authentic. This is what I say on those days. "Please God (or you could say source, universe, light, sun, or a word that brings the same spiritual meaning) give me the courage, grace, strength, and dignity to get through this."

This is being real. You just put one foot in front of the other so to speak. You are back out on that track and you are showing some love for yourself even when you least feel like it.

The act of self-care on days that challenge you are doubly good! And I can promise it helps you navigate the world of pain and fear, back to a place of love and compassion more quickly and more effectively than anything else I know. It's that powerful.

I have asked people in my audiences: "Who in the room, honestly, does not like their boobs?" I get a serious number of women putting up their hands with a muffled giggle. Next, I ask: "Who in the room doesn't like their legs or their stomach?" Again, another great show of hands. Then: "Who in the room doesn't like their hair or their bottom?" More hands rise. And to the men: "Who doesn't like their chest?" Not as many put their hands up.

I mention to the audience, "You may not know the story of the person next to you, or certainly not everyone in the room, you don't know what everyone has been through or how they feel. The throw-away line of, "I hate my boobs" could mean very little to you, but to the woman who has just survived breast cancer, or just been diagnosed, that could be a massive kick in the guts. She would give anything to have healthy boobs, even saggy boobs, any boobs that were healthy. Mums who hate the stretch marks their children have left as a legacy could be the contrast for the woman spending tens of thousands of dollars on IVF (In Vitro Fertilisation) attempting to fall pregnant. These women spend month after month on an emotional rollercoaster, desperate to hold their own child close, and would trade their stretch marks in an instant. Those 'stripes of honour' are the mark of an extraordinary blessing."

Now, let's look at the traits of someone who constantly fills their love tank and what those attributes look like:

- They don't blame others for their issues or challenges.
- They will work on healing wounds and changing dysfunctional patterns or behaviours that don't serve them.
- They have learned to follow their heart and gut as opposed to their ego.
- They speak with integrity and mean what they say and say what they mean.
- They take responsibility for their experiences and the outcomes they create.
- They don't label themselves or look to the opinions of others. They have the courage to look within.
- They don't look for approval to be themselves.
- They are the greatest observers of themselves in what works and what doesn't. They embrace what works and adjust what doesn't.
- They know how to spend emotional, mental, and financial energy. Whether this brings joy, connection, nurturing, rest, creativity, and love, they know it is worth spending time on all these areas.

- They allow themselves to dream big with no judgement or perceived limitations or lack of deserving.

Who says that we can't be a millionaire at the age of eighty?

Who says that we can't run a marathon at ninety?

Who says that we shouldn't have a better life, or want for more?

Now I'm not going to say this is going to be easy, but I will say that once you master this practice of self-love, you'll find yourself more confident, resilient, open, empowered, inspired, and most importantly, free! Doesn't that just sound miraculous?

I've popped a few of my favourite how-to steps here for you so that you can select at least one of these rituals each day and use them to top up your own love tank. I recommend you do a 'self-love-tank' inventory at least once a week so that you can be aware of what you need to do to stay in the warm embrace of the self-love circle:

- **Practice, Practice, Practice.** Loving the self doesn't come easily if you're used to making your life about others, including your kids. Putting yourself first is going to take practice and willingness to do things a little differently. If you're open to new habits, you'll find your practice will come with excitement and joy. So, let's decide right here, right now, that you're committed to loving yourself as much as you love others, and as you work your way through this list daily, you'll find self-love will become a natural condition in your life and you won't even need to think about it.

- **Self-Reflection.** Take the time to reflect each day on what you did for yourself that made you feel loved by yourself. Begin a journal of self-love and be sure to make a note of what you do and how it makes you feel so that you're bringing your mental and emotional awareness together. This process helps to rewire the neurological connections towards the feelings of self-love, which is what makes practice effortless over time.

- **Meditation.** I have said it a number of times already but create a sacred space in your home, even if it is a corner in your bedroom where you can retreat to meditate and quiet the mind. This brings peace and calm to your daily practice, which refuels the love tank automatically.

- **Be honest** about your choices and thoughts and adjust your practices, rituals, and ideas to make sure they reflect self-worth. Pay attention to your own thoughts and how they affect you from the inside out. When you recognise a sensation inside that feels heavy or dull, be willing to make adjustments to ensure that you're not leaving your suffering unattended.

- **Be present to the NOW** moment and surrender to whatever is currently occurring for you. Understand that you are only powerful to affect change in yourself or the circumstances around you, in the 'now' moment. When we are worried about the past or future, we are impotent to create change, and we are also absent from the loving or nurturing our spiritual selves is calling for. The only time that exists is NOW.

- **Be willing to choose yourself first,** even if it causes upset. Sometimes saying no is the best yes you could ever give. Saying yes in a situation that you mean 'no' only causes resentment and disconnection, both inside yourself and to the circumstances you have agreed to, which were created under duress. By putting yourself first, you are creating an inner dialogue that says, "I will listen to myself and honour my own standpoint, even if it doesn't meet with others' expectations of me". This can be challenging, I'll agree, particularly if you're used to conforming to keep the status quo, so get ready to feel a little uncomfortable for a little while, but I promise, the rewards will be worth it!

- **Say what you mean and mean what you say.** Similar to our previous point, begin to experiment with saying only what you mean and then always following through with what you've said. Another word for this is integrity.

- **Give your body nurturing,** rest, exercise, and nourishment so that you can be the best version of yourself more often. The physical body is the vehicle you use to make everything possible in your world, so taking care of it daily, hourly, minute-by-minute, is crucial if your intention is to experience a healthy, vital, and outstanding existence.

- **No matter what your story,** history or experience, self-love is building a life we love regardless of who is in it. Everyone has various reasons why they make the choices they do, or behave in the manner they do, and it is important to the experience of self-love to always use our past as a platform to create a better future. Sometimes we can feel that our story about ourselves is too debilitating to move beyond, and this usually occurs when self-love has not been created as a priority. Instead, what takes up residence in our cellular memory is fear. With a little attention and self-awareness, we can turn our disempowering experiences into the very reason we are transformed.

- **Do what you love and love what you do.** We are here for such a short time, and to waste precious moments on things we don't enjoy—or love—compromises our own self-love. So, if you're in a job or situation right now that doesn't benefit you, consider what else is possible or, if you can't alter the outer world, consider what you can do to alter your inner state so that the circumstances can be more tolerable to you. I've listed some oils here that can help you to alter your state of mind instantly which can support this objective.

- **Own your inner and outer beauty.** It's the only vehicle you will have this time around, so make the most of it. Be open to 'Brettisms' and appreciate everything you have and don't have, both inside and out. This is the body and soul that you have been given, and wishing it were different in any way means you're out of gratitude and also, out of the self-love circle. Finding at least three things about yourself each day that you can be grateful for keeps you focused and owning the magic of your existence and beauty.

- **Be willing to ask: "What's right about this situation."** We usually look for what's wrong with life and then set about fixing it. Instead, try looking through a different lens and ask yourself, "What's right and what's perfect about where I am right now and what is occurring?" Be prepared to give up the need to fix everything and instead, just BE with what is because if it were meant to be different, it would be. Set yourself and everyone around you free from the expectation that things should be different to what they are. If you want to change anything, by all means, go for it, but change only occurs in the present moment so dwelling on what already is, or what happened in the past won't serve the change you're trying to make.

I love how my dear friend, Pete Evans, believes in the power of self-love. He says making time to do something like a tea ceremony with your partner, going for a surf, or nourishing your body with food that is not inflammatory, are acts that will make a huge difference to your life physically, mentally, and emotionally.

*"Find yourself something to do, that you can do often,
and doesn't require the input of someone else."*
–Helen Padarin

Self-love is your birthright and the most natural part of being human but unfortunately, not the most common conversation we have. If we can discover and embrace the secrets to self-love and then share them openly with our children, it's likely that they will experience life with far greater confidence and self-assurance than we ever knew ourselves.

It is thanks to the great technological evolution that we are connected more than ever. Instant text messages, live video and global conferencing are all a part of our everyday world. And it's thanks to these advancements we have been able to create new communities that would never have happened even two decades ago. We can reach out and feel a part of a group, we can find people with similar interests and we can support one another from afar better than ever. And here's the beautiful part, it only takes one person in any of those communities to say, "I see you", or "I understand", or "I care" to feel we are not alone.

One of the main reasons I wanted to create the Health & Lifestyle Education program was to create a community. A beautiful group of souls who originally enter a program to learn about essential oils, low toxin living, healthy eating and mindful movement, only to discover this common interest creates more knowledge around relationships, passion, purpose and drive as well as a beautiful tapestry of friendships and lifelong connections.

If I could give you just one piece of advice here and now it would be you must put yourself out there. Get involved. As scary as it might seem you get back what you give out. I was advised as a teenager if you do not know what your passion or purpose is then serve. Serve others. Get into community work, follow someone you admire and offer to help. Work in the hospitality sector. Help the elderly and disabled. Reach out. It's not always easy finding your tribe or putting yourself out there but I have learned for myself the more I give the more I receive. That doesn't mean its not tough some days but my goodness it helps you to get through them with more grace.

Whether it is on social media or in our own local community, our workplace or home, we all have the opportunity to BE that person for someone in need. We all know how good it feels to help another human being, and we know how much we love to feel good.

But feeling good doesn't just happen. We know now that it takes awareness, care and discipline, and gratitude will prolong it.

I know that a Mack Truck can strike everyone at some point in their life; sadly no one escapes it. If that is the case, then maybe reading this book will help to prepare us better and create a gentler personal awakening. Maybe it will be a chance for us to all become a part of a greater conscious awareness around the forces of fear and love and how much they each impact the way in which we live our lives.

I do believe that love conquers all. I know that together we can change the world and make this journey through life a rich, wondrous experience. And I know we each have the power to make a difference and get through anything.

It might not always be perfect; some days it might be best to get lost in the lyrics of 'Lost' by Cold Chisel, which was written by a very special friend, Wes Carr. The pathway back is the discipline of self-care, that is at the heart of the work and creates the foundation for us to navigate up, over, and through all experiences. This, coupled with the belief that this too shall pass, and most importantly, to know *you've got this*!

Essential Oils for Self-Love:

Frankincense Oil: Your personal coat of armour! This oil protects you and keeps you safe. Powerful to use when life gets too busy and emotional and physical reserves are low. It is the oil for personal growth and expansion especially when the past is holding you back. Enjoy feelings of acceptance, clarity, enlightenment, focus, forgiveness, love, peace, and wisdom.

Application: Massage, spritz, diffuse, bathe, inhale, compress.

May Also Benefit: Anti-aging, circulation, arthritis, respiratory conditions, digestion issues, wounds, inflammation, acne, large open pores, dry and mature skin, and wrinkles.

Jasmine Oil: Considered to be the 'King of Flowers', you can draw on its strength to let go of the past and adapt to what is present. Become confident, content, fulfilled, grateful, passionate, positive, sensual, uplifted, and trusting. Release deception, depression, distance, disconnection, fear, rigidity, sorrow, and worthlessness.

Application: Massage, bathe, spritz, compress, inhale, and diffuse.

May Also Benefit: Muscular cramps and spasms, coughs, colds, and flus. Relieve insomnia, muscle tension, dry skin, eczema, dermatitis, infertility, and pre-menstrual syndrome. Can also be used as an aphrodisiac!

Lavender Oil: This oil is like having your 'dream mum' in a bottle. Comforting you with generosity, gratitude, kindness, love, nurturing, protection, and relaxation, your feelings of anxiety, hurt, irritation, judgement, neglect, worry, sadness, shock, stress, vulnerability, and feeling overwhelmed will melt away with ease.

Application: Inhale, massage, spritz, compress, direct application, diffuse and bathe.

May Also Benefit: Coughs, colds, catarrh and fever. Great for burns, bites, stings and rashes (direct application works well here). Keep handy for headaches, muscle tension, asthma, respiratory conditions, and all skin conditions.

Marjoram Oil: This oil is perfect if you're trapped in obsessive thinking and negativity. Ease anxiety, defeat, frustration, neglect, stress, and tension with ease as you ground yourself with love, openness, strength, and warmth.

Application: Massage, bathe, compress, inhale, diffuse, and spritz.

May Also Benefit: Muscle aches and pains, respiratory conditions, coughs, constipation and flatulence. Great for pre-menstrual syndrome, menopause, headaches, insomnia, and muscle tension.

Note: Be careful with topical application during first trimester of pregnancy.

Rose Oil: The 'Queen of Flowers' has long been a symbol of love. Through her nurturing properties, you'll enjoy abundance, compassion, creativity, connection, courage, enlightenment, joy, kindness, love, nurturing, passion, and peace. Release anger, defeat, depression, fear, heartache, sorrow, worry, and worthlessness.

Application: Spritz, massage, compress, bathe, diffuse, inhale.

May Also Benefit: Broken capillaries, inflammation, hormone support, menopause, dry, mature skin, wrinkles, scars, weight loss, cellulite, and even and aphrodisiac!

Sandalwood Oil: This wonderful oil is best on those long busy days when you want to feel grounded and centred without feeling sedated! A popular choice for meditation as It's renowned for bringing quiet to a busy mind along with balance, acceptance, compassion and confidence. Wash away anger, depression, grief, nervousness, rigidity, and feelings of being unattractive.

Application: Massage, sitz bath, compress, spritz, inhale.

May Also Benefit: Cystitis, urinary tract infections, dry skin, eczema, dermatitis, acne, oily skin, inflammation, respiratory conditions, sore throats, and can even act as an aphrodisiac!

SUMMARY

So, where do we go from here?

We've explored the most common ways that you can be pulled away from the self-love circle and we've investigated the miraculous pathway back in. So, what does this all mean and how can you begin to apply it to your life in a way that transforms the way you think, feel, and act?

How do you share this with your kids, family, friends, work colleagues, and partners so that they can speak the same language that you do, or at least watch your growth and expansion with interest and intrigue?

Where do you see these changes making the greatest difference in your life and what are your greatest visions? What are your dreams, wishes, deepest desires, and aspirations? What would be possible if you embraced love instead of fear?

Let me ask you this: Have you tried other ways to enhance your life? Have you tried to bring peace of mind, and quiet the noise and constant chatter in your head? And have you found that everything you've tried has worked temporarily but you've slipped back to your old ways too soon, only to be disappointed because you wish you'd persevered?

What's on offer here, is the opportunity to become mindful of your 'self', and conscious of the footprint you leave for others on this planet. The strategies to create the experiences you dream of are right here in these pages and the invitation to love yourself unconditionally is calling you to answer right now!

In life, we always have choices. We can take the road less travelled and enjoy the adventures that come with challenge, opportunity, growth, expansion, and joy, or we can choose to stay in our old habits, creating the same experiences we've always had, blaming others for the reasons why our lives are not the way we want them, while feeling helpless to effect meaningful and lasting change for ourselves and those we love.

To put it simply, I am asking you to choose. Which life is more compelling for you? The one you know and can't control and that leaves you exhausted trying, or the one you dream of that is full of love, bliss, and mystery?

I have included one of my favourite programs here for you as a bonus, to help you take the first steps towards an implementation plan: *The 28-Day Self-Love Jump!* This step-by-step guide to creating simple rituals in your life will keep you in the circle and mindful of when you've fallen out of love. By following this guide, you are invited to take tangible steps for 28 days, effortlessly developing your new, self-love habit.

I've also included an Essential Oil Self-Love Index and my very own 'Scentual' Blending Schedule, available here for reference and in alphabetical order. Turn to this index and schedule any time you're feeling overwhelmed and need an instant rescue remedy to clear the fog, lift the pain, and shower yourself with love and bliss. And promise me, the last thing you do before closing this book is go back to the beginning pages and re-read the poem I wrote just for you – The Art Of Self Love.

In a world where mental health and emotional instability is desperately high, I have to please stress that I have not written this book in place of professional advice or support.

I don't have all the answers. We are all unique individuals and in life as we know there are many, many influences at work, and so many factors that affect how we feel on a daily basis.

But what I do know is that we need to talk more about 'wellness'; mental and emotional wellness. And I do think we need to honour the fact that sometimes it is the small things like self-care rituals done on a daily basis that can help build resilience inside ourselves, maybe even touchstones, that we can refer to each and every day. It is my hope that this then may be the foundation that we can fall on, not only on the happy days but especially on the tough ones.

It has been both an honour and a pleasure to serve you with these words and support you, my beautiful friend, and it is my wish that self-love follows you everywhere you go and is the guiding light that illuminates your adventures!

Fall in love with taking care of yourself;
mind, body and soul.
Kim Morrison

Black Dog Institute

Information on symptoms, treatment and prevention of depression and bipolar disorder: www.blackdoginstitute.org.au

Carers Australia

1800 242 636

Short-term counselling and emotional and psychological support services for carers and their families in each state and territory.

Headspace

1800 650 890

Free online and telephone service that supports young people aged between 12 and 25 and their families going through a tough time.

Kids Helpline

1800 55 1800

A free, private and confidential, telephone and online counselling service specifically for young people aged between 5 and 25.

MensLine Australia

1300 78 99 78

A telephone and online support, information and referral service, helping men to deal with relationship problems in a practical and effective way.

Head to Health

An innovative website that can help you find free and low-cost, trusted online and phone mental health resources: www.headtohealth.gov.au

MindSpot Clinic

1800 61 44 34

An online and telephone clinic providing free assessment and treatment services for Australian adults with anxiety or depression.

National Aboriginal Community Controlled Health Organisation (NACCHO)

Aboriginal Community Controlled Health Services and Aboriginal Medical Services in each state and territory: www.naccho.org.au

QLife

1800 184 527

3pm-12am

QLife is Australia's first nationally-oriented counselling and referral service for LGBTI people. The project provides nation-wide, early intervention, peer supported telephone and web based services to diverse people of all ages experiencing poor mental health, psychological distress, social isolation, discrimination, experiences of being misgendered and/or other social determinants that impact on their health and wellbeing.

Relationships Australia

1300 364 277

A provider of relationship support services for individuals, families and communities.

SANE Australia

1800 18 7263

Information about mental illness, treatments, where to go for support and help carers.

New Zealand

Lifeline (open 24/7) - 0800 543 354

Depression Helpline (open 24/7) - 0800 111 757

Healthline (open 24/7) - 0800 611 116

Samaritans (open 24/7) - 0800 726 666

Suicide Crisis Helpline (open 24/7) - 0508 828 865 (0508 TAUTOKO). This is a service for people who may be thinking about suicide, or those who are concerned about family or friends.

Youthline (open 24/7) - 0800 376 633. You can also text 234 for free between 8am and midnight, or email talk@youthline.co.nz

0800 **WHATSUP** children's helpline - phone 0800 9428 787 between 1pm and 10pm on weekdays and from 3pm to 10pm on weekends. Online chat is available from 7pm to 10pm every day.

Kidsline (open 24/7) - 0800 543 754. This service is for children aged 5 to 18. Those who ring between 4pm and 9pm on weekdays will speak to a Kidsline buddy. These are specially trained teenage telephone counsellors.

Your local Rural Support Trust - 0800 787 254 (0800 RURAL HELP)

Alcohol Drug Help (open 24/7) - 0800 787 797. You can also text 8691 for free.

For further information, contact the Mental Health Foundation's free Resource and Information Service (09 623 4812).

TWENTY8 ESSENTIAL OIL INDEX

Hippocrates, the father of modern medicine believed that the use of herbs was essential to health in daily life. Many of his prescriptions included various plants, oils, and fragrant crushed herbs. By the tenth century, books were being written in Arabia, dedicated to the use and benefits of certain aromas.

In 1910, French cosmetic chemist René-Maurice Gattefose discovered the healing and therapeutic properties of lavender after burning his hands severely in a laboratory explosion. Gattefose was so impressed he dedicated the remainder of his life to the study of essential oils and has been credited for coining the term 'aromatherapy' in 1937.

Modern research has indicated that certain essential oils and herbs do indeed have therapeutic and healing properties. Lavender is still used for burn victims and the scent is used widely to treat depression and anxiety.

Many aromatherapy essential oils are used for the benefits of their smell alone. Eucalyptus is an example of this, as the scent of this plant is said to relieve chest congestion. Other essential oils are used for their antibacterial, anti-fungal, or anti-inflammatory properties. Tea Tree and Manuka (New Zealand tea tree) are time-honoured remedies for ringworm, athlete's foot, and other fungal infections. Rosemary can be used to treat arthritis and muscle pain, and when used in a morning bath or shower, is said to revive energy and memory recall with its stimulant properties.

It seems that many practitioners of aromatherapy concur that there are a few healing and potent essential oils that should be in all medicine chests; these include: chamomile, clove, eucalyptus, frankincense, geranium, lavender, lemon, orange, oregano, peppermint, rosemary, and tea tree (or manuka).

Essential oils and aromatherapy tools like blending bottles, diffusers, vaporisers, and books are available for purchase from qualified therapists, directly through an essential oil distributor, in some health food and independent stores, or online. The key is to ensure that they are of the highest quality to avoid any contamination.

For more information on essential oils and education, go to: www.kimmorrison.com or www.twenty8.com

Basil Oil: When you want to feel more abundance, clarity, strength, worthiness and less apprehensive, chaotic, confused, exhausted, fatigued, forgetful, insecure, overwhelmed, and sensitive.

Application: Compress, diffuse, inhale, massage, bathe, spritz.

May Also Benefit: Headaches, muscle tension and cramps, sinusitis, bronchitis, congested skin, varicose veins, digestion issues, and hormone support.

Self-Love Affirmation: *I have the mental strength to continue, my mind is clear and focused.*

Bergamot Oil: Helping you release suppressed feelings of sadness, sensitivity, shock, self-deception, which can often lead to anxiety, nervousness, and depression. This is the oil that will lift your mood, bring you balance, clarity, ease, fulfilment, joy, and motivation.

Application: Spritz, compress, bathe, massage, inhale, and sitz bath.

May Also Benefit: Wounds, fever, digestion issues, acne, eczema, dermatitis, hormone support, urinary tract infection, and cystitis.

Note: avoid exposure to the sun after using bergamot in a massage or bath, as it's considered phototoxic.

Self-Love Affirmation: *Mastering my nerves, I relax into every situation life presents.*

Black Pepper Oil: This revered, spicy oil helps to activate and excite the body! Think energy, endurance, enthusiasm, focus, vitality, warmth, and stimulation as you wash away feelings of defeat, fatigue, mental lethargy, nervousness, sensitivity, and worthlessness. This oil has a powerful kick so only small amounts are needed for great results!

Application: Inhale, massage, diffuse, spritz, massage, bathe, and compress.

May Also Benefit: Colds, flu, rheumatic pain, muscle aches and pains, bruises, oedema, circulation, liver detoxification, and digestion issues.

Self-Love Affirmation: *I ignite a fire within to warm my heart, recharge my body and light my soul.*

Cardamom Oil: When you feel like you're in a rut, cardamom reminds you of all that is possible leaving you feeling content, fulfilled, generous, and warm. Leave behind feelings of depression, disheartenment, mental fatigue, judgement, lethargy, and tension. This precious oil eliminates fears and worries and helps to restore your appetite for life.

Application: Massage, compress, inhale, diffuse, bathe, and spritz this supporting and inspiring oil.

May Also Benefit: Digestion issues, flatulence, monthly feminine balance, immune support, coughs, bronchitis, nausea, circulation and is even an aphrodisiac!

Self-Love Affirmation: *Inspiring my appetite for life, I connect to my inner truth.*

Cedarwood Oil: Release the strains of chaos, mental fatigue, negativity, neglect, sensitivity, stress, and withdrawal and embrace courage, focus, inspiration, purpose, worthiness, and wisdom.

Application: Massage, compress, bathe, inhale, diffuse, spritz, and sitz bath.

May Also Benefit: Eczema, dermatitis, respiratory conditions, urinary tract infections, cystitis, acnes, oily skin, greasy hair, cellulite, and oedema.

Self-Love Affirmation: *As I willingly surrender and let go, Mother Earth grounds my energy relieving me of all stress, tension, and worry.*

German Chamomile: A very calming and healing oil to ease anger, irritation, nervous tension, stress, and hopelessness, instead inducing feelings of harmony, joy, and relaxation.

Application: Massage, bathe, compress, spritz and diffuse.

May Also Benefit: Inflammation, arthritis, dermatitis, muscle aches and pains, sensitive skin, dry skin and rashes. Great for bruises, burns, acne, psoriasis, and feminine balance. Dilute to 2.5% to help heal inflamed skin conditions. A high content of the active compound azulene give this oil its deep blue colour.

Self-Love Affirmation: *The calm, quiet space in my heart creates healing that balances and soothes my whole body, releasing inflammation.*

Roman Chamomile Oil: One of the best oils to use when feeling grumpy, agitated, or irritated. Ideal for hormone support and relieving stress. It is a wonderful oil to reinstate a sense of comfort and belonging and one of the safest oils to use on children. You'll experience calm, expansion, peace, relaxation, and a sense of worthiness instead of anger, anxiety, heartbreak, impatience, negativity, sorrow, or worry.

Application: Compress, spritz, massage, diffuse, inhale.

May Also Benefit: Acne, boils, cuts, sensitive skin, dry or red skin, insomnia, muscle tension, nausea, digestion issues, menopause, endometriosis, pre-menstrual syndrome, and infertility.

Self-Love Affirmation: *I focus my sensitivity and connect with a deeper love amidst the disharmony, enhancing a feeling of comfort and belonging that shines from within.*

Cinnamon Oil: This warm, spicy oil is best when you're feeling emotionally separated or fragile. It can help alleviate fears, worries, lethargy, rigidity, feelings of withdrawal, and disheartenment. Reach for this oil to feel connected, energetic, expansive, passionate, vital, and comforted.

Application: Massage, compress, bathe, inhale, diffuse and spritz.

May Also Benefit: Muscle cramps and spasms, fever, headaches, bronchitis, coughs, colds, flu, digestion issues, weight loss, and even as an aphrodisiac!

Self-Love Affirmation: *Stepping into my powerfully warm and comforting heart centre, I ignite my senses and release worry and fear.*

Cistus Oil: When you want to feel more expansion, grounded, open, strength, and warmth, and less heartbroken, hurt, shock, and stressed.

Application: Compress, massage, bathe, spritz, inhale.

May Also Benefit: Eczema, dermatitis, psoriasis, acne, oil skin, mature skin, wrinkles, anti-aging, pre-menstrual syndrome wounds, and oedema.

Self-Love Affirmation: *I am grounded as I step into deep concentration, release the clutter that fills my mind, and connect to the inner wisdom that guides me.*

Clary Sage Oil: Considered the 'champagne' of essential oils, clary sage calms anger, anxiety, irritation, judgement, nervousness, stress, and feeling overwhelmed. Strengthening and fortifying the mind with clarity, creativity, enthusiasm, inspiration, intuition, and strength, this oil can help you become joyful and intoxicated with life.

Application: Massage, compress, bathe, diffuse, and spritz.

May Also Benefit: Keep this oil on hand for monthly feminine balance, labour, childbirth and infertility, asthma, bronchitis, muscle aches and pains, and even oily hair.

Self-Love Affirmation: *I am the sacred feminine as I harmonise, balance, and uplift my energy field.*

Clove Oil: You'll feel confidence, courage, creativity, focus, openness, strength and warmth instead of confusion, depression, lethargy, and negativity. When mixed with peppermint oil, clove oil is well known to ward off fatigue.

Application: Diffuse, inhale, spritz, massage, bathe, direct application (for mouth ulcers and dental issues only - dip a cotton bud into the undiluted oil and apply to the surface and surrounding areas of the aching tooth).

May Also Benefit: Colds, flu, arthritis, rheumatic pains, digestion issues, parasites, mouth ulcers, muscle aches and pains, insect repellence, and air freshening.

Note: Use in moderation as considered a potential skin irritant. Be careful with topical application during first trimester in pregnancy.

Self-Love Affirmation: *I surround myself with a barrier of loving protection that repels the darkness and nourishes all that supports life.*

Cypress Oil: If you're challenged emotionally, mentally, physically, or feel as if you're about to fall apart, cypress will help you pull it all together. Diffuse in times of change and transition from chaos, defeat, grief, judgement, sadness or sorrow to acceptance, balance, expansion, protection, and vision.

Application: Massage, compress, sitz bath, spritz, diffuse, or inhale this reviving and cleansing oil.

May Also Benefit: Varicose veins, haemorrhoids, acne, oily skin, broken capillaries, asthma, coughs, colds, weight loss, cellulite, bruises, oedema, and excessive perspiration.

Self-Love Affirmation: *The time to cleanse has arrived. I wash away the old and transition to the new.*

Eucalyptus Oil: Renowned for reviving the spirits and restoring vitality, this refreshing oil will bring you clarity, expansion, focus, strength, and vision, where previously you grappled with anger, distance, exhaustion, lethargy, and sadness.

Application: Inhale, massage, diffuse, spritz, bath, compress.

May Also Benefit: Asthma, colds, flu, catarrh, immune support, sinusitis, headaches, muscle tension, burns, cuts, wounds, insect repellence, air freshening. Blend with lavender and tea tree when colds and flus are prevalent, as a potent chest rub. Combine one drop of each into a teaspoon of carrier oil and rub on the back and chest.

Self-Love Affirmation: *As I create the space to revive the spirit, I restore vitality to my soul.*

Fennel Oil: With its cleansing and energising properties, fennel encourages you to be more productive, creative, and on-task to meet your highest aspirations. You'll enjoy compassion, courage, fulfilment, and strength in the place of chaos, frustration, insecurity, negativity, and stress.

Application: Massage, compress, bathe, inhale, diffuse, spritz.

May Also Benefit: Constipation, diarrhoea, flatulence, indigestion, nausea, headaches, pre-menstrual syndrome, hormone support, fluid retention, varicose veins, weight loss, and respiratory conditions.

Note: Be careful with topical application during first trimester in pregnancy.

Self-Love Affirmation: *Cleanse, clear, energise, and balance as I move on to better things.*

Frankincense Oil: Your personal coat of armour! This oil protects you and keeps you safe. Powerful to use when life gets too busy and emotional, and physical reserves are low. It is the oil for personal growth and expansion especially when the past is holding you back. Enjoy feelings of acceptance, clarity, enlightenment, focus, forgiveness, love, peace and wisdom.

Application: Massage, spritz, diffuse, bathe, inhale, compress.

May Also Benefit: Anti-aging, circulation, arthritis, respiratory conditions, digestion issues, wounds, inflammation, acne, large open pores, dry and mature skin and wrinkles.

Self-Love Affirmation: *I breathe deeply, I am aligned with the healing powers of inner peace, I embrace this with love, compassion, and kindness.*

Geranium Oil: Call on this delicate yet potent oil when life feels like a continuous rollercoaster ride. When you're feeling chaotic, deceived, distant, moody, negative, or sensitive, Geranium will bring balance, calm, connection, focus, harmony, and protection.

Application: Compress, massage, bathe, spritz, diffuse, inhale.

May Also Benefit: Acne, eczema, dermatitis, congested skin, mature skin, broken capillaries, pre-menstrual syndrome, hormone support, infertility, menopause, wounds, bruising, and oedema.

Note: Be careful with topical application on hypersensitive or overly red and inflamed skin.

Self-Love Affirmation: *Now is my time to steady, nurture, and love myself unconditionally.*

Ginger Oil: Brings clarity, confidence, courage, endurance, motivation, and strength to situations when you're feeling trapped by mental fatigue, forgetfulness, grief, lethargy, and worthlessness.

Application: Inhale, massage, bathe, compress, foot bath, spritz, and diffuse.

May Also Benefit: Digestion issues, indigestion, bruising, muscle aches and pains, cold hands and feet, arthritis, nausea, travel sickness, catarrh, coughs, and sinusitis.

Self-Love Affirmation: *I have the strength to do anything I set out to do with loving intention.*

Grapefruit Oil: Call on this oil with euphoric properties when you're feeling tense, overwhelmed, under pressure, defeated, depressed, overwhelmed, weary, or frustrated. Enjoy the feelings of focus, clarity, joy, positivity, strength, and trust as you're gently uplifted on the delightful citrus scent.

Application: Compress, inhale, massage or spritz this zesty, uplifting, and revitalising oil.

May Also Benefit: Oily, congested skin, acne, weight loss, cellulite, muscle aches and pains, headaches, insomnia, and muscle tension.

Self-Love Affirmation: *I recognise my self-worth and step into my power with love, grace, and ease.*

Immortelle Oil: This oil helps clear the mind, awaken the senses and promote inner peace, bringing the qualities of adapt-ability, connectivity, forgiveness, positivity, strength, warmth, and wisdom when you're feeling disheartened, sorrowful, heartbroken, hurt, insecure, negative, stressed, or worried.

Application: Compress, massage, bathe, spritz, inhale, diffuse.

May Also Benefit: Bruises, scars, stretch marks, anti-aging, mature skin, sensitive and dry skin. A great liver detox and terrific for inflam-mation, muscle aches and pains, bronchitis, coughs, and colds.

Self-Love Affirmation: *Forgiveness allows me to release and clear the ties that no longer serve me, awakening my inner strength, and finding acceptance for what is.*

Jasmine Oil: Considered to be the 'King of Flowers', you can draw on its strength to let go of the past and adapt to what is present. Become confident, content, fulfilled, grateful, passionate, positive, sensual, uplifted, and trusting. Release deception, depression, distance, disconnection, fear, rigidity, sorrow, and worthlessness.

Application: Massage, bathe, spritz, compress, inhale, and diffuse.

May Also Benefit: Muscular cramps and spasms, coughs, colds, and flus. Relieve insomnia, muscle tension, dry skin, eczema, dermatitis, infertility, and pre-menstrual syndrome. Can also be used as an aphrodisiac!

Self-Love Affirmation: *I am living gently by releasing the past, allowing the future, and trusting my ability to connect to, and transform, the deeper aspects of self.*

Juniper Oil: Helping to clear your mind from negative thoughts and mental clutter, this purifying oil will bring confidence, focus, joy, openness, relaxation, and clarity. Dust off apprehension, chaos, exhaustion, negativity, and weariness.

Application: Massage, bathe, diffuse, spritz, compress, inhale, and sitz bath.

May Also Benefit: Liver detoxification, muscle aches and pains, oedema, inflammation, cellulite, varicose veins, oily skin, pimples, cystitis, pyelitis.

Note: Be careful with topical application during first trimester of pregnancy.

Self-Love Affirmation: *Events from my past positively influence my present and future, I embrace change wholeheartedly.*

Lavender Oil: This oil is like having your 'dream mum' in a bottle. Comforting you with generosity, gratitude, kindness, love, nurturing, protection, and relaxation, your feelings of anxiety, hurt, irritation, judgement, neglect, worry, sadness, shock, stress, vulnerability, and feeling overwhelmed will melt away with ease.

Application: Inhale, massage, spritz, compress, direct application, diffuse, and bathe.

May Also Benefit: Coughs, colds, catarrh, and fever. Great for burns, bites, stings and rashes (direct application works well here). Keep handy for headaches, muscle tension, asthma, respiratory conditions, and all skin conditions.

Self-Love Affirmation: *I feel nurtured and loved as I sink into my heart space where it is always calm and comforting.*

Lemon Oil: This fresh and stimulating oil is an instant pick-me-up, leaving you with energy and mental clarity. You'll feel less confused, defeated, disheartened, exhausted, weary, and worried.

Application: Massage, compress, diffuse, or spritz. This oil makes a refreshing addition to your bath, opening the heart, alleviating exhaustion, and creating self-confidence.

May Also Benefit: Anti-aging, nausea, cellulite, weight loss, oedema, varicose veins, warts, colds, flu, immune support, and a liver tonic.

Note: Avoid exposure to the sun after using lemon in a massage or bath as it is phototoxic (will cause a sunburn like skin condition when exposed to sun light).

Self-Love Affirmation: *I wash away the past and uplift the spirit by embracing the moment and shining my light brightly for all to see.*

Lemongrass Oil: Bring balance, clarity, endurance, energy, enthusiasm, expansion, motivation, and vitality to your days as you say goodbye to apprehension, depression, mental fatigue, impatience, lethargy, negativity, stress, vulnerability, and feelings of worthlessness.

Application: Massage, compress, bathe, spritz, inhale, diffuse.

May Also Benefit: Muscle aches and pains, bruising, oedema, inflammation, indigestion, fever, headaches, weight loss, and cellulite. Works wonderfully as an insect repellent and air freshener, and when used in massage boosts energy and endurance.

Self-Love Affirmation: *I increase my endurance by focusing on the path and allowing the energy to flow.*

Lime Oil: When you want to feel more abundant, alert, celebratory, energetic, enlightened, focused, inspired, joyful, nurtured, uplifted, vital, and less anxious, chaotic, confused, fearful, heartbroken, irritated, unattractive, weary, and worthless.

Application: Massage, bathing, compress, spritz, inhale, diffuse.

May Also Benefit: Muscle aches and pains, congested and oily skin, cellulite, weight loss, digestion issues, indigestion, coughs, colds, flu, and sore throats.

Self-Love Affirmation: *I have boundless inner peace and joy, as worry and stress just melt away.*

Mandarin Oil: This is your 'lighten up and enjoy life' oil, and the one to call on to bring out your softer and more playful side, connecting you with your inner child. Sweet and uplifting, this oil will transition your experience of chaos, depression, fear, grief, rigidity, shock, stress, and worry into calm, inspiration, celebration, and trust.

Application: Massage, compress, inhale, bathe, spritz, diffuse.

May Also Benefit: Digestion issues, indigestion, muscle cramps, stretch marks, scars, insomnia, nausea, muscle tension, acne, oily skin, and wrinkles.

Self-Love Affirmation: *Happiness flows to me, around me, and within me.*

Manuka Oil: This healing, cleansing, and uplifting oil is right there for you to call on when you're feeling emotionally low, and negative feelings are getting the better of you. When apprehension, confusion, defeat, depression, mental fatigue, irritation, lethargy, shock, vulnerability, or weariness sets in, this highly medicinal plant is at the rescue. Instantly feel more balanced, cleansed, energetic, protected, and vital.

Application: Foot bath, spritz, massage, direct application (for abscesses, ringworm, corns, warts and cold sores only). Bathe, compress, diffuse, inhale, and sitz bath.

May Also Benefit: Bacterial and fungal conditions, wounds, and bites. Healing for candida, urinary tract infections, coughs, colds, and flu.

Self-Love Affirmation: *I trust in the ebb and flow of life, and love with ease and vitality.*

Marjoram Oil: This oil is perfect if you're trapped in obsessive thinking and negativity. Ease anxiety, defeat, frustration, neglect, stress, and tension with ease as you ground yourself with love, openness, strength, and warmth.

Application: Massage, bathe, compress, inhale, diffuse, and spritz.

May Also Benefit: Muscle aches and pains, respiratory conditions, coughs, constipation and flatulence. Great for pre-menstrual syndrome, menopause, headaches, insomnia, and muscle tension.

Note: Be careful with topical application during first trimester of pregnancy.

Self-Love Affirmation: *I draw my energy inwards, I trust myself, I create a sense of calm, peace, and sincerity.*

Melissa Oil: When you want to feel more acceptance, balance, expansion, gratitude, trust, vitality, and less anger, deception, depression, forgetfulness, heartbreak, irritability, judgement, lethargy, sadness, sensitivity, sorrow, and stress.

Application: Inhale, spritz, massage, diffuse, direct application, compress, bathe.

May Also Benefit: Heart palpitations, circulation, digestion issues, indigestion, cold sores, acne, oily skin, headaches, migraines, and hormone support.

Self-Love Affirmation: *I reach my full potential effortlessly by reconnecting with my heart, my truth, and divine self.*

Myrrh Oil: Rejuvenate yourself with rituals that include myrrh to create a feeling of abundance, connection, expansion, patience, grounding, peace, trust, and wisdom. Allow neglect, sadness, vulnerability and feelings of worthlessness to fade away.

Application: Massage, bathe, foot bath, spritz, compress, inhale, diffuse, and direct application (to mouth ulcers and cold sores only).

May Also Benefit: Bacterial and fungal conditions, dry, aging, and mature skin, eczema, acne, diarrhoea, flatulence, respiratory conditions, arthritis, mouth ulcers, and cold sores. Blend myrrh with frankincense, pine and orange, and use as a perfume or add to your facial regime to reduce wrinkles and preserve youth.

Self-Love Affirmation: *My connection to intuition is empowering and I follow the guidance that comes with ease and grace.*

Myrtle Oil: Cleansing, positive, harmonious, and peaceful, kindness and sensuality replace anxiety, chaos, fear, tension, hurt, hopelessness, and feelings of worthlessness. Supporting deep inner wisdom and knowing, calm the busy mind, and feel reassured that we are all supported and connected.

Application: Inhale, diffuse, spritz, massage, sitz bath, bathe, compress, and hair rinse.

May Also Benefit: Bronchitis, catarrh, coughs, urinary tract infections, haemorrhoids, acne, oily skin, open pores, hormone support, and head lice.

Self-Love Affirmation: *As I forgive myself, I can forgive and release others. We are all doing the best we can with what we have been given.*

Neroli Oil: Considered a wonderful rescue remedy oil, making it an ideal choice if suffering from shock or hysteria. It is one of the best oils to enhance creativity, trust intuition, and to connect to your higher self. Enjoy calm, contentment, courage, joy, nurturing, passion, peace, strength, and trust. Support depression, fear, grief, moodiness, negativity, sadness, shock, sorrow, and worthlessness.

Application: Massage, compress, spritz, diffuse, bathe.

May Also Benefit: Sensitive and dry skin, insomnia, muscle tension, diarrhoea, digestion issues, scars, broken capillaries, stretch marks, and is even an aphrodisiac!

Self-Love Affirmation: *I trust my intuition and allow the gentle integration of peace and calm, as nervous tension and fear is released.*

Orange Oil: Just like its flesh, the oil promotes health and vitality. It's uplifting, radiating, relaxing, calming, and soothing properties bring contentment, creativity, ease, joy, kindness, and warmth. Let go of distance, hopelessness, irritation, moodiness, negativity, nervousness, obsessiveness, and sadness.

Application: Massage, bathe, compress, inhale, spritz.

May Also Benefit: Stretch marks, cellulite, arthritis, digestive issues, large open pores, acne, dry skin, liver detoxification, weight loss, insomnia, and muscle tension.

Self-Love Affirmation: *I celebrate life, embrace the moment, and spread my light out into the world.*

Oregano Oil: A beautifully purifying oil that warms to the skin during massage. Feelings of frustration, hopelessness, lethargy, impatience, negativity, procrastination, and rigidity will be replaced with clarity, openness, protection, safety, and strength.

Application: Massage, compress, inhale, and spritz this warm and stimulating oil.

May Also Benefit: Staving off colds, flus and sore throats, digestion issues, urinary tract infections, asthma, bronchitis, bacterial, and fungal conditions.

Self-Love Affirmation: *I am self-motivated, strong, confident, and unwavering in my mind, body, and spirit.*

Palmarosa Oil: Encouraging a sense of balance, security, compassion, confidence, creativity, forgiveness, and generosity, this oil melts away anxiety, deception, hurts, hopelessness, insecurity, obsessiveness, and vulnerability.

Application: Massage, compress, spritz, inhale, bathe.

May Also Benefit: Oily or dry skin, broken capillaries, rashes, eczema, dermatitis, pre-menstrual syndrome, hormone support, scars, wrinkles, anti-aging, and digestive issues.

Self-Love Affirmation: *I regenerate and restore my connection to self by moisturising my soul with love.*

Patchouli Oil: This enduring and sensual oil makes for a hypnotic aroma when blended with ylang ylang and orange, increasing intimacy and passion. Attract abundance, confidence, courage, enlightenment, expansion, focus, grounding, peace, and sensuality. When you're feeling anger, anxiety, controlling, disheartened, distant, hopeless, stressed, or tense, keep this harmonising and regenerative oil on hand.

Application: Massage, compress, spritz, bath, inhale.

May Also Benefit: Cracked and dry skin, stretch marks, fluid retention, cellulite, dermatitis, eczema, inflammation, wounds, and guess what? It's even an aphrodisiac!

Self-Love Affirmation: *I ignite passion and intimacy. I relax into the harmonising pleasure of standing in my sacred energy.*

Peppermint Oil: This fresh, minty oil is both warming and cooling at the same time! A perfect remedy for chaos, confusion, depression, fatigue, procrastination, and forgetfulness. Instead, experience being alert, clear, connected, enthusiastic, motivated, and vital.

Application: Inhale, massage, compress, massage, vaporise, or spritz.

May Also Benefit: Indigestion, flatulence, colds, flus, coughs, fever, headaches, nausea, muscle aches and pains, asthma, bronchitis, and sinusitis.

Note: Be careful with topical application during the first trimester in pregnancy, if you have hypersensitive skin, and within twenty minutes of taking any homeopathic remedies.

Self-Love Affirmation: *It is in the overload that I am able to activate and balance my energy, as the warmth of love fills my soul.*

Petitgrain Oil: The orange tree produces three essential oils. Orange from the fruit of the tree, neroli from the flower and petitgrain from the leaves. Hence why so many of their qualities overlap. Petitgrain is uplifting, refreshing, and an emotional comforter in times of anger, exhaustion, mental fatigue, and frustration. Be nourished with balance, calm, creativity, and gratitude.

Application: Compress, spritz, massage, inhale, diffuse, and bathe.

May Also Benefit: Acne, boils, pimples, digestive issues, dry skin, mature skin, insomnia, muscle tension, inflammation, and arthritis.

Self-Love Affirmation: *I am soothed and nurtured as my heart opens to the divine love that surrounds me.*

Pine Oil: This cleansing, refreshing and invigorating oil can have the same effect as if you were standing in a pine forest. A fabulous oil for clearing the air, improving alertness, and increasing inspiration.

Application: Inhale, vaporise, bathe, spritz and compress this motivating and intuitive oil.

May Also Benefit: Coughs, colds, flu, asthma, cystitis, pyelitis, inflammation, muscle aches and pains, headaches, arthritis, rheumatic pain, and liver detoxification.

Self-Love Affirmation: *Feeling inspired, I go into today invigorated and alert, ready for anything.*

Rose Oil: The 'Queen of Flowers' has long been a symbol of love. Through her nurturing properties, you'll enjoy abundance, compassion, creativity, connection, courage, enlightenment, joy, kindness, love, nurturing, passion, and peace. Release anger, defeat, depression, fear, heartache, sorrow, worry, and worthlessness.

Application: Spritz, massage, compress, bathe, diffuse, inhale.

May Also Benefit: Broken capillaries, inflammation, hormone support, menopause, dry, mature skin, wrinkles, scars, weight loss, cellulite, and even and aphrodisiac!

Self-Love Affirmation: *Loving myself is easy because I am beautiful. I attract love, joy, and happiness into all of my being.*

Rosemary Oil: Known to have a very stimulating effect on the mind, a cleansing effect on the emotions, and is renowned for being the oil for memory. This energising oil improves mental clarity, focus and intuition while calming exhaustion, mental fatigue, neglect, procrastination, and feeling overwhelmed.

Application: Enjoy this delightful oil in a bath, compress, diffuser, spritzer, or massage.

May Also Benefit: Liver detoxification, weight loss, cellulite, muscle aches or pains, respiratory conditions, sinusitis, heart palpitations, circulation, and hair growth.

Note: Be careful with topical application during first trimester of pregnancy.

Self-Love Affirmation: *I breathe with ease, cleansing, and connecting to this beautiful mind and body.*

Rosewood Oil: Uplifting and enlivening, this oil is wonderful for meditation and can help restore emotional balance and enhance spiritual healing. Trade your depression, insecurity, procrastination and moodiness for balance, confidence, courage, energy, peace, and joy.

Application: Massage, diffuse, inhales, compress, bath, or spritz this regenerating and balancing oil.

May Also Benefit: Acne, dermatitis, sensitive skin, dry mature skin, bronchitis, respiratory conditions, headaches, nausea, and inflammation.

Self-Love Affirmation: *Steady head and centred heart, I stand strong throughout the challenges life presents.*

Sage Oil: An excellent physical detoxifier and emotional cleanser. It is also known to help enhance intuition and develop innate wisdom. This beautifully regulating oil will bring trust, confidence, adaptability, and energy as the antidote to anxiety, depression, grief, hopelessness, and negativity.

Application: Massage, bathe, compress, direct application (for cold sores only), spritz, inhale.

May Also Benefit: Muscle aches and pains, cold sores, loss of appetite, digestion issues, hormone balance, pre-menstrual syndrome, menopause, and excessive perspiration.

Note: Be careful with topical application during first trimester in pregnancy. Use in moderation.

Self-Love Affirmation: *I cleanse, clear, and release all negativity that surrounds me, and I protect my energy now.*

Sandalwood Oil: This wonderful oil is best on those long busy days when you want to feel grounded and centred without feeling sedated! A popular choice for meditation as it is renowned for bringing quiet to a busy mind along with balance, acceptance, compassion, and confidence. Wash away anger, depression, grief, nervousness, rigidity, and feelings of being unattractive.

Application: Massage, sitz bath, compress, spritz, inhale.

May Also Benefit: Cystitis, urinary tract infections, dry skin, eczema, dermatitis, acne, oily skin, inflammation, respiratory conditions, sore throats, and can even act as an aphrodisiac!

Self-Love Affirmation: *I am grounded, as my mind is clear and open to new possibilities; I am a miracle worker.*

Spearmint Oil: Brings comfort to the mind and a sense of relief to the body as it calms mental fatigue and exhaustion, confusion, forgetfulness, lethargy, and weariness. Enjoy clarity, energy, enthusiasm, focus, motivation, and a feeling of being uplifted.

Application: Compress, massage, inhale, spritz, direct application (for wounds, cuts, and mouth ulcers only) and bathe.

May Also Benefit: Digestive issues, indigestion, wounds, cuts, mouth ulcers, sinusitis, catarrh, asthma, acne, dermatitis, psoriasis, nausea, and travel sickness. Spearmint shares similar properties to peppermint, with only trace amounts of menthol, making it gentler on the skin. Ideal for children with digestive upsets.

Self-Love Affirmation: *My mind and body are at one with my soul, aligned with my purpose.*

Tea Tree Oil: Highly recommended for those who struggle with their body, depression, victimisation, and a sense of doom and gloom. Feelings of confusion, mental fatigue, irritation, lethargy, negativity, and shock will be soothed instantly. If you're wanting to feel protection, strength, vitality, energy, and wisdom, this is your oil.

Application: Massage, bathe, spritz, compress, diffuse, inhale, and sitz bath.

May Also Benefit: Bacterial and fungal conditions, colds, flu, immune support, candida, cystitis, acne, pimples, rashes, burns, wounds, cuts, bites, and stings. The most antiseptic of all oils!

Self-Love Affirmation: *I acknowledge the negative and draw energy by focusing only on the positive to heal and energise my life.*

Thyme Oil: This cleansing oil helps to generate strength and enthusiasm, adaptability, focus, vitality, and warmth. Eliminate exhaustion, mental fatigue, stress, vulnerability, and feelings of withdrawal.

Application: Massage, diffuse, spritz, inhale, and bathe.

May Also Benefit: Immune support, bacterial and fungal conditions, acne, oily skin, eczema, dermatitis, digestion issues, parasites, and respiratory conditions.

Self-Love Affirmation: *Strength is within my power. I revive enthusiasm with passion for life.*

Vetiver Oil: When you want to feel more abundance, balance, calm, connected, generous, grounded, strength, uplifted, and wisdom, and less controlling, depressed, distant, grief, lethargic, obsessive, sensitive, sorrow, stressed, tense, and withdrawn.

Application: Massage, compress, spritz, inhale, diffuse, and bathe.

May Also Benefit: Dry skin, mature skin, scars, stretch marks, pre-menstrual syndrome, menopause, inflammation, and even an aphrodisiac!

Self-Love Affirmation: *My unique and special nature creates abundance in my life.*

Wintergreen Oil: The sweet and minty scent of wintergreen is a powerful antidote to stressed muscles and head tension. Replace feelings of hurt, negativity, procrastination, and rigidity, with energy, endurance, motivation, positivity, relaxation, and heal those deep-down emotional wounds. As an added bonus, this oil has the ability to act as a natural pain reliever! It is also antiseptic, anti-arthritic, and an astringent.

Application: Massage, compress, diffuse, spritz, and bathe in this relieving and warming oil.

May Also Benefit: Colds, flu, muscle aches and pains, digestion issues, inflammation, bacterial, and fungal conditions.

Note: Avoid topical application during pregnancy. Always use diluted as the methyl salicylate content can cause skin irritation.

Self-Love Affirmation: *The warmth of love flows through me, stimulating growth on my journey of self-discovery.*

Ylang Ylang Oil: Meaning 'flower of flowers' and often referred to as the Perfume Tree. This oil creates a sense of peace, harmony, and passion as it dispels anger, anxiety, and shock. Along with rose, orange, and patchouli, it is an exquisite aphrodisiac! And is a beautiful love-making oil!

Application: Inhale, spritz, massage, diffuse, compress, bathe.

May Also Benefit: Heart palpitations, circulation, dry skin, oily skin, anti-aging, pre-menstrual syndrome, menopause, and hormone support.

Self-Love Affirmation: *I create the space for intimate connection by releasing tension and inviting peace and self-confidence.*

DAILY BODY BOOST

The Daily Body Boost is a daily ritual that can change your life. It is a treatment for your mind, as the oils you use can be specific to your needs, enhancing the way you think and feel in seconds. It is a full body treatment, connecting us to its beauty, not its issues! And it is a full skin treatment that assists the circulatory and lymphatic systems to increase blood flow and eliminate toxins. The best part is it only takes one or two minutes every morning. No excuse that you haven't enough time! Commit to it fully for the whole twenty-eight days and you will see the phenomenal results. It is fantastic for both men and women; even your kids will love getting in on the act! We constantly receive feedback on what the Body Boost is doing for people all around the world. How much better they feel, how much they crave their two-minute ritual, how important it is to set themselves up for a great day, and how much they love making themselves a priority first thing in the morning. As simple as this ritual seems, it can be life-changing so don't ever miss this self-care opportunity out.

You will need:

- Your favourite synergy blend or three single essential oils.
- Cold pressed massage carrier oil or everyday body lotion.
- Magnesium health spray.
- A small glass or ceramic bowl.
- Your wonderful, naked body!

Place just over one teaspoon (6 ml) of massage carrier oil and three drops of your chosen essential oils or synergy blend into the small glass or ceramic dish along with three sprays of magnesium health spray.

If you would prefer you can add three drops of your chosen essential oils into the everyday body lotion instead of the carrier oil. You can mix this blend in your hand if easier and then pat onto the body in key spots and then massage it in over the whole body. Either way, it is quick to do and easily absorbed into your skin.

If using the oil, mix the blend using your fingertips in the bowl and inhale the aroma to make sure it feels right. Lightly dry yourself off after your morning shower, rub a little oil blend between your hands and working from the feet up start massaging briskly over your entire body continually dipping back into your bowl for more oil until a fine film has you covered. Apply the blend to as much of your body as you can reach (except the face), finishing by stroking down the neck, then cupping both your hands over your face to take 3 deep breaths to inhale the aroma. This is the perfect time to create an affirmation or positive statement for the day. For example,

"I am fit, strong and healthy, and I am up for an incredible day!", "I am an amazing, positive person who loves life", or "I am grateful to be alive".

The best times to perform your Daily Body Boost are after your morning exercise and after your shower in the morning. You can perform this ritual in the evening, allowing an hour or so before bedtime so that the oils can be fully absorbed. Try to limit the stimulating oils at night time if rest is your priority.

Detoxifying oils for your morning body boost are black pepper, cypress, fennel, grapefruit, juniper, and rose.

Stimulating oils are basil, black pepper, cardamom, fennel, ginger, lemon, peppermint, pine, rosemary, and thyme.

Calming oils for your evening blend could be lavender, chamomile, geranium, orange, and cedarwood.

You can choose any three of these oils to add to your carrier oil of cold-pressed sweet almond or macadamia, or a natural body moisturiser.

The benefits of your daily body boost are numerous. It:

- Allows you to take a moment to nurture and honour yourself.
- Wakes your body up in the morning.
- Stimulates the lymphatic and circulatory systems.
- Gives your skin a full nourishing treatment.
- Creates a beautiful, lasting body aroma.

- Affects the way you think and feel with the psycho-therapeutic properties of the oils.

- Can be a very calming and relaxing way to set yourself up for sleep if done in a gentler manner in the evening.

This could become one of the most symbolic self-care rituals you could ever do for yourself.

METHODS OF USE

Bathing: Fill a bath with water, add a cup of magnesium salts, light natural candles around the room, roll a towel as a neck support, put on relaxation music. Just before you immerse yourself add a total of 3-6 drops of your chosen essential oils and thoroughly agitate the water.

Body Boost: A daily, two-minute, full body, ritual using three drops of your chosen essential oils into a teaspoon of carrier oil and massage all over from toe to head. See page 331 for more information.

Body Brush: Place 2-3 drops of your chosen oil or oil blend onto a natural bristle body brush and take into the shower. Add some water and exfoliate the whole body with brisk circular motions. You can dry body brush, too.

Compress: Fill a bowl or sink with warm or cold water. Add a total of 3-4 drops of essential oils. Immerse a face cloth. Wring excess water and then gently compress onto the face or affected area. Repeat 3-4 times.

Diffusing: Fill the electrical unit with water to the specified level. Add a total of 6-10 drops of essential oils. Replace the lid and turn the unit on.

Direct Application: Place one drop of your chosen essential oil onto a damp cotton bud and apply to affected area.

Foot Bath: Fill a large stainless-steel bowl with warm water. Add 3-6 drops of your chosen essential oils. Agitate the water and immerse your feet for ten minutes. Place two large marbles on top of a face cloth to massage the soles of the feet.

Hair Rinse: Fill a 50ml bottle with water. Add 3-4 drops of your chosen oils. Wash hair as normal, then on the final rinse squeeze excess water, shake the bottle and pour over the head, massaging the scalp and hair.

Inhalation: Fill a bowl or sink with warm to hot water. Add a total of 3-4 drops of essential oils. Place a towel over the head, close your eyes and inhale slowly in through the nose and out through the mouth. Alternate in through the mouth and out through the nose for 5-10 minutes. This is a wonderful steam treatment for the face too.

Massage: Make a massage blend by filling a 100ml glass bottle with a carrier oil like sweet almond, macadamia or jojoba. Add 50 drops in total of your chosen essential oils. Shake the bottle and use as required.

Sitz Bath: Fill your tub or basin with just enough warm water to cover your bottom. Add a total of six drops of essential oils into one teaspoon of quality milk of choice. Add to water, agitate to disperse then soak for 10 to 15 minutes.

Spritzer or Aroma Mist: Fill a 50ml spritzer bottle with water. Add a total of 3-6 drops of your essential oils. Always shake before using your spritzer. Close your eyes and breathe in as you spritz a few times around and over your head.

Tissue: Place 1-3 drops of your chosen oils onto a tissue and tuck into your top or bra so you can enjoy its aroma throughout the day.

Vaporising: Fill the crucible at the top of the unit with water. Add a total of 6-8 drops of your chosen essential oils. Place a candle at the bottom of the unit, light and enjoy. Do not let the water run dry.

THE SAFETY OF ESSENTIAL OILS

Just because essential oils are natural does not mean that great care should not be taken. They are a potent, complex mixture of organic molecules that should be used with the utmost respect. Most safety claims are based on isolated chemical component studies, yet an essential oil is a complete synergy containing many chemical components that work harmoniously all together. Therefore, common sense should prevail with the theory that less is more. If you follow the number of drops to use on page 343 (The Quick Reference Blending Guide), and adhere to the following cautions, then essential oils can indeed be used safely and effectively.

Oral Administration

Essential oils should NOT be taken internally unless under the care of a qualified specialist, aromatherapist, or medical herbalist.

Poisoning

Most essential oils are sold in 5-15ml bottles which is a lethal amount if consumed orally by a young child. Keep out of the reach of children. Seek medical attention immediately if swallowed.

Skin Problems

Due to skin sensitivity and irritation always use essential oils diluted and never directly onto the skin. Exceptions can include lavender, chamomile, tea tree, and manuka if applied on a damp cotton bud in small areas. If a reaction occurs remove with warm, soapy water immediately.

Pregnancy Risks

Research suggests that most essential oils are safe to use during pregnancy. Do not take them orally, follow the pregnancy ratio on page 49 and for extra precaution avoid topical application in the first trimester.

Serious Medical Conditions

It is extremely important to note that oils are NOT a substitute for allopathic (scientifically proven medical) treatment of serious diseases. The use of essential oils with medical conditions such as cancer, epilepsy, high blood pressure, heart, or liver damage should only ever be used as a complementary treatment, under the care of a qualified medical practitioner, and in conjunction with allopathic medical treatments.

Phototoxicity

Some essential oils like bergamot, lemon and cold pressed lime are known to have phototoxic reactions with the sun; that is, become toxic after exposure to sunlight. As a general rule, be careful after topical application of citrus oils for up to twelve hours before exposing the skin to the sun.

QUICK REFERENCE BLENDING GUIDE

Massage	100ml = 50 drops (2:1 ratio, 2.5% dilution)
Body Boost	3 drops
Vaporising	6 - 8 drops
Diffusing	6 - 10 drops
Spritzer	3 - 6 drops
Bathing	3 - 6 drops
Compress	3 - 4 drops
Inhalation	3 - 4 drops
Foot Bath	3 - 6 drops
Sitz Bath	6 drops
Hair Rinse	3 - 4 drops
Body Brush	2 - 3 drops
Tissue	1 - 3 drops
Direct	1 drop on a damp cotton bud

Children (2 - 12 yrs), Elderly, and Pregnant Women

Massage	100ml = 20 drops (5:1 ratio)
Vaporising	3 - 4 drops
Diffusing	4 - 6 drops
Spritzer	2 - 3 drops
Bathing	3 - 4 drops
Compress	1 - 2 drops
Inhalation	1 - 2 drops
Foot Bath	2 - 4 drops
Hair Rinse	1 - 2 drops
Body Brush	1 - 2 drops
Tissue	1 - 2 drops
Direct	1 drop on a damp cotton bud

Note: Always measure accurately, label all blends, and store the oils correctly using glass bottles (preferably amber or cobalt) away from light and heat.

Babies (3 months - 2 yrs)

Massage	100ml = 10 drops (10:1 ratio)
Vaporising	3 - 4 drops
Bathing	1 - 2 drops
Compress	1 drop
Inhalation	1 drop

Newborn (0 - 3 months)

Massage	Use plain massage base oil
Vaporising	3 - 4 drops

Avoid all topical applications of essential oils

Twenty8 Synergy Blends Created by Kim

Balance & Harmony

This blend will bring stability, balance, and strength. A beautiful combination of clary sage, geranium, lavender, lemon, neroli, and rose that will help balance emotions and regulate body cycles.

Celebrate & Uplift

The perfect blend to honour and celebrate life and uplift your spirits. An exquisite combination of clary sage, sweet orange, rosewood, ylang ylang, and grapefruit. This is your 'happy' blend. The one to promote joy and celebration into your life. A fantastic 'pat on the back' blend too!

Courage & Confidence

To elevate self-esteem, increase courage, and boost confidence, this beautiful blend of grapefruit, bergamot, sweet orange, geranium, clary sage, and rose is the perfect combination to take on warrior status!

De-stress & Revive

A powerful blend of oils to de-stress the mind and body and revive the soul. A wonderful combination of petitgrain, bergamot, rosewood, pink grapefruit, sandalwood, and neroli. A great blend when things are getting on top of you or deadlines are looming. A positive start to your day and perfect to use when you have a lot on your plate.

Detox & Strengthen

Juniper, rosemary (Spanish), cypress, lemongrass, pink grapefruit, black pepper, and Rose are all activating oils to help boost the body's ability to cleanse and detox. It is the kick-butt body and mind blend for supporting weight-loss and toning. It is also a wonderful muscle ease blend and combined with one cup of Epsom salts in a bath post exercise is very rejuvenating.

Energy & Vitality

A blend to revitalise and energise at any time, this uplifting combination of rosemary (Spanish), basil, lemon, lime, and black pepper is the perfect pick-me-up. The best blend when you want to get yourself up and out of bed with vigour and into your exercise regime with ease. A great afternoon blend when it is common to feel most lethargic and you need a pep up!

Focus & Clarity

With oils of grapefruit, rosemary, myrtle, and spearmint you will find the Focus & Clarity blend an incredible one for studying, focusing, mindfulness, and for being truly present. Perfect when feeling clouded or unable to make decisions and ideal for an instant pep-me-up!

Immune Boost

This potent combination of eucalyptus, lavender, tea tree, cedarwood, and pine is perfect for strengthening the body's immune system to get you back on top fast and feeling great. Use if you are feeling slightly under the weather, if you feel a sore throat coming on or you are not feeling 100%.

Instant Calm

This rescue remedy blend of oils uses the soothing properties of lavender, mandarin, orange, frankincense, roman chamomile, and neroli to strengthen an overburdened nervous system and restore calm. A great oil blend if you need to calm your emotions and relax before bed.

Peace & Meditation

When a quiet mind, deep awareness, and grounding is sought, this powerful combination of lavender, frankincense, patchouli, sandalwood, and myrrh is ideal. Especially good for prayer and meditation or when one is after a little peace within.

Romance & Intimacy

A sensual combination of ylang ylang, patchouli, rosewood, sandalwood, and sweet orange, which enhances loving re-lationships, romance, and positive communication. It is also the perfect blend to use when you need to show yourself some TLC.

Vigour & Spice

This cheeky blend is the one to create a little fun in your life. With essential oils of bergamot, sweet orange, grapefruit, vetiver, cistus, and jasmine it is the perfect blend to help ignite that inner spark and bring some playfulness and positivity into your life. It is the encouragement oil and definitely one for enhancing sensuality and putting a smile on your face!

Four Seasonal Blends

When my therapist, Jacqueline, said to my husband and I at one point that it was important to take four seasons before making any big decisions, it got me wondering about the different energy of each season. And how we can each feel different levels of energy during each season. I researched what this meant on a personal and emotional level and came up with the following four seasonal blends.

Autumn - Ground Me

The time of year to ground yourself and start winding down. These specially chosen oils of mandarin, lime, rosemary, clove bud, and ginger help to bring more stability, comfort, and grace to your world with a sense of calm and lightness to the soul.

Winter - Nurture Me

Winter is a time to pull your energy in and really focus on healing, warming, and nurturing the spirit. With a combination of cedarwood, patchouli, ylang ylang, ginger, and cinnamon bark, these oils will support purification, inward reflection, and connection with your intuition.

Spring - Inspire Me

As the Earth begins to awaken and expand, spring is the perfect time to focus on opening and expanding your heart. With oils of lemon, basil, ylang ylang, thyme, and jasmine, this combination will help you to increase passion, courage, creativity, and romance in your life.

Summer - Love Me

This beautiful season is a chance for the mind to open and self-awareness to increase. With oils of orange, peppermint, lime, coconut CO_2 extract, and jasmine, this time of year brings an element of freedom, transformation, and power.

REFERENCES

Introduction:

Page xxix   One of the most simple... from the book The 4 Agreements – Don Miguel Ruiz https://www.amazon.com/Four-Agreements-Practical-Personal-Freedom/dp/1878424319

How to use this book:

Page xxxviii   Definition of aromatherapy - Salvatore Battaglia – The Complete Guide Of Aromatherapy

http://www.salvatorebattaglia.com.au/

Page xxx   Robert Tisserand, one of the worlds leading experts...

http://roberttisserand.com/

Page xxx   National Association for Holistic Aromatherapy

https://naha.org/

Page xxxix   Daniel Penoel

https://www.amazon.com/Books-Daniel-Penoel

Kurt Schnaubelt

http://www.kurtschnaubelt.com/

Dr Eric Zielenski and Sabrina Zielenski (Mama Z)

https://drericz.com/

Pat Princi-Jones

https://www.linkedin.com/in/pat-princi-jones-9a310334/

Robbi Zeck

https://www.robbizeck.com/

Megan Larsen – Sodashi

https://www.sodashi.com.au/

Jennifer Jeffries

http://jenniferjefferies.com/

Liz Fulcher

http://aromaticwisdominstitute.com/

Farida Irani

https://subtleenergies.com.au/

Valerie Ann Worwood

https://www.amazon.com/Valerie-Ann-Worwood

Patricia Davis

https://www.amazon.com/Books-Patricia-Davis

Vanessa Megan Gray

https://vanessamegan.com/

Bo Hengden

https://absoluteessential.com

Page xxxix   According to world leading aromatherapist
Shirley Price...

https://www.shirleyprice.co.uk/

Why we fall out of love with ourselves:

Page 3   Since reading a book called The Secret by
Rhonda Byrne

https://www.rhondabyrne.com/

Page 4   According to Clifford Nass...

https://www.nytimes.com/2012/03/24/
your-money/why-people-remember-negative-
events-more-than-positive-ones.html

Page 17   Carren Smith tell her story for the first time...

https://carrensmith.com/

Page 33   And according to Brene Brown...

https://brenebrown.com/

Page 40   ...we explore the work of Byron Katie
           http://thework.com/en

Page 48   ...Cyndi O'Meara - nutritionist
           www.changinghabits.com.au

Page 55   My business coach... Bruce Campbell
           http://www.onlinebusinesscoach.com/

Page 74   ...Marcus Pearce, a fellow podcaster and
           speaker
           http://marcuspearce.com.au/

Page 82   ...by a gentleman called Ian Grant...
           http://www.fatherswhodarewin.com/about-us

Page 85   ...reminded me of a book I read many years ago
           by Jon Kabat-Zinn
           https://www.amazon.com/Wherever-
           You-There-Are-Mindfulness/dp/1401307787

Page 91   ...Law of Precession by Dr Buckminster Fuller
           https://www.bfi.org/about-fuller/resources/ev-
           erything-i-know/session-4

Page 102   Dr Michelle Nielsen ten-step manifestation
           process in Manifesting Matisse
           https://www.amazon.com.au/Manifesting-
           Matisse-Practical-Reality-Creation/dp/1439211620

Page 109   ...The beautiful, late Louise L. Hay
           https://www.louisehay.com/

Page 110   Truth can be defined as...
           https://en.oxforddictionaries.com/definition/truth

           Belief can be defined as...
           https://en.oxforddictionaries.com/definition/
           belief

Self Awareness:

Self Care:

Page 176   According to the Journal of Environmental Health...
https://www.hindawi.com/journals/jeph/2012/291541/

Page 179   Quote: Dr Natasha Campbell McBride says...
http://ecofarmingdaily.com/interview-natasha-campbell-mcbride-on-gut-health/

http://www.doctor-natasha.com/

Page 180   Helen Padarin – 9V9 Vege Challenge
http://padarinhealth.teachable.com/p/9v9

Cyndi O'Meara – Hunter Gatherer Protocol
https://changinghabits.com.au/hunter-gatherer-protocol/

Kirsty Wirth – Kultured Wellness Kickstarter Program
https://www.kulturedwellnesstraining.com/p/optimal-gut-health-program

Page 182   ...sex being a chore to be 'done' Dr Christian Northrup
https://www.drnorthrup.com/

According to 'Gardening Know How' soil microbes...
https://www.gardeningknowhow.com/garden-how-to/soil-fertilizers/antidepressant-microbes-soil.htm

Page 184   Biorhythm curves...
https://www.degraeve.com/bio.php

Self Discipline:

Page 189   Dr Sherrill Sellman quote from Up For A Chat interview
http://thewellnesscouch.com/uc/uc-280-hormone-health-with-sherrill-sellman

Page 191   Self-discipline can be defined as
            https://en.oxforddictionaries.com/definition/
            self-discipline

            Food Matters TV – James Colquhoun and
            Laurentine Ten Bosch
            https://www.fmtv.com/join-today

Page 192   Steve Johns – let's look at using 'up until now'…
            http://stevejohns.com.au/about/

Page 195   Profile Magazine
            https://profilemag.com.au/

            Genine Howard
            https://geninehoward.com/

Page 204   Nikki Parkinson – Styling You
            https://www.stylingyou.com.au/

Page 205   Dare your genius – Bryce Courtenay
            https://www.penguin.com.au/books/a-recipe-
            for-dreaming-9780670028689

Self Control:

Page 213   Bill Phillips – Body For Life
            https://bodyforlife.com/

Page 216   Sharny and Julius Keiser – Fit Mum and Fit Dad
            https://www.sharnyandjulius.com

Page 220   American Psychological Association suggest that
            willpower…
            https://exploringyourmind.com/psycholo-
            gy-willpower-will-way/

Page 227   Transcendental Meditation
            https://tm.org.au/

Page 229 Cyndi O'Meara – Changing Habits
https://changinghabits.com.au/

Helen Padarin
https://helenpadarin.com/

Pete Evans
https://peteevans.com/

Kirsty Wirth – Kultured Wellness
https://kulturedwellness.com/

Jordan Pie – The Life Of Pie
http://www.reallifeofpie.com/

Sheridan Austin
http://www.sheridanjoy.com/

Charlotte and Wes Carr
https://wescarr.com.au/

Luke Hines
https://lukehines10.com/

Ashley Jubinville – The Kitchen Coach
http://thekitchencoach.com.au/

Tania Hubbard – Gluten Free Grain Free
http://www.glutenfreegrainfree.com.au/

Jo Whitton – Quirky Cooking
https://www.quirkycooking.com.au/

Fouad Kassab
https://www.fouadkassab.com

Marnie Perkinson – PerkyNZ
https://perky.nz/

The Merrymaker Sisters
https://themerrymakersisters.com

Self Respect:

Page 249   Self respect can be defined as…

https://www.collinsdictionary.com/dictionary/english/self-respect

Page 250   The Maori dictionary defines mana as…

https://maoridictionary.co.nz/

Self Acceptance:

Page 262   Self-acceptance can be defined as…

https://en.wikipedia.org/wiki/Self-acceptance

Page 263   Florence Littauer wrote a book called Personality Plus

https://www.amazon.com.au/Personality-Plus-Understand-Understanding-Yourself/dp/080075445X

https://www.gotoquiz.com/personality_plus_1

Page 264   …the more commonly known Myers-Briggs

https://www.myersbriggs.org/

…and DISC models

http://www.discprofile.com.au/

Page 271   A dear friend Trevor Hendy…

https://trevorhendy.com/

Page 272   …late author and speaker Wayne Dyer

https://www.drwaynedyer.com/

Self Love:

Page 293   I love how my dear friend Pete Evans…

https://peteevans.com/

Page 295   … lyrics to the gorgeous Cold Chisel song 'Lost' written by the amazing Wes Carr

http://www.coldchisel.com/lost/

https://wescarr.com.au/

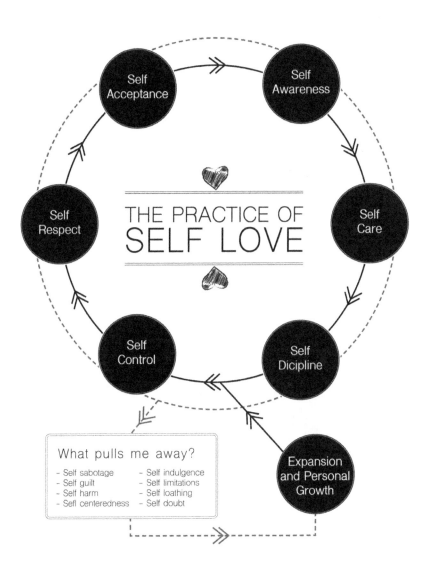

THE PRACTICE OF
SELF LOVE

Self Acceptance

Self Awareness

Self Care

Self Dicipline

Expansion and Personal Growth

Self Control

Self Respect

What pulls me away?

- Self sabotage
- Self guilt
- Self harm
- Sefl centeredness

- Self indulgence
- Self limitations
- Self loathing
- Self doubt

ABOUT KIM MORRISON

There is so much more to Kim Morrison than meets the eye. Tenacity is probably the first word that comes to mind. Her journey and all she has accomplished to date has all stemmed from her unwavering self-belief and her deep understanding that you must also take care of yourself, first and foremost.

Kim set a world record as the youngest female to run 100miles in less than twenty-four hours in 1989. Cliff Young was her mentor at the time and to this day lives by his ethos that success is 90% mental and 10% physical. She has used her running story as a direct metaphor for life - riding the highs, hitting the walls, pushing through the pain barriers, crossing the line and never, ever giving up!

Highly regarded as a presenter, it is Kim's innate understanding of people and what makes them act the way they do that has her in demand as a speaker. Her workshop on personality dynamics will leave you and your team understanding what makes them (and those they work with, live with, or love) tick. Her workshops have resulted in greater team and relationship dynamics, increased productivity in the workplace and have even been accredited to saving marriages.

Kim believes it is your inner power, passion, commitment, and having truckloads of self-belief that distinguishes you as an achiever. It's about visualising your dream and going for it, regardless of the feedback you receive, or the challenges you face. As a five-time best-selling author, creative director of Twenty8, and a multi-tasking mum and wife, Kim shares her essential tools for self-care, discipline, leadership, teamwork, relationships, and of course the art of self-love.

If you would like to make an enquiry to have Kim speak at an event please go to www.twenty8.com/kimspeaking for more information.

Take care
Be kind

Printed in June 2019
by Rotomail Italia S.p.A., Vignate (MI) - Italy